# The Daisy Diaries

A true story of one woman's
unusual journey through tragedy,
transformation, & triumph

Krista Lindquist

***The Daisy Diaries***
*A true story of one woman's unusual journey*
*through tragedy, transformation, & triumph*
By Krista Lindquist

Copyright © 2022 by Krista Lindquist

All rights reserved. This book or any portion thereof may not be reproduced or used in any manner whatsoever without the express written permission of the publisher except for the use of brief quotations in a book review.

# The Daisy Diaries

2-14-23

Every part of your story is important!

♡ Krista Lindquist

This book is dedicated to my daughter and two heavenly heroes, who guided and inspired me to put this story into words.

# Table of Contents

Introduction: *Welcome to My Life* ............................................. 9
1. May 2001: *The Significantly Insignificant Beginning* ............ 12
2. September 2002: *The Blond Boy Returns* ............................ 17
3. March 2004: *New Love, New Heartbreak* ............................ 24
4. July 2006: *Tragedy Strikes* ................................................. 40
5. October 2006: *The Blond Boy Returns... Again* ................... 50
6. December 2006: *Colorado Confessions* ............................... 69
7. March 2007: *The Last Party* ............................................... 79
8. April 2007: *Uncomfortably Numb* ....................................... 91
9. July 2007: *The Life-Saving Surprise* .................................. 101
10. March 2008: *The Day Light Entered My World* .................. 112
11. September 2008: *Growing Pains* ....................................... 121
12. August 2010: *The Fork in the Road* ................................... 128
13. May 2012: *The Visits* ....................................................... 136
14. October 2013: *Waking Up* ................................................ 153
15. July 2014: *The Real Awakening* ........................................ 171
16. November 2016: *A New Path* ............................................ 181
17. January 2019: *The Leap of Faith* ....................................... 201
18. March 2020: *When the World Stopped* .............................. 216
19. August 2020: *Off We Go* .................................................. 222
20. April 2021: *The Intuitive Guide Revealed* ........................... 231
21. May 2021: *The Curtain Close* ............................................ 237
22. August 2021: *The New Story* ............................................ 245

Acknowledgements ................................................................. 252
Connect with Krista ................................................................. 253

# Introduction

## Welcome to My Life

True life: this is the story of a girl and her unusual experiences through first love, heartbreak, and tragedy. That girl was me. Within these pages is my unfiltered, ugly, raw truth, laid across a timeline that quickly crashed with disaster at the age of seventeen.

Though those initial events occurred within twelve months, it took another fourteen years for me to find the courage to face my past, relive every heart-wrenching moment, and share the details in tangible form for the first time. Even if you know me personally or had any part in the series of unfortunate events to follow in these chapters, you will learn details of my personal experience that I have *never* shared before. Many of these details I have only recently discovered through writing this book. Buried deeply within me, even I wasn't aware of their existence. Until I finally surrendered to face my truth through writing, I didn't realize their impact on my life and sense of self-worth.

After the tragedies concluded, I spent the next decade hidden underneath a false veil of strength and optimism. I even earned an engineering degree, succeeded in a corporate career, and then walked away to start my own business. Yet the traumatized young girl inside me continued to cry silently in pain for my attention and healing throughout my outward successes. Unannounced waves of depression and anxiety have drowned me in turbulent seas of silent suffering over these last fourteen years. I often crawled into countless deep, dark holes of guilt and self-sabotage, denying myself the love and healing I have become so passionate about sharing with others.

Almost immediately after the actual events occurred, I felt a calling to write my story. Many people who learned of my experience responded by saying, "Wow! This should be a book! Or a movie!" I dismissed the potential importance of sharing my story for the entire decade I spent distracting myself with challenges and opportunities to "prove" my worth. Behind closed doors, I continued to indulge in self-loathing and deny myself the healing I needed from writing these words.

I finally committed to writing my story by taking a massive leap of faith with my career. No longer able to ignore my calling to write and help others heal, I quit my job and started a business. I took my first month of freedom off to relax from the corporate rollercoaster I exited, with full belief that I could write my entire book within that free time. I mean, I already had the whole story; all I had to do was put it into words!

Eighteen months later, I'd hardly made it past the outline and first few chapters.

Upon my new freedom of self-employment, I suddenly realized that I had stored insurmountable pain within me from those tragedies. Now it had the time, space, and solitude to finally reach the surface for my full attention. Stricken by a shockwave of depression and anxiety, I found myself paralyzed in pain and shock for the next few weeks. Inconveniently during the coldest, darkest months in Minnesota (remember the Polar Vortex of 2019, anyone?), I slipped into darkness and isolation. I suddenly found myself hardly able to get out of bed in the morning, putting all I could into just getting my daughter up and off to school each day. Many days, I crawled back into bed to sleep and cry until my daughter came home from school. From there, I faked a smile to get through each evening of my motherly duties until I could retreat to the depressing comfort of my bed.

*Write a book? What book? My story is too shameful to share,* I told myself. *I'm not a writer. I shouldn't have survived my past. I'm unworthy of life altogether.*

Within the first weeks of building my story's outline and facing its details, my writing came to a screeching halt for months. I let myself silently suffer until I couldn't physically stand it anymore. After making confessions to my mom and best friend, I was able to climb far enough from the darkness to set a new goal: take the time I needed (and deserved) to heal myself so that I could genuinely help others heal through my experience. Instead of writing, I spent those months diving deeper into self-exploration and uncovering the roots of my old pain, guilt, and suffering. And when I finally returned to these pages, I realized that I never "lost time" from finishing the book.

*I was still living the story.*

After another eighteen months of intertwined healing, failing, teaching, writing, facing a pandemic, giving up my entire life for a new one, again, and rediscovering my most authentic self, the grand finale of my one-of-a-kind story is finally here. Up until the last pages, I continued to heal, grow, and flourish all along the way.

What lies ahead is a collection of my most absolute, raw truth to the best of my memory. It is a roadmap of the mistakes, lessons, Divine interventions, and personal evolution that allowed me to heal from my past, love myself, and manifest a deeply fulfilling life. Some names and situations have been changed to protect the identity and privacy of those involved in my experiences. If you recognize yourself as one of these unnamed individuals in my story, I thank you for helping to shape the most important, and often hardest, lessons I needed to learn, and I remind you that these words are simply honest reflections of my younger self's perspective. I have no intentions of offending or undermining anyone who anonymously made a cameo appearance within these pages.

In sharing my darkest, most vulnerable experiences, I hope you might find compassion for yourself in your own story. I put mine into words to reach out to others suffering out there, in hopes you might be able to relate and feel less alone. I pray you find some valuable insights in these words that might inspire you to make better, more self-loving choices in your own life. No matter your age or gender, I genuinely hope my words rekindle a liberating sense of understanding and compassion for your own darkest truths. May you find gratitude for your life's lessons so that you, too, can find ultimate healing, freedom, and the power to manifest the dream life that you deserve. If I could do it, then you can, too.

Are you ready? You're about to step into one real and raw journey, from trauma and surviving to ultimate freedom and thriving, all road bumps, highlights, and lessons learned included.

But before we dive into all the juicy details, let's begin at the beginning. Back to May of 2001, when a 12-year-old girl met the boy who would change her life forever.

# Chapter 1

## May 2001:

### The Significantly Insignificant Beginning

Where I grew up in the Upper Peninsula of Michigan, twenty miles from the shores of Lake Superior, there is an annual tradition that local sixth-graders spend three days and two nights at Camp Superior.

Right alongside the greatest Great Lake, the camping experience may be just as you imagine: gatherings in the large recreation hall, sleeping in tents, nature hikes, team building activities, and the greatly awaited Ropes Course. Two stories high in the trees, the Ropes Course was the final activity of camp to test our physical and mental ability to rough it in the woods!

I attended the small Catholic grade school in my town, which was grouped with the only other Catholic school in the surrounding area, along with the smallest local public school about fifteen miles away. We piled on the bus with our camping gear, and I was filled with excitement and anxiety about this unknown experience ahead of me. New kids to meet, new experiences, and new challenges to face. This was most every sixth-grader's dream and fear, all bundled into one!

As we picked up more kids from the other schools, the excitement rose. Everyone was happy; the contagious energy spread across the bus. My nerves faded quickly and shifted into straight excitement, too.

We finally got to camp and rushed off the bus, hauling our gear into the giant camp lodge. As more pulled in, other buses had already arrived. Kids buzzed around everywhere in a chaotic bliss. The exuberant sounds of laughing and shouting were echoing off the walls.

Being slightly shy, I tried to stick close by my best friend since she was the funny and outgoing one who would break the ice and introduce us to everyone. Yet I quickly realized that every new kid I encountered was just as nervous and excited as I was, *and* really nice. I felt my anxiety melt away and started to think, *I could get used to this!*

I looked across the vibrating energy of the room full of kids, and something caught my eye. I met and locked eyes with a tall blond-haired boy. It felt like we both looked up and directly at each other simultaneously from across the room. My heart immediately skipped a beat and proceeded to flutter, sending tingles up my spine and down every limb.

*Woah, what is this feeling? And who is that boy?* I thought. I had never had a boyfriend. I'd certainly had many major crushes by then, but this felt different. This wasn't the feeling of tiny butterflies in my stomach; it felt more like an electric shock that closed a circuit between this mysterious boy and me.

Who knows how long I stood lost in thought, mesmerized by the stranger across the room, before I suddenly realized I was still staring at him. *Oh my God! Look away!* I thought. *Don't stare or look obvious.* I snapped my head like a whip to look away, with a bashful smile on my face. *Yeah, way to play it cool, Krista.* Blushing, I returned to my circle of old and new friends.

My heart continued to pound with electricity as my eyes kept a secret watch out for that boy. *He's so cute!* My heart fluttered. *Will I get to meet him? Was he looking at me like I was looking at him?*

As the crowds of kids shuffled and danced around, we were ushered to our assigned cabins. The squeals of excitement continued as I gathered into my cabin, thankfully with my best friend and some of the girls I had just met. We all picked our bunks and unloaded our bags, dishing about who snuck in candy and where they hid it. I was only half paying attention at this point, in the back of my mind wondering, *where is that blond boy?*

A few minutes later, we were called back out into the Great Hall to receive our group assignments for the next three days. I could feel an electric shock pound through my heart in anticipation of who I might be grouped with. As my name was called, a rush of relief washed over me, joining others from my class and some of the kids I had just met and made friends with.

And then *he* was called over. My heart nearly leaped out of my chest this time. *The blond boy is in my group!* We locked eyes again as he walked over. I felt a charge of energy that surged even stronger between us as he walked closer from across the room. We both blushed and looked away. *He did it, too; I know he feels it!* I thought. My sheer excitement for the next three days nearly blew me through the roof.

Through the agonizingly long group introductions, I finally learned the blond boy's name, Cody. *Of course, what a perfect name!* Ok, I was totally crushing at this point. My wildest (and unbeknownst until that moment) romantic camp dream was just beginning before my eyes.

Through every activity during camp, I couldn't keep my eyes off him, though I pretended to "play it cool." Yeah, I'm sure I really pulled that off well. Whenever I couldn't see him, I practiced fielding my energetic radar for his presence. I couldn't make sense of it; it just felt so good to be near this strange blond boy I hardly knew. Finally, during downtime between activities, we got the chance to break the ice and get to talking.

We first made small talk, sharing our names and what schools we came from, while bashfully batting eyes at one another. Butterflies danced through my belly as we chatted. *Oh my God, Cody's so cute!* I kept thinking to myself. Forget Taylor Hanson; I suddenly had a brand-new crush right here in person!

Before the end of the first day of camp, boys and girls that had just met from different schools were paired up as "boyfriends and girlfriends." You know, as seriously as sixth-grade relationships can go. I can't remember who orchestrated this assignment, but low and behold, Cody and I were paired together in this magical nonsense. Yes! My campground fantasy was unraveling before my eyes!

The magic continued over the next few days, through group hikes to the lake, doing the "trust fall" and other team-building activities, and finally, the Ropes Course.

Our camp counselors had us line up in alternating girl/boy order to start the course, and I was thrilled to get right behind Cody. I watched in admiration as he effortlessly made his way across each obstacle, and I followed in excitement (and some nerves) to get across each section just as gracefully. At one point, a boy further ahead got himself stuck on an obstacle. Being behind him, we had nowhere to go. But being stuck in the trees next to my adorable blond crush? I could have stayed there all day! For about an hour or so, we sat up in the trees, singing songs and encouraging our poor friend ahead to untangle himself and continue the course.

By the time we got moving again, we were almost to the last and best obstacle: the zip line. Cody zoomed down the line like a blond Tarzan ahead of me, and I couldn't wait to follow. Once it was my turn, my heart jumped with me off the platform as I flew through the trees. And at the end of the line, Cody was standing on the ground looking up at me. My heart fluttered as I was lowered to the ground in front of him. He smiled at me before bending down and picking a wild daisy from the ground.

"Here, this is for you," he said bashfully, handing me the bright little flower.

"Aw, thank you," I replied. I could feel my cheeks turn red. *How sweet!* I thought. My little young heart was head over heels in love!

As we approached the end of the sweet escape of camp, I started sensing a rough edge around Cody that I couldn't quite understand nor find the guts to ask him about. I mean, we'd only known each other for a whole three days. Plus, he was so cool and made me so nervous! I ignored the mild pang in my gut and settled back into the warm electricity between us.

On the bus ride home from camp, we sat together. We even held hands. I sat feeling light and bubbly at his side until I suddenly wondered, *Wait, are my palms sweaty?*

Almost as quickly as that disturbing thought popped into my head, I felt a shift in energy, like Cody was vacuuming in his radiant, warm energy. He got quieter as the bus drove closer to his school. Yet his mesmerizing deep blue eyes seemed to hold stories of a thousand lifetimes. Painful ones, it felt.

My heart sank as the bus stopped. Cody gave me a quick, awkward hug. I felt the electric circuit between us break as he turned and got up, walking off the bus. I suddenly fell back to earth from my romantic camp cloud. He lived fifteen miles away from my home. The odds of us seeing each other again anytime soon were very slim. I mean, unless we became avid bike riders.

As the rest of his classmates shuffled off the bus, one of them paused to tell me, "Oh, by the way, Cody had a girlfriend in the eighth grade. But I think he still totally likes you!"

I was crushed like someone had dropped a brick on my chest. This was my first official heartbreak!

*The Daisy Diaries* | 15

*Ugh. He has a girlfriend?! How stupid could I be? No wonder his energy changed so much. Of course, he didn't actually like me.*

Within a mere three days, my little 12-year-old heart had experienced its first dose of love and heartbreak. I was utterly swept away by this mysterious blond boy and had been dumped by him already. For the next few days after camp, I listened to sad 90s pop/rock hits on my Walkman CD player, sulking in the devastation of my lost hope of love with the blond boy from Camp Superior.

Though the next few weeks felt like utter middle-school misery, it didn't take me long to "recover" from my crushing romantic camp crusade with Cody. I mean, I was already a master of boy crushes by the time I went to camp. Growing through pubescence in the days of JTT, NSYNC, and Hanson, I had already married Justin Timberlake, Taylor Hanson, and the cute boy in school in my mind hundreds of times.

That fall, I entered the seventh grade and my first "real" relationship with another cute blond boy. I quickly fell head over heels all over again and experienced my first kiss and cuddles. We gained super middle school couple status by the end of spring and enjoyed a summer of fun with friends and my family.

Though we seemed to be perfect together, by summer's end, I suddenly found myself questioning how young we were and how serious our relationship was. *Was this really it? Already?* I was only thirteen, after all! Plus, the new school year was approaching, and it would be completely different. My boyfriend was entering high school, and I was still in middle school; we knew we would be far more separated than the year before.

My picture-perfect teeny-bopper relationship slowly faded away, and I was about to be served surprising news at the dinner table…

# Chapter 2

## September 2002:

## The Blond Boy Returns

Just before my eighth-grade year, my family was eating dinner together on one very ordinary night. The usual "how was your day?" made its way around the table between my mom, dad, sister, and me. I tuned in and out of the conversation until I stood up to clear my plate, then my mom asked, "Did you know that you'll have a new classmate this year?"

"Who?" I asked.

My mom replied, "I work with his family. Since birth, I've been his little sister's physical therapist, and now she's six. His name is Cody Southwell."

My heart skipped a beat. That same electric current from Camp Superior rushed through my entire body. *He's moving here?* I asked myself in shock. *I can't believe it! I wonder if he still has that older girlfriend.* Snapping back to reality, I played it cool like I didn't care, although my heart and mind raced with wonder.

On the first day of school, I was already filled with the annual first-day butterflies. This year, my butterflies turned into giant flapping birds each time Cody came to mind.

Thrilled to see my friends upon entering the building, I walked with them up all three flights of stairs, around the corner, and down the hallway toward my new locker. Suddenly, an intense rush of chills struck through my body. A familiar electric energy made my hair stand on end. I looked up and further down the hallway, immediately locking eyes with the blond boy. It was Cody.

He quickly looked away, playing it cool. So did I. But shoot, we were walking towards each other. *What do I do?!* I panicked. *Most of my friends don't know that I know him. They have no idea that he was my "boyfriend." How awkward!*

As we walked closer, our eyes darted all over the hallway and back like ping pong balls. Both blushing and locking eyes for the five hundredth time within fifteen seconds, Cody and I smiled bashfully and turned to our lockers... that were right across the hall from each other.

I continued to "play it cool" as I fumbled with my lock. But good Lord, I couldn't hide my awkwardness to save my life! *What the heck is my combination again?!* My mind went blank as I tried my hardest to grow eyes in the back of my head and see what the blond boy was doing behind me. *Does he feel what I feel?* After about six failed attempts, my lock finally popped free, and I swung my locker door open, slamming it on the next locker. *Get it together, Krista; way to be cool about it!*

I scrambled to gather my books for my first class, half hoping I was grabbing the right books, as my entire day's schedule blanked out of my mind. I slammed my locker shut, pretending to carry on with my friends, but I looked back at Cody to shoot him a shy smile as I walked away. *Alright, that was cool. Way to be mysterious!*

A buzzy crowd of eighth-graders shuffled into my first classroom. As the dust of commotion settled, in walked Cody. My heart fluttered. *Play it cool, Krista. Play it cool.* Yeah, we know I was great at that.

The teacher immediately assigned us seats in alphabetical order. So, wouldn't you know that fate aligned our last names and the number of desks in the room to seat Cody in the next row just behind me?

*Can he see that I'm sweating?* I was so nervous. But really, I was so excited. I now knew I'd get to see him in class every day! Then fate continued to have its way with me. Throughout the day, the same scenario kept repeating in each new class. Cody was nearly the last person to walk in the room before being assigned to a seat near me.

I couldn't pretend to be cool and not notice him for long. That same old electric energy was so strong, I felt like everyone in the room could physically see it! By the third common class period, we finally re-broke the ice, chit-chatting about how our summers went and why he moved to Ironwood. *I wonder if he still has that girlfriend,* I couldn't help but wonder. Though acting cool on the outside, I was totally heating up on the inside!

Since Cody was the new kid, I took the opportunity to introduce him to all my friends in the "preppy" popular crowd. Now, imagine what our "crowd" was like; we all got good grades, played all the sports, participated in extracurricular activities, and made up all the Student Council members. Cody sure looked the part with his tall and fit physique, thick blond hair, and piercing blue eyes, and most of my crew immediately welcomed him into the group.

As the school days moved on, the magnetism between Cody and me continued to intensify. I quickly found myself crushing on him all over again. I tried to hide it around my friends, but I secretly developed my blond boy radar. I looked for him in the hallways and anxiously anticipated seeing him in our classes together. I became excited to go to school every day just to be near him and feed off the energy between us.

Nearly every Friday night, my friends would all go to the movies and walk to the bowling alley or someone's house afterward. Many times, it was my house. Cody started joining us as he and I unofficially became a couple again. After he came to our house a few times and it became evident that we liked each other, my mom spoke up.

"I don't want to mix my work life with my home life," she said. "I do weekly home visits with his sister. I don't want him in my house anymore, and I don't want you dating him either. You have no idea what his home life is like, and I don't want you mixed up with it."

I was devastated by her command. But my stubborn nature refused to let her control who I spent my time with. It wasn't my problem who she worked with! Plus, I had been upsetting my mom with my strong will since I could walk and talk, so what did I have to lose?

Since I can remember, I never felt very close to my mom. Even so, as a child, my world revolved around mom and dad. I instinctually believed that they were the most intelligent and amazing people in the world. They both had answers to my every question, spoke in confidence, and knew what to do when my sister and I were hurt or in trouble. I had no doubt that mom and dad knew everything, and everything they said was right.

My calm and quiet father was always kind and easy-going; I can't remember him ever yelling at me as a child, not even out of anger or frustration. My mom, on the other hand? I seemed to have a knack for pushing her buttons. Especially since my dad was so thoughtful with his words, it never occurred to me that my mom might say words she didn't mean. Everything they said was the truth, right? Including the first time she called me a selfish little brat.

Of all people on earth, I thought that no one knew me better than my own mom. Not even my dad, since he was always so busy running his electrical business. So, if she said I was a selfish little brat, it must be true. Maybe dad was just being too nice to me. He must not know me as well. I must be a bad person who needed to be punished.

I must admit that I've always been stubborn. I guess little strong-willed Krista needed more explanation of why she should obey and that when you upset someone, they're going to react out of anger. And that those words in anger aren't necessarily a reflection of who I am, but what I did. I guess my mom didn't have time for that. Instead, I just remember being told I was a selfish little brat and feeling misunderstood. My mom always seemed to think I was too wild and out of control. Was I really that bad?

By age fourteen, the bull in me had grown stubborn and rebellious. I was already tired of being corrected and controlled. When someone told me I couldn't do something, I reacted oppositely. So naturally, my mom telling me not to see Cody just made me want to see him more.

To hide that I was seeing Cody, I stopped inviting my friends over to my house. However, there weren't many places in our small town for tweens to "hang out," besides the movie theater or the bowling alley. I wanted to hang out at someone's house and hope for the chance to sit and snuggle up to him on a couch! However, he lived far out of town, and the welcoming of the "preppy" crowd was starting to fade…

It was just becoming apparent that Cody didn't share a similar background to my "preppy" friends. Most of us came from relatively "stable" homes, didn't get in trouble (yet), and had most of our needs well taken care of. Cody didn't have that and couldn't fake it either. He didn't quite fit in, and we experienced that awkward realization together. He started to make friends with more of the cool "rebels," "slackers," and "troublemakers" in school, and together we attempted to blend somewhere in the middle.

Since I wasn't allowed to invite him to my house, I got clever in sneaking around to see Cody. I'll never forget the night that a girlfriend of mine slept over, and we snuck out the basement window of my parents' house to meet Cody and his friends. In the late evening and wee hours of the morning, all we did was walk around the streets. Really cool and exciting, I know. But what else could a bunch of middle schoolers possibly do at that hour with nowhere to go and no vehicle to get them there?

There were about five or six of us, having a blast sneaking around in the darkness and stopping in the 24-hour gas station since it was the only place open. With nothing to do and nowhere to go, we found simple bliss in walking the streets together, laughing, and telling stories. Though most of the evening consists of blurry bits of memory, one moment still stands my hair on end.

Cody was walking ahead of me, so I quietly snuck up behind him. I wrapped my arms around him, breathing a soft giggle into his ear before giving his neck a gentle kiss. I could feel *and* hear him shudder, and the most intense energy surge yet ran through my body. He stopped walking, frozen by this overwhelming feeling for a moment, before turning around to slide his hands around my waist.

Cody leaned in closer, making my heart skip out of my chest as he kissed me on the lips for the first time. Shockwaves tingled up and down my spine. *I hope I'm doing this right!* I wondered. His lips felt so soft on mine. This time, it felt like the energy field around us was as visible as a neon sign.

"Ooooohhhh! Look at the love birds!" called one of his friends from further up the street, as the whole group paused to look and join the gushy rounds of "ooohs" and "aahs."

Cody and I pulled away from our innocent and breath-taking kiss, blushing and giggling like the middle schoolers we were. We continued down the street, hand in hand. As we passed a little white house nearly hidden behind a vast wildflower garden, Cody suddenly paused and pulled me with him toward it. He bent down and picked a flower. Then, turning back to me and holding his hand out, he said, "Here, this is for you."

I looked in his hand. He was holding a daisy. Déjà vu struck as the image of him handing me a daisy at Camp Superior flashed in my mind. A huge smile spread across my face.

"Remember Camp Superior?" he asked with a smile just as big as mine.

"Of course, I do," I replied. I softly took the daisy from his hand and stuck it behind my ear. "How do I look?"

"Like the most beautiful thing I've ever seen," he replied. Butterflies stirred in my stomach. *He's so sweet,* I thought. *Does anyone else know he has such a soft side to him?* Time stopped as I got lost in his deep blue eyes for a moment, or maybe minutes.

Suddenly, our friends from down the street yelled, "Hey, are you love birds coming?" Our eye lock broke as we turned to our friends, now nearly two blocks ahead of us. We laughed, smiling back at each other before continuing down the street.

"Yes, we're coming," he yelled to them. Then, turning back to me, he said softly, "But as long as I'm with you, I'm in no hurry to get anywhere." The butterflies in my stomach flapped wildly again. I smiled.

"Me either," I replied. Still hand in hand, and my hair adorned with the precious daisy, we carried on down the street, floating on Cloud Nine.

From that moment, Cody and I were serious. Especially Cody. Surprisingly serious, really. Since I couldn't let my mom find out he was my boyfriend and didn't have the heart to tell Cody how my mom felt about him, I gave him my own room phone number.

Yes, my separate phone line. My friends, this was the early 2000s, back when the internet needed its own phone line. I somehow lucked out in having a phone jack connected to that line right in my bedroom, thus granting my very own private phone line! *Perfect,* I thought, until Cody started calling me... and kept calling... multiple times... Every. Single. Night.

I had never experienced a boy fall so hard for me so quickly. I mean, I knew I was pretty cool, but come on now, we were fourteen! I began wondering if I enjoyed his dedicated attention or if I was starting to get plain old annoyed by it.

Hindsight is always 20/20, isn't it? Now that I look back, I'm not sure if I was genuinely annoyed by his love for me or genuinely brainwashed by my mother's and friends' opinions of him.

How could I continue dating Cody without my own family knowing? I couldn't possibly keep that secret very long! Especially not with the number of times my phone rang each night. I found myself wanting to hide him from my friends, too. They seemed to notice his rough edges as he drifted further away from the "preppy" group and closer to the "bad boys," for lack of better cliquey terms! I felt the pressure building in me until I couldn't stand it anymore. Cody kept calling after school, so I started ignoring his calls. Once he tried saying "I love you," I called it quits... over the phone.

*We're only fourteen! We're too young for love,* I justified in my mind. *Cody is crazy to think he's in love with me. He can't be. And I can't be around him anymore if he thinks he does,* I convinced myself, still under the heavy influence of my mom's orders and peer pressures. *It will be much easier if we go with our separate crowds and move on.*

After crushing his heart, I suddenly dreaded seeing him in the hallways and in all the classes we had together. I could feel him watching me. I could still feel our energy. But I cut myself off from it. I couldn't be with him and convinced myself that he wasn't even attractive to me anymore through my new eyes of social status and judgment.

Cody was devastated. He was convinced that we were meant to be, but I wouldn't hear it. So I dismissed him as crazy and avoided him as much as possible.

However, avoiding him altogether was impossible; we still had several classes together, sitting awfully close to each other! So I went back to "playing it cool" and putting him in the "friend zone." Eventually, the awkwardness faded between us, at least to a tolerable level. Or maybe it just did for me, as I trained myself to dismiss our connection.

Cody and I continued to chit-chat politely in classes, pretending to be friends. Still, we drifted to our separate crowds and carried on as unlikely friends.

I don't think I saw Cody at all that summer. By summer's end, I believed the time and distance away would clear the energy between us. But come fall, entering our freshman year of high school, we were in just about the same boat as the previous year. In any class we had together, our desks were always nearby. We also had gym class together, which put me in competition mode, trying to strut my stuff and secretly impress him. I sensed he was doing the same.

As much as I ignored and denied it, the electricity between us was still visible to me. Without a doubt, in a crowded room or hallway, we'd always manage to lock eyes from any distance. I just trained my reflexes to look away faster.

My boundaries of the "friend zone" got stronger, too. Although I must admit, I enjoyed knowing that he still had a crush on me. I loved the attention. But we both knew it wouldn't happen, and he politely gave up and moved on, settling into a new relationship that would last for the next few years.

# Chapter 3

## March 2004:

## New Love, New Heartbreak

Enter Jake. The boy that would rock my world, shatter my heart into pieces, and change my life forever.

Spring forward to my second semester of freshman year, sitting in computer class. Yes, with the old desktop computers. Those big and boxy Dell monitors with gigantic clunky-buttoned keyboards. Real keyboards, not screens. Anyway, in passing to and from this ecstatic computer class, I occasionally smiled and said hello to our Teacher's Assistant, who was two grades above us, and carried on without a thought. Until one day, he approached me and said, "Hey, my friend Jake thinks you're cute."

At first, I didn't know who Jake was. I recognized him once he was pointed out to me, but I had never thought about attracting the attention of an older boy. I learned Jake was two and a half years older, even a few months older than my older sister, who was also in his class. This was certainly awkward, but I was quickly blinded and swept away by the idea of being "cool" enough for an older boy to like me.

Soon enough, Jake and I were paired up to hang out with our mutual friends. We later learned that this was indeed a game of blind matchmaking, as his friend (the Teacher's Assistant) had a crush on *my* friend and decided that pairing us together would work wonders in his own conquest to win over my friend. *How lucky for me!* Jake was cute, funny, and popular. I was quickly flying high on a new crush.

Within a few weeks of spending time together, Jake asked me to be his girlfriend. Not long after that, I was wearing his old softball T-shirt in gym class. Our gym teacher, who Jake worked for part-time, found great joy in teasing me every day in that shirt. Telling stories about my future marriage with Jake, having ten kids, and living in a trailer. I openly received his jokes and kept wearing the shirt, all in good fun. I could see Cody cringe every time he heard Jake's name or looked at my shirt. Maybe I wore it just to rub it in his face. *Look at me now, with this cool older boy.* It was official now; Cody and I were really done for good.

However, the timing of Jake and I getting together was not ideal. Just before our matchmaking, he agreed to go to prom with a girl from another school. Since they were in different schools with different proms, they signed up for both.

Upon learning this rather threatening detail, Jake assured me that he wasn't at all interested in her and felt obligated to accept her invitation and invite her to his prom in return, only because he didn't yet have a date at that time. Unfortunately, it was too late to go back and change plans, so we moved forward with our relationship and let prom come as they planned.

When the first prom arrived, nausea grew in my stomach throughout the day and reached its peak as I waited with my friends at the prom's Grand March. I knew his date had a crush on him, and I was immensely worried that she might be able to steal him from me that night. I tried to be at his side through the public event and take as many pictures of us as were taken of him and his date.

I don't think she and I ever spoke at that point. There was an unsaid and extreme tension between us, the young girlfriend vs. the hopeful prom date. I couldn't even look at her without my heart leaping up into my throat. I kept trying to soothe the sickening pit in my stomach with reassurance that I'd be going to the after-party with Jake and all would be okay from there.

During the prom, I went to my friend's house for a sleepover and planned to attend the after-party with Jake and his friends. They were supposed to let us know on MSN Messenger when they got to the party for us to come. I pretended my stomach wasn't twisted in knots all night waiting for that message to arrive. And when it finally did, from Jake's friend, it wrote:

*Sorry, there's already too many people out here, so you can't come anymore, or we'll get in trouble. I'm sorry.*

"What the fuck!" my friend exclaimed.

I felt like I was going to throw up. My gut was screaming what I didn't want to believe or accept: *Jake is cheating on me.*

My friend tried to reassure me with every possible excuse for the sudden change in plans and Jake's inability to speak a word to me all night. But, as I tried to deny reality in my anxious mind, Jake was already drunk and about to lose his virginity to his prom date.

After a sickening, sleepless night, I finally heard from him the following day, promising me that nothing had happened. I tried to convince myself that I believed him, but I knew in my gut that it was a lie. Still, I wanted to give him the benefit of the doubt since he *swore* he was faithful.

After several days of rumors flying around our school and anxiety swallowing me whole, a mutual friend of Jake's and his prom date stopped me in the hallway to tell me what she knew. Here, the truth came out for the first time: Jake not only messed around with this girl, he had sex with her.

I might have blacked out at that moment. On the inside, it felt like my chest exploded. On the outside, I choked down tears, thanked her, and continued down the hallway with an attitude ready to kill.

Completely shattered and outraged, I confronted Jake after school through a storm of tears. And he still continued to deny it! But I wouldn't have it. I knew the truth and refused to stop the accusations until he confessed. Eventually, he did.

"I'm so sorry. I didn't mean to. I promise I will never do it again!" Jake claimed in guilty tears. I wasn't sure if his tears were from genuine guilt or just from getting caught, but I wanted so badly to believe he was truly sorry. *Who could hurt someone they care about this badly?* Certainly not such a nice guy like Jake. He had to be uncontrollably wasted to do such a hurtful thing. I even wanted to believe he couldn't remember a bit of what happened.

Regardless, my heart was broken. This time, that 15-year-old heart felt shattered. *How could anyone do something so hurtful and disrespectful to anyone? Why did he start dating me in the first place if he knew he was going to do this?* I couldn't make any sense of it. I cried in my room for days, howling tears, as my mom described, although, at the time, she had no idea what had hurt me so badly. I refused to tell her. I was embarrassed and knew she'd try to make me break up with my boyfriend again if she knew what he did.

You would think this would have been the end of a very short relationship. But remember, there was still another prom *the very next day* for Jake and his date to attend. And have I mentioned that I am bull-headed? A true Taurus from birth, I wasn't about to let him go to another after-prom party with this girl, so I stayed with him. I made sure to get to the party this time, praying that I would ruin that girl's prom for the evil act she imposed on me.

The next few weeks were a broken record of uncontrollable tears and apologies. Honestly, as I write this, I'm baffled by how Jake and I stayed together. I no longer trusted him, and I can't imagine he found any enjoyment from my frequent emotional outbursts.

Then I remembered, when things were good, they were *so good*. Jake was hilarious and charming; we could spend hours laughing together. Our precious moments alone made our troubles seem to disappear. We cared too much about each other to let it go, so we stuck it out, and Jake promised and proved (for a little while, at least) to be faithful.

As the next few months rolled by, I lost count of how many times I cried and he settled my tears with promises that he wouldn't be able to keep. It appears to be true insanity as I look back now, although it fills me with so much compassion and sorrow for my young, naive 15-year-old heart, who wanted so desperately to love and be loved that she would take such treatment as if she deserved it.

What a sad girl my younger self was, who let her guard down and threw her morals to the wayside to be wanted and accepted by this boy who stole her immature heart. And that stubborn bull that I was (and must admit, still am) would tough through such heart-breaking betrayal just to make sure that no other girl could steal him again.

Jake and I continued dating, somehow managing to deepen our relationship. We were together daily after school, driving around in his tiny Toyota truck and either hiding away in his bedroom with movies and laughter or exploring ways to find trouble with our friends. Since his friends first experimented with drinking at their prom, the curiosity and thrill of alcohol became the latest fascination and quickly influenced my younger friends and me.

A pattern soon developed of partying nearly every Friday and Saturday night. But, since I had a strict curfew enforced by my mom, who I'm sure could sense what I was getting into without obvious evidence, I had to get creative. So, I cleverly asked for sleepovers every weekend. First at other friends' houses, particularly those crushing on Jake's friends, and especially those with less strict parents than my own.

Until that is, the latest party location settled at Jake's friend's house, just four blocks away from mine. Since I had an earlier curfew than everyone else, this convenient location required more creativity after hours. I kept asking for sleepovers, now at my own house. After my parents went to bed and it was quiet throughout the house, my most mischievous friends and I would sneak out and run a few blocks to the party.

At this point, I wasn't pulled too far into drinking, but I sure was wrapped around Jake's finger. Well, more like we were both tangled in each other's webs. I was willing to do whatever it took to be in his arms as much as possible, especially when he was drinking. I convinced myself it was because I cared about him so much, and he cared about me just the same, but looking back now, it's clear how consumed I was by making sure he wouldn't get "too drunk" and cheat on me again.

The parties became a predictable scenario of passion and pain each night. Jake and I quickly disappeared into a bedroom upon my late-night arrivals and swept into a passionate whirlwind of kissing and fooling around. Until the passion got too hot and heavy, that is. As soon as I felt an inkling of the heat rising too high, I burst into a sobby mess of tears. I suddenly felt cornered by an unspoken pressure to go further with him sexually than my immature mind and body were ready to go.

"I feel like I have to sleep with you now that you've done it before," I'd choke out through ugly tears. "How could you do this to someone you think you really care about?" Then, exhausted by the tidal wave of betrayal that repeatedly washed over me, I buried my sobbing face in his chest, soaking his shirt in tears, if he was even wearing one. I needed to know that he was genuinely sorry for hurting me, not just for getting caught. I needed a guarantee that it would never happen again.

Jake always remained patient and consoling. Even though they sprung right at the peak of our passion, he always stopped to hold me and let me cry. He often cried, too. *He must be really sorry if he's crying*, I reassured myself. Yet I couldn't hear him say "I'm sorry" enough times; the words alone were never enough.

Jake unwaveringly denied any intention of laying pressure on me and promised that we could move as slowly as I wanted to. But now that he was no longer a virgin, I didn't know how long I was able to wait anymore. My screaming insecurity warned me that if I didn't sleep with him soon, he'd do it with someone else. Again.

I mean, who were we trying to kid? He had sex already. As a hormone-raging 17-year-old, of course he'd want to do it again. So, I kept giving him a little more every time, eventually exploring every possible intimate alternative to sex in an attempt to keep him satisfied. I didn't know if I really wanted to be doing these things; I just knew I wanted him to stay with me and no one else.

A few months later, once I felt my body had run dry of tears, Jake was living up to his promise of loyalty to me. It finally felt like we were back to where we started, with moments full of laughter and fun, especially when just the two of us. When we were sober, we really were the perfect couple. Time stood still when it was only he and I. I didn't care where we were or what we were doing; if I was with him, I felt happy and complete. Finally, I started to feel confident that we were truly in love with each other and decided I was ready for Jake to take my virginity.

I was only fifteen that summer. Jake and I went swimming at Lake Superior with friends earlier that day. After whispering in his ear that I was ready, we drove out to his dad's hunting camp. To say the least, it was a much less magical environment than I dreamed about for my first time. In the heat of a stuffy wooden cabin, we nervously got to business.

As the moment came, my body felt numb from the waist down. *Is this really happening?* By the time it was over, mild nausea washed over me; *I just got her sloppy seconds.* Yet I still convinced myself that I was ready and meant to be with Jake. I hadn't felt this crazy about anyone before, not even Cody.

Suddenly, it seemed like all our previous intimate encounters were just warm-ups. Now, we entered the Olympic Games of raging teenage hormones. Jake and I were going at it whenever and wherever we could find any glimpse of privacy, exploring each other's bodies like our lives depended on it. We couldn't keep our hands off each other; it had to be true love, right?

As our sexual exploration continued, so did our experimentation with alcohol. If we weren't alone in Jake's bedroom on the weekends, we were at parties getting wasted with our friends. And by wasted, I mean entirely shit-faced. My girlfriends and I would get cheap gallons of Carlo Rossi wine from friends of friends who were over twenty-one, then chug the entire jug like water. Mixing liquor, wine, beer, anything with any alcohol content was fair game. The more we drank, the more reckless each party became.

Of course, my mom couldn't know about this. She'd kill me. And ground me forever, as she often did already. So, I mastered the art of my weekly sleepovers. Sneaking out of different friends' houses to escape to the latest party. Each weekend was a quest to get more drunk than the weekend before, do more stupid shit we wouldn't remember, and puke a time or two during trips to pee in the woods before eventually crawling into someone's bed with Jake.

As we partied harder, I fought harder to protect my relationship. Besides Jake's ever-lurking prom date, there were always plenty of others present and eager to play in the game of breaking us up. Drunk boys began approaching me as drunk girls flocked to Jake, and I soaked up the attention.

It wasn't that I really wanted to make Jake jealous, at least not when I was sober. But the more I drank, the angrier I felt, and the more I wanted him to know how badly he hurt me and make sure he'd never hurt me again. One night, in the wee morning hours at the end of one of my hardest (and most embarrassing) nights of partying, I finally acted on my revenge.

Let me paint this hot mess of a scene for you. My friends had convinced one in our group to have a party while her parents were out of town. We went all out with a "Pimps n Hoes" themed party. Because that was totally cool and acceptable: to dress slutty, get shit-faced, and let the belligerence commence.

Not far into the evening, my best friend, Mel (all five feet and 100 lbs. soaking wet of her), and I drank straight from a bottle of Bacardi… and finished it. Dressed in skanky tank tops and skirts, we danced on the kitchen countertops and ran wild all over the place. I don't remember much (thank God), although I do know I fell straight on my ass down an entire flight of stairs, which led me to be carried to a bathtub as a safety precaution, you know, in case I threw up; it was the only logical place for me to rest. However, my wasted bestie found it hilarious to turn on the bathwater, which fired me up for the next round of obliterated nonsense.

I was falling all over the place. Until I briefly (or perhaps for a very long time, who knows) passed out on the kitchen floor, spread eagle with a short skirt on, with everyone at the party to sit back and take in the view. I vaguely remember Jake making an appearance at this gong show, though I tried to defer him from coming just so I could rage in all my drunken revengeful glory.

To say the least, Jake was not impressed with my level of intoxication. I believe I repeatedly questioned why he came, and after failing to coax me into leaving the party to settle down and sober up, he finally went home in frustration. But one of his friends stayed and got just as drunk as I did. After I took another break or two to pass out on a couch or the floor,

I woke up with the desire to finally give Jake a taste of his own medicine, and it filled me with a disgusting level of excitement.

Around three or four in the morning, those who lingered at the party found places to crash, and I landed in the basement with Jake's friend, alone. To be honest, I wasn't really attracted to him, nor do I think he was to me. We were attracted to the carelessness of intoxication, and I was obsessed with revenge.

Nevertheless, we kissed. And before either of us knew it, I had experienced my second sexual partner: one of my boyfriend's friends. I don't believe, nor hope, either of us remembers much of the awkwardly sloppy experience; it sure wasn't a proud moment by any means. At the time, though, it didn't matter; I claimed my vengeance. I triumphantly tied up the score. Now we were even, and the pain game could finally be over.

Although my soul felt guilty for acting against my own morals, I felt justified. If Jake experienced how painful being cheated on was, then he wouldn't do it to me again. I honestly believed this would be the end of it, and we could live happily ever after in reconciliation and peace.

Well, that might have been an almost logical scenario in a slightly less sick and twisted way had I not picked his good friend as my partner in crime. What I served back to Jake was a double stab in the back, not only by me, but also by his once-innocent friend.

Jake still forgave us, knowing first-hand exactly how drunk we both were that night. It seemed that our infidelities were cleared and behind us now… at least while we were sober. But the partying continued to get further out of control every weekend.

My mom [finally] started catching me sneaking out of the house and grounding me for it. She knew I was getting in trouble with Jake and was trying her hardest to influence me (with force) out of my relationship with him. But my stubbornness protested. *Not again! No way in hell will she tell me who I can and cannot be with.*

My mom and I quickly moved into a routine of regular screaming matches over my going out with friends. Little did she know that my anger at her was only bursts of anxiety from my need to be where Jake was. If I wasn't there, someone else would be, and I couldn't trust him to not get drunk enough to cheat on me again. It was never about the "fun" of the party; it was all about making sure that no other girls were trying to take my place. But I couldn't explain that to my mom.

To her, I seemed to be a wild and selfish little brat. Now that I was a teen, I was promoted from brat to bitch. I had no concern for anyone other than myself and my own selfish motives. And now that I had been caught lying and sneaking out of the house multiple times, I certainly couldn't be trusted.

"What the hell is wrong with you?" she'd ask in a rage every time I got caught in another lie.

Inside, my heart was screaming with anxiety. *But you have no idea what will happen if I don't go out,* I thought. *I'll lose my Goddamn mind staying locked up in this house without Jake.* I could never tell her what was really happening in our relationship; I knew she would freak out. I had to deal with it on my own. Instead of confessing my honest, heart-wrenching anxiety, I screamed back at her.

"What the hell is wrong with YOU? All of my friends' parents let them stay out late on the weekends," I shouted at her. "All my friends think you're a crazy and controlling bitch, and you know what, they're right."

"I don't give a shit what your friends' parents let them do. You're a 15-year-old, and there's no way I'm going to let you go out and run around at all hours of the night doing God knows what," she declared. "I don't know what the hell makes you think you can just do whatever you want. You're so inconsiderate of everyone else around you; I can't believe it."

These words, and many other versions like them, comprised the almost daily fights between my mom and me. And no matter what version played out, they always seemed to burn a little deeper each time. "You selfish little bitch" always stung, signaling an alarm inside the back of my brain that repeated back continuously, "You selfish bitch! You selfish bitch!"

In the moment, I never could stop and just say out loud to my mom how badly those words made me feel; I only responded with more anger and attack.

"I fucking hate you," I'd shout at her. *How are you my mother?* I thought to myself as I glared into her eyes, unable to recognize the stranger she appeared to be. *How the hell is it so hard to communicate with you?* I couldn't build the nerve to tell my truth to her out loud to her face. It felt forbidden. I had grown up with an understanding that I must do and say what pleases her to avoid her disapproval.

If I told her exactly what I was thinking or feeling in the moment, would she freak out and yell at me? Or will she just give me the silent treatment, huffing and puffing in my presence while darting around the house doing all the chores no one else helped her with? The negative energy she emitted when upset or irritated was so strong it was hard to be in the same room with her. The feeling was so unpleasant, I never found it worth it to "intentionally" upset her with my truthful words I knew she would disagree with.

Just thinking about telling her something difficult filled me with sickening anxiety. Every time, I got ridiculously choked up trying to spit my words out to her and would instead get angry and yell at her. Yet I knew I wasn't just mad at her; I was mad at myself for my inability to speak or explain myself clearly.

Instead, I did the next best thing, I tried my best to organize my words on paper so that she might understand what I was trying to explain. The words poured straight from my vulnerable heart. I cried and spent many hours writing each long letter, and as cell phones became more popular, every long text. Before sending them to her, I prayed that they might finally hold the right words that my mom could understand. Unfortunately, every time concluded with a defensive reaction that ultimately made me feel ten times worse than I did before saying anything.

My growing fear of her reaction developed a personal habit of holding things in, letting them go unheard and unaddressed until they finally burst out of me in unexpected and unpleasant ways, like screaming "I fucking hate you" in my mother's face.

And so, I was often grounded, and in my absence, it didn't take long for Jake to cheat on me again. Though we stayed together, the battle of revenge continued by taking shots, both of liquor and at each other, one drunken night at a time.

It eventually got to the point that it didn't matter if I made it to the party; infidelities happened anyway. Enemies, acquaintances, best friends... no one was off-limits when it came to the heart-breaking game of battleship between us.

We continued to steer our emotional train wreck on and off the tracks while managing to maintain a "picture perfect" appearance as the cutest high school sweethearts in public, the football player and the cheerleader. Yet every weekend, we took 'shit-faced' to a new level, both frequently crossing a new girl or boy that was just as drunk and willing to join the game of retaliation.

So, here's how our loyalty appeared to lay out: as long as we were too drunk to take responsibility for our actions, we could forgive each other and master the art of making up.

Though we couldn't control ourselves on the weekend, our relationship was completely different during the week. When it was just the two of us, sober, we *did* make the perfect couple. We played and laughed together in our own little world, where no one else seemed to exist. During the week, Jake and I got along perfectly. He treated me like a princess, always picking me up, bringing me wherever I wanted to go, and going out of his way to make our private moments together fun and romantic.

During the week, I was in love with my soul mate. He took care of me and protected me. I felt safe and secure in his presence, enough to truly make me believe that we were destined to be together. I daydreamed about our future marriage and wondered what our kids would look like. *How many kids would we have? Where would we live? What will our future look like?*

During the week, it didn't matter what we did to each other at the last out-of-control party. Our connection felt unquestionable. Jake didn't want to be with anyone else but me, and I felt like the luckiest girl in the world. For a few weeks or months at a time, at least. Before the next swing of the cheating ax struck.

Another year passed while Jake and I continuously cycled through love and laughter to betrayal and tears. Then in 2005, Jake graduated high school and left for college two hours away that fall. I was only entering my junior year of high school, yet we ignored our past's apparent warning signs and stayed together.

The distance quickly grew painful for me; I knew Jake could party even harder in college, and I couldn't be there. And, of course, my mom refused to let me go visit him. "Absolutely not. A high schooler doesn't belong on a college campus," she demanded. No matter how much I argued, screamed, and completely shut down on her, there was no convincing her.

"You selfish little bitch!" she and the voices in my head would shout back at me.

I felt like I was drowning in anxiety over not being where Jake was and keeping other girls away from him. To this day, I still don't know how often he cheated on me while he was at school. Yet every time he came home, I'd play the hopeful card of ignorance, and we'd dive right back into our romantic reunions.

Let's not forget, though, I was a master at partying and revenge myself. Although I was frequently confined to my home on the weekends by my mom, I never gave up my determination to sneak out of the house for a good party. To justify my fear of Jake's unknown infidelity, I partied with the new senior boys and my friends, carelessly soaking up the attention of the latest boy that dared to give it to me.

Eventually, the truth of Jake's college adventures slipped out one at a time, as did my own collection of dirty secrets. The stress of our distance reached a peak by mid-fall, and for the first time, we officially broke up. Well, for a few weeks at least, or long enough for me to give someone else half a chance before Jake came home again. Because every time he did, we both couldn't resist the pull right back into our old, tangled webs.

*We are just meant to be together,* I concluded. I couldn't resist falling back into Jake's comfortable and strong arms. Though I chased and had flings with a handful of other boys during our blurry break-up, I felt certain that there was no one else I truly wanted to be with but Jake. No one made me feel like he did... when we were sober, that is. Everyone else only sounded like a good idea while I was drunk and lonely at parties, or after I knew Jake hooked up with someone else.

Through it all, no one had my heart like Jake did. No one had his like I did either. If we could have only been able to resist the temptation of underage drinking, we might have had a great and stable relationship. At least we did during the week...

Two years after we first met, Jake and I were "on again." This time, my own junior prom was quickly approaching. After some resistance and resentment, I decided to take Jake to my prom. An entire group of my friends made dates with Jake's crew, including a couple of his new college friends.

We planned to pick out his tuxedo for prom during one of Jake's weekend visits. I had just finally picked out my dress, a slinky strapless lime green one, exposing under layers of vibrant pink and purple chiffon at the big slit running up one leg. Ignoring the nightmarish memories from Jake's junior prom, I focused on how damn good Jake and I were going to look together at *my* junior prom.

The day we picked out his tux was like any other ordinary day. Except when we walked into the shop (the *only* one in the area that rented prom tuxedos). We walked in to see none other than… Cody.

Cody and his date, and my fellow cheerleader, dancer, and so-so friend in our class, were also there picking out his tux. Standing right inside the door, we nearly plowed them over upon our entrance. First stunned by our coincidental timing, I then felt a wave of jealousy wash through me. *She's like his sister, and her own boyfriend won't go to prom. I* reassured myself about Cody's date. *Wait, why do I care? I'm here with Jake. Be cool.*

We politely exchanged hellos and quickly turned to page through a catalog of color swatches for vests, ties, and bows. We paused on a page of lime green as I pulled color swatches of my dress out of my purse. Suddenly, Cody's date exclaimed from behind us.

"Wait! What color is your dress?" she huffed, coming closer to get a look. "Lime green?! Ugh! No way. My dress is lime green, too!"

*Oh great,* I thought.

"Cody's wearing lime green, too. You guys are going to match!" she continued. *Are you kidding me?* I thought. *This can't be happening!*

"Well, there's pink and purple on my dress, too," I reassured the group. "We'll do pink instead." *Jake will be sexier in pink, anyway,* I thought to myself.

Cody was silent, standing back slightly with what felt like a repelling fear to get too close to me. Jake felt relaxed about it, even a bit noticeably more affectionate towards me. *Marking his territory*, I figured. I marked mine, too. *We're still together, see?* I thought, as if I were speaking telepathically to Cody. *Look how great my boyfriend is.*

After a brief exchange of comments and complaints between us girls over our dresses being the same color, Cody and his date wrapped up their rental and headed out the door.

I soon forgot about this incident in the weeks leading up to prom; I was too busy keeping tabs on Jake while he was away at college during the week and drinking until I blacked out on the weekends. By the time prom rolled around, Jake's and my friends were ready to party in style.

We passed around mini bottles of liquor before entering the prom, slamming shots as quickly as we could. The buzz kicked in as we all lined up for the Grand March, and Jake and I strutted down those stairs like we owned the place. Once the flashing cameras and crowds of family and friends left, prom-goers scurried around and took the first steps onto the dance floor. About to cross the floor, I saw Cody walking towards me.

Just like old times, the awkward eye-darting ensued. Unable to turn around and pretend I wasn't walking in his direction to begin with, I sighed with surrender and smiled at him.

"You look good tonight, Cody," I said. "And since we match so nicely, we should probably take a picture."

Bashfully looking down, he replied, "Yeah, thanks. You look nice, too. I guess we can take a picture."

I passed my camera to a nearby friend, and we hesitantly wrapped an arm around one another, faking a smile for the camera. He could barely stand next to me. I felt like an explosion went off between us. I was pulled in and blown away at the same time. As soon as the camera flashed, he stumbled away quickly, locking eyes one more time.

"Have fun tonight, Krista," he said before looking down and walking away.

I didn't see much of Cody the rest of the night. I was quickly enthralled with sneaking shots from the flasks hidden in the boys' pockets. Before long, we were drunk and dancing dirty. Our group took off to the after-party within an hour or so, where the shenanigans continued. I finally had my prom and after-party with Jake, and we had the best time together. No drama, no pain, just fun. Jake and I were back on. For good. Again.

As the school year ended, Jake surprised me with a sudden uncertainty of his future and a need to know that we would stay together. "Jake, if we're meant to be together, we'll be together. It will just work out. Don't worry about it," I assured him. For the first time, I felt relaxed, finally no longer clinging to a need to control or confirm our relationship.

Jake came home for the summer, and we returned to our old routines like they had never stopped. I felt a new confidence in our relationship, some sort of comfort that released my fears for our future. I wasn't attracted to anyone else and finally didn't feel the need to pry for others' attention out of jealousy.

Well, until we collided with my old world one night at a party. I couldn't believe I had avoided this situation until now for all the reckless parties and people that came between Jake and me. At this particular party, who did we run into? Cody.

By that time, Cody had well-established a "bad boy" reputation of his own: partying, doing drugs, skipping school, and dropping out of all the sports he was so naturally talented at. As our cliques and interests grew distant, Cody and I stopped crossing paths over the years, or perhaps my tunnel vision on Jake just blinded me from noticing him anymore. From time to time, I would hear about Cody's latest run-in with the school principal or local police, always concluding that I had "picked the right guy" in staying with Jake and his squeaky-clean reputation.

So now, at this summer party, I found myself walking next to Jake and approaching a circle of people, including Cody. I was stung with an old and familiar feeling upon entering that circle. This time, I immediately dismissed it as awkward tension between Cody and me, just like our awkward run-in at prom a few months earlier.

As we stood in that small circle in the evening darkness, I was tuned into the unspoken tension, sprinkled with a pinch of mutual respect, between Cody and Jake. However, Cody had had the same girlfriend just about as long as Jake and I had been dating, so I also sensed relieving ease as we broke the ice and got to chatting. Of course, we played it off in good fun, and plus, Cody had a joint for us to smoke.

Though the moment itself was fleeting, I'll never forget the feeling of two worlds colliding inside me. On the outside, I played it off carelessly in front of Cody, even hugging and hanging on Jake, as if to show him off as a fancy "better than you" ornament. We passed the joint around the circle, got high and giggly, and carried on our merry ways to enjoy the rest of the party.

I quickly dismissed this coincidental crossing until another chance meeting took me by surprise a few weeks later. This time, I didn't cross paths with Cody, nor did Jake. Yet our webs of relationships were entangled again…

Imagine this: there was yet another party that I couldn't get to. Our relationship felt stable for the first time, and I thought nothing of Jake drinking with his friends. That is, until he confessed a few days later.

He wanted to openly admit that he had fooled around with another girl before I heard it from anyone else. Initially repulsed that he "did it again," my anger dissolved as he dished out the details. For another first, I was delighted to hear who it was: Cody's girlfriend. I literally laughed out loud. I knew I didn't have to get revenge on Jake this time; Cody's tough-guy rage would kill him for me. Perhaps I felt a sense of comfort knowing that I shared the role of "The Betrayed" with Cody.

For a moment, I contemplated contacting Cody to discuss our shared betrayal. But I didn't. Something told me I didn't need to. I felt enough of a connection to Cody through the situation anyway; we didn't need to say words to communicate it. So I let it go, laughed it off, and continued enjoying the summer, keeping Jake by my side.

# Chapter 4

## July 2006:

## Tragedy Strikes

On an ordinary summer day, I made plans with my girlfriends to see the latest *Pirates of the Caribbean* movie at the matinee. Jake and his friends were heading out to Saxon Harbor at Lake Superior to go swimming. My friends and I were more interested in getting our Johnny Depp fix first, so we agreed to meet them afterward at the lake.

The movie ended, leaving us with a satisfying dose of sexy man pirates, and we hopped into my friend's car to meet the boys. We each tried calling one of them during our drive without any luck. They had no signal. This was no surprise; most areas near Lake Superior don't have cellular service. As we approached Saxon Harbor, our cell phones lost service, too.

Once we reached the final hill down to the harbor, we came upon a swarm of cars, people, and even an ambulance and helicopter in the harbor bay.

"Wow, what's going on?" we all asked simultaneously. We had no idea what had happened, nor who it happened to. We got out of the car and cautiously stepped closer towards the scene. I turned to ask my friends, "Do you think the guys left already?"

A split second after, I heard a voice calling my name from behind me. "Krista! Krista, do you know what happened to Jake?" I heard the voice call.

The words pierced through my chest as I turned around to a woman I had never seen before rushing towards me. I immediately teared up as my heart leaped up into my throat. *Holy shit, what is going on?!* My mind raced in panic.

"No," I spit out with a tremble in my voice. I had no idea what happened, but reality suddenly dropped on me like a bomb. The helicopter was obviously here for Jake, and it couldn't be good.

The woman introduced herself as Jake's friend's mother. "He's hurt really badly," she said carefully. "The helicopter is about to leave for Duluth. Here, follow me to the boys." She put her hands on my shaking shoulders and guided us to a vehicle with Jake's friends sitting inside.

Both boys were both crying hysterically. I had never seen either of them cry before, and their obvious shock and pain was excruciating to see. Upon being ushered into the vehicle, my friends and I burst into tears with them, still utterly clueless about what had happened.

*What in the hell is happening?! What happened to these guys?* My mind was racing just as fast as my heartbeat, which pounded a deafening beat in my ears.

"What is going on?" I finally choked out through my confused, sloppy tears. "Did you see him?"

"No," the mom replied. "They wouldn't let any of us near the ambulance, and they're about to take off."

She continued to explain, "Jake dove off the break wall and hit his head. He's hurt very badly, but I don't know how much." All of us seemed to sob harder with every word. "He's unconscious. They're airlifting him to Duluth for an MRI."

A numb daze clouded through my body as the details settled in. *This can't be real. Jake's fine. He's got to be okay.*

"I need to see him before he goes!" I blurted out. My inner bull came out after the initial blow washed through me. I demanded to see Jake and understand what was happening, but he was already going into the helicopter. No one was allowed anywhere close.

"Then I need to get to Duluth!" I declared. Though blinded in a storm of shock and confusion, I was ready to drive straight to the nearest major hospital in Duluth, Minnesota, where Jake was heading. Instead, the rest of the group in the vehicle coaxed me back down, convincing me to settle down and call my family before I went anywhere.

My friends and I got out of the car and walked to the harbor restaurant, the only place for miles with a landline. I called my mom, who had already been called and was trying with countless others to reach my cell phone that had no service. Reluctantly, I agreed to stay put until she could pick me up and drive me to Duluth herself.

The fifteen minutes I waited for my mom felt like fifteen hours. My anxiety was about to blow through my chest by the time she arrived. The next hour and forty-five minutes to Duluth were more than I could bear.

Luckily, my mom knew the Duluth hospital well, as my aunt was the head nurse of the Intensive Care Unit, exactly where Jake was. As soon as we arrived, we were told Jake was being assessed by the doctors, and we were guided to a waiting room until we could see him.

The waiting room door opened before me to reveal Jake's parents and aunt standing inside, pacing back and forth. They looked up, and we all burst into tears, rushing to each other with open arms. I had always been shy around Jake's family, but no barriers existed as we embraced one another tightly, sobbing uncontrollably.

Another eternity passed before the door opened again. All of us immediately froze. It was the doctor, with a calm and serious look on his face. He opened his mouth to begin, "The good news is that Jake is not going to die."

*What?!* My mind screamed. *That's the good news?! I didn't know that death was an option here!*

"The bad news is," the doctor continued, "that he broke his neck and severely damaged his spinal cord. He is paralyzed from the chest down…."

The entire world as I knew it froze with me. I think the doctor continued explaining Jake's condition, but I couldn't hear a thing. With my back pressed against a wall, I slowly sank down to the floor, burying my head into my knees. I could do nothing but sob as shock stabbed me from every angle.

*Paralyzed? Fucking paralyzed?!* My thoughts scrambled to analyze the reality of paralysis like I had never heard the word before. *This can't be! Not Jake! He's too big and strong to be broken. What happens now?* I was so lost in the shock of the moment; it didn't yet occur to me that this could be a permanent affair.

My consciousness returned to the room when I heard the doctor ask Jake's parents if they wanted to see him. "He's unconscious and won't likely respond, but he can hear you," the doctor warned. "If he does, be sure he doesn't turn his neck; he could do worse damage before surgery."

Both parents looked back at me, and Jake's father said, "If we can see him, Krista can come, too." He then reached out for my hand, filling my heart with overwhelming love and reassuring acceptance, and we followed the doctor into the hallway.

Our tears poured as we were guided through another doorway into a narrow room. There was Jake, lying motionless with a large brace on his neck and a breathing tube in his mouth. I let his parents walk up to either side of the bed while I stood down at his feet, unsure whether this was reality or a dream.

Jake's parents took turns talking to him, with no noticeable reaction from Jake. The nurses in the doorway reminded us that he was highly sedated and would likely not open his eyes or answer us, but he could certainly hear us. His parents continued to speak, pouring their love and promises out to Jake that everything was going to be alright. We couldn't see much more than a twitch of Jake's eyes. Then, his father looked at me and said, "Come on up here, don't you be shy."

I tried to swallow as I hesitantly stepped forward to Jake's side. I felt paralyzed myself, with no clue what to do or what to say.

"Hi, Jake," I stuttered out with a quiver in my voice.

Immediately, Jake's eyes opened wide and looked over, sending waves of awe and tears around the room. He turned his head to look at me, and the room swirled into a panic.

"Jake, don't move your head! You need to keep your neck straight!" the nurses and his parents exclaimed in unison. But every time I spoke, he kept turning to look at me. I leaned in as close as I could without falling on top of him to help keep his neck straight.

Jake attempted and struggled to speak with the breathing tube in his mouth. I read his lips, saying, "I'm sorry."

The room roared in tears.

"It's okay, Jake! Don't be sorry." My heart sank in guilt that these were his first words after such major trauma. "You're going to be okay, and I'm going to be right here," I assured him through stammering tears.

After what only felt like a few seconds, the nurses said it was time for us to go and that we could see Jake again once he was settled in the Intensive Care Unit. After another agonizing wait, we were finally led to his new room, where I immediately pulled up a chair to the side of his bed, staring at him in disbelief.

*This can't be real*, I thought to myself. *How could my big, strong Jake be paralyzed?*

His surgery was scheduled for early the following day, which turned out to be the longest day ever. I don't remember exactly how many hours his surgery lasted, but to me, it felt like it took until the end of eternity. I sat in a waiting room with his mom and aunt, sometimes pacing anxiously back and forth or sitting silently with a blank stare of fear and disbelief.

*Is this really happening?* I'd ask myself in my head each time I came to and realized again where I was. *Is Jake going to be okay?*

Just when I thought I would die from anticipation, a nurse came into the room. "The family of Jake Gertz?" she called out.

"Yes, yes! That's us!" Jake's mom exclaimed.

"Jake is just getting out of surgery now; it went very well," the nurse said. "They were able to take bone from his hip and replace part of his vertebrae. He's got a large scar down the back of his neck and a smaller one from the front. They also put a halo on him to hold his neck straight while it heals. Don't be alarmed; there are four screws into his head to hold the halo in place."

*Holy shit*, I thought to myself. *I can't believe this is happening. Are we sure we're talking about my Jake?*

"Are we able to see him yet?" his mom asked through soft tears.

"Yes, please follow me," the nurse replied, slowly turning to open the doors behind her and leading us down another hallway.

As we came to Jake's doorway, my heart was beating so hard, I was sure that everyone across the building could hear it. With no idea what kind of condition he would be in, I braced myself and followed his parents into the room. My heart dropped to the floor as I laid eyes on Jake, who lay motionless in the bed before me.

I had never seen a halo before, and it looked terrifying. A colossal harness wrapped around Jake's chest and held metal bars connected to the "halo" around his head. My eyes drew straight to the screws of the halo that embedded into his forehead. *Wow, this can't be real,* I thought again. *But it is real. What the hell really happened out at that lake to do this to him?*

Over the next few days, I collected the details of the accident. The boys dove off one of the harbor break-walls to swim to the opposite side. Jake dove in last and happened to hit his head on a sandbar about five feet below water level that had recently formed during the ongoing reconstruction of the harbor's pier.

Realizing that Jake did not come back up from his dive, his friends first thought he was joking. When Jake still didn't come to the surface, the boys swam back to where they dove in to find him. One of them was able to stand on that same sandbar and look down into the water, finding Jake drowning below.

In shock and instant survival mode, the boys lifted Jake's head above water, screaming for help. By the grace of God, a boat was entering the harbor, and its driver happened to be a paramedic on vacation that day. Immediately coming to their rescue, the boat's passengers helped lift Jake onboard.

The angelic paramedic captain gave Jake CPR as they rushed to the nearest dock. Calls for help gathered nearby boaters and campers; many were also paramedics and nurses on camping vacations. These angels in disguise continued CPR tirelessly, losing Jake's heartbeat several times before an ambulance arrived about twenty minutes later.

As phone calls were made, including to me, my friends and I were already past the point of no cell service on our drive to the lake. By the time Jake's parents were reached, they were told to drive straight to Duluth, where I eventually met them in the waiting room of excruciating suspense.

I stayed by Jake's side in the hospital for the next two months, literally sitting at his bedside day in and day out, only leaving to spend the evenings at various local hotels and campus dorm rooms with his parents and aunt.

I never thought I could get so close to his family so quickly. Once known as Jake's shy and quiet girlfriend, they watched me break out of my shell over the months we unexpectedly lived together. Experiencing this shocking wake-up call to the fragility of life and physical mobility, my walls came crashing down. I suddenly couldn't think of anything to hide or be shy about anymore. Experiencing this together, both of our families united unanimously to support each other and help take care of Jake.

The last three years of drama with Jake instantly dissolved. The silly games of drinking and cheating were rendered insignificant. I couldn't be mad at him anymore, and neither could my parents. Their worries over Jake and I partying and having sex came to a screeching halt. Without hesitation, my parents did all they could to support Jake and his family, including letting me live in Duluth to stay close to the hospital. I know they hated it, but you know me, I was too stubborn to move. I refused to leave Jake's side. This time, my mom let me do what I wanted, and felt I needed, to help Jake.

I was quickly introduced as Jake's girlfriend to all the family, friends, and community members who came to visit Jake and wish for his recovery and healing. Every new introduction made me realize, *this is it*. The more people I met, the more I felt destined to take care of Jake for the rest of his life. At seventeen, the fate of this accident convinced me that I'd undoubtedly marry Jake, take care of him, and see him through total recovery.

Still in disbelief of our new reality, I fully intended to see his complete healing. I wasn't ready to face the truth of this permanence. Especially after I learned that Jake didn't completely cut his spinal cord, I sought relentless optimism. *Jake will walk again, and we'll be just fine*, I constantly reassured myself.

I promised myself that Jake would be a living miracle. I believed that his spinal cord would heal itself. In hindsight, it's debatable whether that optimism was true faith or my own selfish wishes. Jake was the one who drove me around and helped me do all the tough, manly things. But now, the roles reversed, and I wasn't sure that I was strong enough to take on this role. However, this bull never turned down a good challenge. I sat by his side tirelessly, confident that my support would heal him.

The strength of the bull drained out of me at an alarming rate, though. Maintaining my initial level of optimism grew more difficult as each long day dragged on. Every day played out a traumatic version of *Groundhog Day*, repeating the same experience of fear, sorrow, and resistance to reality over and over again.

Day in and day out, Jake's family and I settled into a routine. I spent all day in the hospital on the same chair next to Jake's bed for most of my waking hours. I was seen at his side so often, the chair was named my "perch" by nurses and family. I occasionally switched it up and moved my chair to the other side of his bed before returning to curling up in a ball on my seat, leaning against the bed rail, and praying silently that this, too, shall pass.

From my perch, I sat and watched my boyfriend deteriorate before my eyes. At 6'1", Jake was about 220 lbs. of husky muscle on the day of his accident. Since then, I witnessed his body shrink day by day until his arms were smaller than my own. Jake often refused to eat from nausea and pure misery, and as his weight continued to drop, I became the staff's helpful "assistant" as the only one who could occasionally get him to eat.

Eating wasn't the only sore subject I was tasked to handle with Jake. I was his girlfriend, and therefore the person he felt most comfortable confiding in. And Jake had a lot more on his mind than the hospital food. He was angry. He was robbed of his freedom. He was depressed about his hopeless future. And he had no way to escape; he was literally paralyzed and trapped in a hospital bed, at the mercy of strangers to take care of his most basic needs.

My "perch" also served as my new therapy office. Each day, I sat and listened, letting Jake release his pain by yelling at me with his frustrations whenever we had a moment of privacy in his room. These "vent sessions" blurred right into the repetition of our *Groundhog Day* routine. Though my own empathic and guilt-stricken consciousness has since blocked out full memory of many of Jake's heart-breaking rants, I can still feel the following words cut right through my heartstrings:

"If I have to live in a wheelchair, I'm going to kill myself," he growled.

Hearing these words hurt so bad that I couldn't stop myself from crying. Though I had trained myself to dish out words of support and encouragement tirelessly, I don't remember how I responded to this one. I'm not sure that I ever actually did. It stunned me. Every time. Because if I were in Jake's place, I would want to kill myself, too.

How do you comfort someone who has just lost their most basic human capabilities with mere words? I don't think any words can provide that comfort. That kind of comfort doesn't even exist. And though I wasn't the one permanently immobilized, the idea of life-ending, at this point, started to sound more tempting to me, too.

Our *Groundhog Day* story dragged on through the summer until it was time for me to prepare for school again. I was about to enter my senior year, yet the excitement I had my entire life for this year was now non-existent. I couldn't think about focusing on anything other than Jake. I was permanently attached to my perch at his side. Nothing else could be more important than making sure Jake healed.

My stubbornness couldn't hold up to reality, though. I had to go back to school. This meant no more living near the hospital. I had to go back home and to school five days a week. I promised Jake I would come to Duluth every weekend until he could go home, too.

I reluctantly entered my last year of high school. By this point, our entire small community was aware of Jake's accident. Plus, our relationship was very well-known through the school, and I appeared to be the key person to ask about Jake's condition.

I was immediately approached by teachers and staff, asking how Jake was doing. The response in my mind always went something like this: *Are you kidding me? He's fucking paralyzed! And telling me every day that he will kill himself if he has to live in a wheelchair. He's miserable, I'm miserable, and I wish I could strangle you for even asking!*

However, the words that filtered through my thickening mask of optimism went something more like this, "Oh, he's doing great, given the conditions. He's still alive, he's healthy, and hanging in there. We can't wait for him to come home!"

About twenty times a day, I was confronted by this question, and every time, my chest tightened. Heartbeat racing. Palms sweating. I thought my nerves over parties and Jake's cheating were terrible, but now, anxiety swallowed me whole. Every morning filled me with fear of having to face that question again with a smile on my face. As the questions and overwhelming sense of being watched and gossiped about continued, my anxiety skyrocketed until my body felt ready to explode through my skin.

After several emotional breakdowns in front of my parents at home, they suggested that I talk to my doctor about options to help my anxiety, who quickly prescribed me an antidepressant. She warned me that it may take a while for my body to adjust to it, and she was right. The first week was rough; my mind seemed to be spinning out of control with intense up and down mood swings. *This is making me feel even worse!* I thought to myself. I couldn't handle feeling any worse; I needed an escape and just wanted to be numb.

Since I knew I couldn't hide and drink all day to numb myself, I started smoking pot regularly. I adopted a routine of getting high with a close friend before school. Every day. I didn't think I could handle walking into the building without the high to pad my anxiety. I became afraid of sobriety altogether; it made me face reality. Reality was no longer something I could accept or handle, so neither was sobriety.

My weekends remained dedicated to returning to my perch at Jake's side. Except now, I smoked pot in my car the whole drive to Duluth and back. At least now that I was high all the time, and my antidepressant seemed to be slowing down my inner emotional rollercoaster, the sharp pain of reality became fuzzy enough to daze my way through.

Now let me tell you, this new weekend routine of sitting in a hospital instead of going to parties was unfamiliar. Especially now that I was constantly craving any kind of buzz to free me from my living nightmare, I let resentment begin to build towards Jake's unfortunate fate. Not only did I have to deal with the demands of his caregiving, I had to miss out on all the opportunities to drink until I couldn't feel.

By the end of September, I was burnt out. Literally. Exhausted from school and being high around the clock, I tried to maintain my involvement in dance classes and as captain of the cheerleading team during the week before heading back to the hospital on the weekends, feeling angry at the world through it all. I felt bitter with Jake for getting hurt. Though looking at him made my heart break with compassion, love, and hope for his future, I wanted to be mad at him for trapping me in this fate, especially after all the pain he put me through before getting hurt. I felt locked in a cage of my own life, with no way out.

# Chapter 5

## October 2006:

## The Blond Boy Returns... Again

Later that fall, Jake's condition wasn't improving much. He still could hardly eat and continued disappearing before us, losing about eighty pounds during his three-month hospital stay in Duluth. His family started contemplating other options; there had to be somewhere to access the best care available for his injury.

Jake's doctors informed us of a Colorado hospital that specialized in brain and spinal cord injuries. There was no other hospital in the country with their experience and specialty. After a couple weeks of difficult discussions, decisions, and more tears, Jake was loaded on a stretcher into a small private plane and flown to Colorado.

I was a nervous wreck the day of Jake's flight. Already conditioned to a constant state of anxiety, processing another sudden change just wasn't possible. My internal "shock tank" had overflowed, and anything new just spilled over, trickling numbness through me instead. I was also conditioned to take care of Jake around the clock. I needed to be at his side to ease his angry and troubled mind. I believed my love and support could help him heal. I couldn't grasp the concept of him moving one thousand miles away. But when I tried, I admit to feeling a fleeting relief, too.

It was pure waterworks as the flight paramedics rolled Jake's stretcher outside to his private plane. I marched alongside, holding Jake's hand with tears running down my face. Time slowed down to sloth speed, and I felt an unbearable pressure building throughout my body. The nightmare of reality reached a new climax. And all the uninvestigated emotions I stuffed down were ready to explode.

Jake's family and I stood there, hugging one another as our tears poured out, watching his plane take off into the distance. One by one, we slowly turned back toward the door we came out of. As I stepped inside, it was like I stepped into another dimension. The chains holding me to the side of Jake's bed were broken. I was free.

Free to completely crumble, that is.

No longer driving to Duluth every weekend, I ran straight into a race against reality and sobriety as fast as possible. As I delved deeper into partying, I slowly drifted from my "normal" clique of friends and closer to whoever had drugs to numb me with. Besides the second antidepressant I was prescribed by this point, a new concoction of Klonopin, Xanax, and Adderall frequently swam with the alcohol through my bloodstream.

Then somewhere in the blur of a Friday or Saturday night, I eventually ran into a wall of my past I couldn't ignore. At the parties with all the best drugs, who else was there, but Cody.

From across the dim room, Cody and I shared a look that seemed to acknowledge our past and traumatic paths that had led us to the present moment. A new buzz washed over me, one not induced by drugs. It was familiar. Electric. For the moment, at least, until I was passed a joint and took the biggest rip my lungs could handle to float me back to my cloud of darkness.

My hazy path continued crossing with Cody's. I soon found myself shifting into a long-lost pattern, looking for him at school and parties. I wanted to know where he was, even though he was always running from his own life, a moving target that was hard to find.

One night, I was with a small group of friends, Cody included, that dwindled as the night went on. When the wee hours of the morning approached, the last few of us wandered over to our friend's apartment in town. Eventually, everyone else left or fell asleep, leaving Cody and me alone on the couch.

As our whispering discussion quieted, the attraction between us grew. Every few minutes, Cody leaned in closer to me. Butterflies flapped in my stomach. Guilt rose as the compromising situation I willingly put myself in dawned on me, but that guilt grew slower than the overwhelming return of electricity between Cody and me.

Mid-sentence, we both lost focus on the conversation, locking eyes without looking away for the first time in years. Cody leaned in closer. My heart pounded through my ears. The magnetic field around us pulsed as the distance between us disappeared. The force became too strong to resist; I surrendered to an impulse, wrapping my arms around his neck, pulling him in for a kiss. *Oh my God*, did his kiss feel *good*.

The sensation of Cody's arms around me and lips on mine sent bone-chilling waves down my spine. I completely lost myself in the moment, suspended in this electrical connection, until my guilty conscience yanked me back down to earth.

Reality suddenly slapped me in the face; I was kissing someone who was *not* Jake! I pressed my hands against Cody's chest and pushed him away in panic.

"Oh my God, I can't do this!" I exclaimed. "I'm with Jake; I can't do this. I can't do this to him. We have to stop."

I watched his eyes as my words struck him. He backed off slightly, and I felt his energy sink in disappointment. "Shit, I'm so sorry," he apologized, "I just couldn't help it. I don't want you to do anything you don't want to do."

This shouldn't have been anything new for me. You already know that drinking and cheating was no new rodeo. But this time was different. My relationship with Jake had changed so much since his accident. Our reckless past dissolved away, and now, I was obligated to Jake for the rest of my life. This drunken carelessness wasn't allowed to happen anymore. I was going to marry Jake, and that was final; we couldn't continue this unrealistic fantasy. But every time I looked straight into Cody's eyes, I lost myself.

*His eyes are like bottomless oceans of seduction. What was I saying again?* I wondered. *I have no idea, and I don't care. This high just feels too good.*

Instead of standing firm and removing myself from the situation, I kept leaning in for another passionate kiss. I let the current of attraction pull me in further before my next guilt-stricken objection broke the circuit. Yet every time I pushed Cody away, I got lost in his eyes and pulled him back in. This game of push and pull became one of the most intense experiences in my memory. I don't know who won; I pulled just as much as I pushed until there was only pulling him closer.

Then Cody slipped his hand around my waist, pulling my hips up to his, and laid me down on the couch. The weight of his body on top of mine felt like a magical sandbag of bliss! I forgot how comforting the weight and embrace of a body felt on top of me. The heat rose like an inferno between us. Time seemed to stop; I was entirely consumed by the moment. The sensory overload shot me higher than any buzz had done before. It was breathtaking. Until I felt something fall within my consciousness and crash to the rock bottom of reality.

"Holy shit, what are we doing?!" I panicked, pushing Cody away from my body. I burst into tears. "Oh my God. I can't do this to Jake. This will kill him."

Taken aback, Cody looked stunned. "I'm so sorry, Krista," he apologized, choking back his own guilt. "This is my fault. I don't want to hurt you. I don't want to hurt him. I just couldn't help it."

"I need to get the fuck out of here!" I demanded. We shuffled around gathering pieces of clothes before slipping out of the apartment in silence. I got into my car, looked back at Cody standing in the doorway, and drove away.

After sneaking back into my parents' house, I laid in bed and stared at the ceiling. Thoughts of despair and disgust torrented my mind. *I'm the biggest piece of shit,* I told myself. *I can never see Cody again.* Then with a breath of hope, I thought, *at least I stopped it before it finished,* as if Jake might appreciate that sliver of distinction. *Ugh, I'm disgusting.*

Yet I couldn't deny a deep longing inside me. I saw something inside Cody that I was longing for within myself. But that longing triggered nauseating guilt in my stomach. *What am I going to do?*

The following Monday, my Cody radar was on an all-time high. I jumped out of bed, excited to go to school for the first time in what felt like forever. I couldn't wait to feel that electric energy again. It was such a breathtaking experience; the rest of the world seemed to freeze around us. It dissolved my deeply depressing reality. It was a greater escape than any drink or drug had yet given me. I didn't care what else happened through the day; I couldn't pull my focus away from wondering where he was, what he was doing, and when I could get him alone again.

I'm not sure what motivated my urge to see Cody more: to feel our electric energy, or just to know where he was, out of control like my typical behavior with Jake. Part of me was terrified that Cody had just used me for the sake of evening entertainment and that I had cheated on my paralyzed boyfriend for nothing. But another part of me held a spark of hope, longing to feel that connection again.

Cody remained a moving target, though. And this was before everyone had cell phones. He didn't have one. So, unable to contact him, I could only rely on my Cody radar to sense and attract him.

I only saw him once as he walked past my classroom that day. My anxiety shot up as I recognized him, and it took all I had to contain myself from running after him. A few more days passed without any opportunity to talk about the weekend before. In the silence of those few days, I spiraled down a path of self-loathing. *How stupid am I?* I kept asking myself. *Of course, he used me. We all know that I haven't gotten any action in a long time; I was an easy target. I bet he just used me to get back at me for our past, too.*

I didn't see him again until later that week at a blood drive. I assume we both signed up to donate blood just to get out of school for a few hours, not that they would use our drug-infused blood, anyway.

I knew he was near when I felt the familiar old shock of energy, this time with an extra jolt of anxiety. Looking through the crowd, I spotted Cody walking from the opposite direction.

My heart skipped. He was with another friend. *Play it cool, Krista. But shit, I need to talk to him before I burst!* We hesitantly approached one another, making small talk with his friend for a few minutes. Finally, after being assigned to new waiting lines by name, I was able to catch a private word with Cody before parting.

"So, we really need to talk. I feel terrible," I said, looking straight into those deep blue eyes. I immediately forgot all the words I wanted to say to blame him for using me and ruining my relationship.

"I know we do, Krista. So do I," he replied, keeping our eyes locked. "I'm so sorry. I don't want you to feel bad. Let's talk tonight."

My heart skipped two beats. One in excitement to be with him again. The second in remorse for my excitement. *Ugh, I'm the worst person in the world,* I thought to myself. *I just need to clear the air with Cody and carry on with Jake. Then it will all be okay.*

This plan worked well in my mind until it came time to say the words aloud to Cody. It took yet another day of nail-biting suspense before we found a few moments alone. We took a ride in his latest vehicle, the "Chum Bucket," as he had adoringly named it.

"I didn't want to ignore you all week," Cody began while he parked to roll us a joint to smoke. "I just feel so bad. This is my fault. I couldn't help myself. I mean, it's you. But I know you can't. And I actually just started talking to someone else."

A lump closed my throat. *There's someone else in this mess, too?* I thought. *I can't believe I fell for this and put Jake's heart at stake for it, too!*

"Are you kidding me? You're seeing someone else, and you still went for it with me, knowing Jake's my boyfriend and fucking paralyzed? What the hell did you drag me into this for?" I shouted at him with tears rolling down my face. I felt shattered all over again, though I didn't know whose heart was breaking. Mine? Jake's? The other girl's? Cody's? Perhaps all of the above.

Cody teared up, too. "Krista, I'm so sorry. I never thought I'd ever be in that position with you again, and I couldn't control myself in the moment."

He continued to explain that he felt like he had to stay away from me after our encounter. I wasn't the only one condemned with guilt for what happened between us. He felt sick over the thought of being "the physically capable asshole that stole Jake's girlfriend." Now, clearly learning that he couldn't control himself around me, he thought the best solution was to stay away altogether.

Cody continued explaining that he wasn't actually dating anyone… yet. He was "just hanging out" with another girl he found intriguingly intelligent and comfortable talking to. He claimed they hadn't "done anything yet," though I didn't believe it. I had been partying long enough to know his reputation. Now that he and his former long-term girlfriend were broken up, if he didn't blackout at a party first, he slept with someone.

Nausea churned in my stomach as I listened, deeming myself a disgusting dirty whore and nothing but the latest addition to his fast-growing list of girls. But the nausea disappeared into a glimmer of hope every time I looked into those eyes; I swore I could see something hiding deep within them. Something so pure and innocent, yet so painful, seemed desperate to be seen and kept hidden at the same time.

*He's not the tough, rebellious guy he appears to be on the outside,* I thought. The world around me froze as I stared into the labyrinth of tiny white swirls entangling his dreamy blue eyes. *There's so much more in there; if only he would let it out.* Lost in his gaze, I naturally leaned in closer. *Oh shit, snap out of it!* I suddenly realized, jerking backward in my seat.

"It's bad enough hurting Jake. I can't hurt anyone else," I declared, reaching for the joint and sucking in the largest hit my lungs could contain. "I can't get in the way of you and someone else. I'm already in my own way. We just can't do this."

Cody's eyes sunk, although nodding in agreement, taking back the joint for another big hit. He, too, didn't want to hurt anyone. He admitted the girl he was talking to was really kind, and he didn't want to risk ruining at least their friendship while damaging my relationship with Jake. We agreed to stay away from each other and continue with the people we were clearly meant to be with.

Then we locked eyes again. *God, what is it in those eyes?* I wondered. *They're telling me something, and it's important. Why can't he just say it?* As quickly as I thought it, I knew the answer. He was locked in his own reality, just as I was in mine. Realizing this mutual sense of entrapment filled me with comfort. We sat and stared in silence. Though we stopped saying words, it felt like our eyes spoke a thousand conversations that drew me in like a magnet. Before I knew it, I was sucked into a vortex of overwhelming passion, with Cody's lips on mine.

*God damnit, Krista! Control yourself!* Reality slapped me in the face again. *Think about Jake. He's alone in a hospital bed in Colorado, wanting to kill himself. He needs me. Stop being selfish and do what's right.*

We finally ended another game of push and pull, filling the voids of our truth with apologies and promises that we wouldn't do it again. I filled my mind with thoughts of Jake's pain to distract me long enough until Cody dropped me off, down the street from my home, so my mom wouldn't see.

I got out of the car and looked back at Cody. I could hear those eyes screaming something, but I couldn't make out the words. I turned and walked away; my mind moved me forward while my heart tugged me back.

*Nope, don't do it. Don't look back.* I kept walking until I heard his car drive away. *Let it go. Don't look back. You're doing the right thing.*

After my rendezvous with Cody, I was utterly disgusted with myself. Without the guts or heart to confess to Jake, I couldn't handle being sober at all anymore. I smoked weed and popped pills before entering the school building every morning. I felt so hopeless, unable to help Jake from a thousand miles away, unable to focus on anything at school, and unable to admit how trapped and worthless I felt inside.

I especially couldn't admit how I felt to Jake. Though I was crumbling before the entire community, I was still Jake's rock. Though a thousand miles apart, we talked on the phone every day. Hearing only his voice, I could pretend he wasn't hurt. My mind pictured my once independent and capable boyfriend. I imagined him walking, running, and even carrying me on his back. Until he vented his anger at the world to me, that is, and I drowned in the pain behind his voice. Trying to find words to comfort him was like trying to get out of quicksand, and by this point, I was sinking in over my head.

Still unable to fathom his freak accident and paralysis, my heart ached for Jake. As a natural empath, I couldn't stop my imagination from stepping into his shoes one hundred times a day. Nausea constantly stirred in my stomach as visions of Jake nearly drowning and dying flashed through my mind. From his perspective, I often pictured myself lying in Jake's hospital bed, wondering what it'd be like to have the screws of a halo embedded into my skull. My chest tightened every time I thought about how miserable Jake must be… and how much more heartbroken he would be to know how pathetic I had become.

I lost count of the times I choked back tears at school. All it took was one thought of Jake's accident, which was hard to avoid at school; nearly every person I crossed asked how he was doing. But the tears snuck up most while sitting silently in class. The same image of Jake floating helplessly underwater haunted me, immediately welling my eyes with guilt and despair.

Once my morning high faded at school, and I was left with only the lukewarm numbness of my latest antidepressant, my anxiety rose so quickly that my brain shut down from all comprehension of consequences. I didn't care what happened to me anymore. I had to escape before I exploded, so I walked right out of the building. Outside, I found brief relief in the fresh air and every step I took further away.

I closed the door to my car before opening the floodgate of tears. I sat there, sobbing in a tortuous mess of emotions. Sadness. GUILT. Shame. GUILT. Anger. GUILT. Hopelessness. GUILT.

From there, if I couldn't find someone else skipping school to get high with, I'd sneak home and crawl into bed. My parents sometimes stopped at home from work, initially shocked to find me there during the school day. But upon seeing them, I burst back into tears. They couldn't deny how depressed I was, and they didn't know how to help. My dad was quiet, though his eyes exposed his concern and exhaustion from trying to find anything to help lift me out of the dark, deep hole I was in. My mom tried tirelessly to convince me to speak with a counselor, but the thought of having to explain my situation and problems to a stranger made me sick. Being in school and answering the same questions every day was bad enough. Plus, I couldn't imagine confessing to anyone what was really going on in my mind.

My mind was lost in a daze of shock, still dwelling on disbelief, and replaying the tape like one of those don't-want-to-look-but-can't-stop-watching horror movies. I couldn't concentrate on school or conversations with friends. My body continued going through the motions, but my mind was constantly searching for something to numb and distract it from berating myself... or thinking about Cody.

It didn't take long for Cody and me to meet again. Naturally, I had joined him as a prime participant at the wildest parties. And just as naturally, we couldn't fight or hide our attraction for very long.

One night, my friend and I had a brilliant idea to drive to a nightclub two hours away; the dance floor was open to teens that night. We devised a plan to "sleepover" at her house, even though it was Wednesday. Since we had school the next day, it was no surprise my mom immediately said no.

"I'm just so fucking depressed," I confessed to her. "If you let me sleepover here tonight, I promise I'll finally see a counselor."

My mom couldn't turn down my promise; she knew how desperately I needed help. She reluctantly agreed, told me she loved me, and we hung up the phone. Though I was extremely depressed, I had no desire or intention to talk to a counselor about it; I just needed an excuse to stay out and go to this club... especially because Cody was going.

Four of us drove to the club that night in my little red SUV. We took turns driving as we passed a pipe around until the car was clouded with smoke. A bottle of booze hid under the seat between rounds of shots. Once we pulled into the parking lot, everyone took a snort of Adderall off a paper plate with a rolled-up dollar bill. I think it's safe to say that we all had a strong buzz going as we entered the club, heading straight for the dance floor.

The club was packed with people. Colorful beams of light flashed through the darkness to the beat of the heavy bass pounding through a wall of speakers. The floor was sticky from spilled drinks. The room reeked of sweat and alcohol. I couldn't hear myself speak. Or think. But I had nothing to think about besides getting lost in the sea of strangers and dancing with Cody.

Cody and I were together in public for the first time, and nobody cared. No one knew us here. No one was watching. So, we danced all night like no one was. I lost all sense of time and space as I got lost in Cody's eyes and the sway of his body. Completely consumed by one another, we danced until we were dripping sweat. We didn't leave the dance floor until closing time, which seemed to come way too early.

The drive home sucked. Long and draining, we each took turns driving while the others slept. I had the last shift, hardly able to keep my eyelids open until finally rolling into town somewhere around 4:00 a.m. Exhausted, we all stumbled into my friend's apartment to pass out for a couple of hours before school. Unbelievably, we made it to school, though un-showered and probably still reeking of the sweaty, drunken dance floor from just hours earlier. I didn't care what I looked or smelled like, though; I just had the best night of my life.

However, now I had to see a counselor. My mom immediately scheduled an appointment, and I dreaded every moment leading up to it. My mom insisted she drive me down for the first visit at an office about an hour out of town. I didn't speak a word through the drive and listened to angry rock music on my new iPod the entire way. Finally, we pulled up to a small office building, where my mom led me to a glass door covered with a decal of a cloudy blue sky.

Two couches sat along the walls of the warm waiting room. A round table stood in the corner with piles of coloring books and a bucket of crayons on top. A small bookshelf lined the opposite wall, filled with a colorful array of worn-out books. *Hm,* I thought. *At least it's cozy.* I still felt sick with dread.

My mom and I each sat on a couch in silence for the next few minutes. Suddenly, I heard footsteps and looked up to see a tall woman enter the doorway. Her thick blonde-grey hair danced across her shoulders as a warm smile spread across her round face. A pair of blue glasses slid down her nose as she made eye contact with me. She took a deep breath in and out before speaking. I already felt invaded. *Is she looking into my soul right now?* I wondered.

"Hi, I'm Suzanne," she said. "Are you Krista?"

"Yes," I said coldly.

"And you must be Mom?" Suzanne said, turning to my mother with a smile. They made brief introductions before my mom offered a summary of my backstory for me. *Thank God, spare me from having to say it,* I thought. *And for delaying my interrogation with this woman alone.* The delay was short-lived, though; within minutes, Suzanne invited me into a tiny, private room with only two chairs. My mom said she'd be back in an hour and left.

*Ugh,* I thought. *I can't believe I'm doing this.* I knew Suzanne could sense my resistance. She spoke in the kindest voice and kept looking straight into my eyes. Though her stare made me feel vulnerable and exposed, I sensed she was looking at me like a real human, and not a mess to be worried about like my mom and everyone else seemed to. Still, I dug my heels into my resistance, answering her questions with a sharp attitude.

We didn't seem to get far in that first session. I wanted to hate everything about it and refused to let Suzanne in. If I was going to keep pulling off my sleepovers and sweet escapes with Cody, though, I had to keep my end of the bargain with my mom. So, I reluctantly agreed to bi-monthly sessions, where I slowly opened to Suzanne, who patiently accepted my teenage angst and depression. Though she would eventually soften my edges and become one of my closest confidants to this present day, I fought our destined relationship, kicking and screaming, for another few months. Until I felt comfortable enough to talk about Cody. It wasn't

Jake's accident that was tormenting me now, it was my longing for the person I wasn't supposed to want, and no one knew I had…

In our small town, Cody and I returned to hiding our undeniable attraction. It was no surprise to see us both at parties by this point. But now, we started sneaking away when we thought no one was watching to be alone, smoke weed, and "talk."

I mean, believe it or not, we really did talk. About the twisted truths and pains of our lives, our hopes for the future, and the aspects of ourselves that we felt no one else could see except for each other. And every time we reached that point in our conversation where we felt seen and understood by the other, our eyes locked. And then we "talked."

I couldn't help melting in the comfort of someone who also felt trapped in his own life. Cody had lost his father to cancer just months before we met at camp in the sixth grade. Since then, he became very protective over his mom as his disdain grew for his abusive stepfather, often drawing him into physical fights. The tension at home bled into the rest of his life; he quit playing the sports he was so naturally good at, skipped school constantly, and developed a reputation for his short temper and being the guy you didn't want to get in a fight with.

As we confessed more stories to each other during our private getaways, I learned why my mom tried to keep me away from Cody years ago. Yes, his home life was not healthy. No, he did not have a "good" reputation. *But those eyes.* They drew me into their labyrinth, like a magnet. And the deeper I gazed, the louder they silently cried out to be seen for who Cody was on the inside, not the hard shell he grew on the outside.

Behind those blue eyes, there was an insanely intelligent and sensitive soul. Though he couldn't care less about his grades, the one class he loved was the CAD (Computer-Aided Drafting) class offered at our local community college. Cody would glow with excitement talking about computers, and I would soon watch him take computers apart and rebuild them in pure joy like a kid in a candy store. He would giggle like a small child just talking about it. Cody also secretly loved the game *Dungeons and Dragons*. Though he was embarrassed at first, he glowed just as brightly trying to explain the game to me. This "hard-ass" tough guy was really a sweet super-nerd on the inside, and I couldn't get enough of it.

These "escapes" with Cody became my newest addiction. Alone with him, the rest of the world didn't matter; it stopped altogether. The troubles of my real life temporarily disappeared, and Cody's presence made me feel loved, understood, and worthy of walking this earth. Though his life had always been difficult, he cared so much about bringing me comfort. Someone caring about *my* needs? And not judging or telling me what I should do? I couldn't believe it! His presence and words filled me with peace, a sensation I hardly recognized anymore. But once I did, that peace sank like a giant boulder of guilt in my gut.

"Let's get high!" became my most common phrase. *Get me high until the guilt goes away, so my head can enjoy this moment as much as my heart wants to.*

I was chasing high after high at this point anyway, but I grew a particular need to drink, smoke, or snort pills in Cody's presence. According to the unspoken rule Jake and I had clearly laid over our relationship, cheating didn't count if we weren't sober. I thought I could justify being with Cody by being "too fucked up." It made me feel less guilty. Well, at least temporarily.

Plus, Cody had connections to drugs, so I always knew I could get high with him. However, he *hated* it. He, unlike me, was searching for a reason to stay sober. He wanted to be sober with me. Unlike most of his life, he wanted to be fully present with me. I wanted it, too, but I was too scared. I couldn't live with my guilt in sobriety, so I kept pushing him to find weed, speed, or alcohol whenever we made plans together. He gently tried to steer us away from it or tell me he couldn't get anything. But my stubborn sober ass would push until he caved. And just to make me happy, he'd get it.

My strongest addiction became a blur. Was I addicted to the high of drugs, or being near Cody? Whether high or sober, when Cody wasn't around, I felt like I was flailing around desperately in a torrent sea, searching for a life preserver between the waves. And when he came around, Cody was that life preserver.

In his presence, I could breathe. My head rose above the water. I was supported. When it felt as though everyone else just watched and gossiped behind my back, Cody faced my front. He looked straight through my eyes and into my soul, telling me that he loved me and that

I would do great things in this world. Looking back into his eyes, I felt *understood*. I felt loved, without judgment; maybe I wasn't such a piece of shit after all.

As happy as I felt with Cody, I was still with Jake. The entire community knew me as Jake's girlfriend. What kind of selfish evil bitch would I be if I left Jake for Cody? Thinking about it made me sick, and I thought about it around the clock.

*Could I just turn back time?* Back to the eighth grade, before I pushed Cody away for the first time. Or back to the start of my relationship with Jake, before I forgave him for cheating on me the first time. I'd go back to *any* time before I cornered myself into this cage. Before this cage locked, leaving Jake with the key and Cody outside its door.

Jake wasn't the only one with a key to my cage. My mom possessed the other. We quickly returned to our old busting, grounding, and screaming routine through her desperate attempts to keep me out of trouble and under control. This time, she didn't just catch me drinking; she found my drug paraphernalia. After an evening of "stoney cruising" (i.e. driving around and smoking pot) with Cody and our friends, my mom found two pipes tucked in a seat pocket of my car. And I was actually as shocked as she was!

I mean, come on now, I always kept my weed safely hidden in my purse. I honestly argued that they weren't mine as I tried to remember who was sitting in the back seat of my hazy car the night before. It didn't matter, my mom was furious, and I was grounded. Again.

While hiding from my mom in our own house, I wondered where Cody was and when I'd see him again. He was hardly at school or home, and he didn't have a cell phone. I *had* to bridge the gap in our distance, so I opened Myspace to send him a message. But I also had to play it cool and speak nonchalantly, just in case anyone else saw it.

That night, I wrote:

Date: Nov 7, 2006

From: kris*

To: COdy

*heeyyyyy i'm in hiding right now from my mom and i feel sick and crazy again and can't sleep so i thought i'd surprise you with a little hello! (and if i left you a comment i figured people would be having heart attacks) so yeah... i'm pretty much fucked.. and might have to hurt whoever left those in my car haha. damn its just one thing after another with my mom lately! but whats she gonna do ya know? only live life once haha. but it might put a little damper on us hanging out tomorrow... we'll see, i don't want my wheels taken away! but i'm off to try to sleep again/watching the clock go by :P.. cccccya later*

*- kris*

Cody didn't respond that night. The following day, he consumed my mind as I dragged myself through school. Maybe I shouldn't have messaged him. *What if he ignores me? What will he say if he doesn't?* He was nowhere in the hallways. *Did he make it to school today? Where is he?* I had to find out, so I sat at the computer in the corner during my Teacher Assistant period, looking serious and focused on work, and opened MySpace.

*Notification:* 1 new email. From Cody! My heart skipped a beat as I clicked it open.

Date: Nov 8, 2006

From: COdy

To: kris*

*Hey there, haha thats funny how you can actually hide from your mom in your house, my mom has like some mystical 3rd eye that sees me whereever i go. Cause somehow she always knows how to find me, its sorta creepy :|*

*But yeah seriously i wonder whose pipes those were, i cant believe your mom found them, i feel really shitty cause i know how the relationship with your mom is. Yeah and i figured you wouldnt be able to do anything too so that ruins my day blah, not like this day could get any more shitty and its only like 9:30. My day started off aweful, my parents i just cant deal with anymore they been driven me over the edge for way to long i cant even explain how fucked up my life has felt for the longest time, got like 3-4 hours of sleep cause i could absolutely not sleep last night, there was just far to much to think of and worry about.*

*When i woke up this morning i felt like i couldnt handle anymore, then i came to school late and just started to have a emotional breakdown walking into school, [the principal] stopped me and made me talk to him for the whole 1st period.*

*Honestly, the only thing i wanted to do at the time was just go find you, these burdens dont seem nearly as heavy when i'm with you. It's just my escape. You dont know how much i wish we could have been together long ago, but ya know thats how life can be, some of the best things you gotta wait for, and its been about since 6th grade for you haha. Just your one message you wrote cheered me up so much, just because it showed me someone else is still thinking or caring about me even when i feel like no one is on days like this. I'm here for you in the same way. i dont know what it is about you krista, but you are amazing in my eyes. Truly.*

My heart pounded as I read the last words. *How was this possible? Cody felt the same way as I did when we were together, like the rest of our worlds didn't exist. And even more unbelievable, how did he believe I was so special? Wait, wasn't Jake supposed to think I was special?* At this point, I was sure Jake thought I was a mess and a terrible girlfriend. I mean, I *was* a terrible girlfriend, a cheating one! One that was skipping heartbeats over an old fling that still believed she was amazing underneath the mess. Jake just didn't know that yet, and Cody's words felt too comforting to stop them.

    MySpace emails became my newest addiction. I logged on constantly, with my heart racing in anticipation of having another email from Cody in my inbox. His words were just as addicting as his presence. Every email made my heart break and soar at the same time. He could feel my pain, I could feel his, and I created more pain for both of us by pretending it didn't mean as much as it did in my heart. I wanted him to know how much I cared about him, but I couldn't admit it in words.

*The Daisy Diaries*

Back at school, all my friends were talking about college and plans for next year, but it felt like my entire future stopped when Jake got hurt. Our future looked different now, and I wasn't ready to face it. I was just trying to survive each day. Both of my parents went to college, and I always knew I would go to college, too. Until Jake got hurt, I wanted to go to the same college. But now, we knew he wouldn't be going back, and I lost focus and hope for myself altogether. I was also still denying "how long" Jake would be paralyzed and hoped he would miraculously recover. Then we could go back to our old plans.

Until then, I continued going through the motions of my senior year on autopilot, or more like a zombie. I hated every class, couldn't focus, and wanted to puke every time a teacher or student asked me how Jake was doing. I longed to hide from the world I felt was watching and judging my every move.

Though I felt stealthy in my escapes from school, they quickly caught the principal's attention, who introduced me to my school's version of detention: Saturday School.

Even worse than having to stay after school, we had to show up at 8:00 a.m. on Saturday morning to sit for four hours of painful (and often hungover) boredom. It stung to be punished with Saturday School for the first time. But as I cared less about myself, I cared less about consequences. Plus, I knew Cody was always there, too.

One day, shaking from the day's near panic attack, I asked Cody to skip school with me. I could see his eyes sink in disappointment, but he was having a rough day too, and reluctantly agreed. The next day, the principal called us to his office in a fit of anger, pointing at a small TV screen behind his desk. It was a surveillance camera, showing a frozen shot of Cody and me walking out of the building, smiling at each other.

*What a cute picture! Can this be printed?* I thought to myself. My sweet moment was abruptly interrupted by the principal's lecture of disappointment in us.

"Saturday School for both of you," he concluded sternly. "And Cody, no messing around this time."

Cody and I knew we were pushing our limits and vowed to go to Saturday School together. That Friday, instead of going to the usual parties, we went to his house for a sleepover so neither of us would miss Saturday School. He claimed this was the first time he brought a girl to his home overnight, and we were bashful as all hell introducing me to his mom.

Cody and I spent the evening hidden away in his room talking, cuddling, and taking "selfies" on my Canon digital camera. Though, of course, we got high before arriving, the buzz soon faded, and I found myself slipping into sobriety. I immediately felt an impulse to smoke, drink, anything; that was my normal reaction. Until a new buzz came over me, a new, overwhelming sensation that I had never felt before. For the first time, I was sober, without any anxiety, and slept peacefully in Cody's arms.

We slept so peacefully, we almost missed Saturday School! After waking up in bliss, we raced downstairs. Cody paused and grabbed something out of a jar on the windowsill as we ran out the door. When we got in the car, he turned to me and held out his hand. A fabric daisy was in it. "Here, this is for you," he said with a cheesy smile.

"Thanks, baby," I replied with a childish giggle. I took the daisy from his hand and stuck it behind my left ear. Then, sliding my palm under his hand and intertwining our fingers, we sped to the school. For another first, I walked proudly into the school with Cody, still hand in hand and beaming from the magical evening before. I didn't realize then, nor did I care, that our secret was officially out.

Gossip was hot since Jake got hurt, and now that my secret affair with Cody was out, the talk around me set fire. I felt some tension with old friends, feeling their disapproving stares in the hallway as I walked by with glazed eyes and Cody-sensing radar turned on even higher than I was. Anxiety sickened me as I imagined what others said about my dramatic love triangle. "Did you hear? Krista's cheating on Jake with Cody!"

I often heard whispers in the hallways as I passed. I acted like I didn't care, but every word ate me alive. *They have no idea what I'm going through*, I told myself. *Fuck them if they want to judge me. What do I have left to lose?* Eventually, the whispers crept into my mind, haunting me with fear and paranoia. I felt like my life was on display. *Who's watching me now?* I constantly worried.

Nothing I could get my hands on seemed to free my anxiety. Because of it, I not only skipped school regularly, I started missing my once-beloved dance classes and cheerleading practices. By the way, I was one of the cheerleading captains; I kind of had to be there. But on many days, I couldn't make myself physically show up. My anxiety was, ironically, paralyzing. It often froze me, unable to move or make decisions other than to find a bowl to smoke, powder to snort, or alcohol to burn down my throat... or, even better, find Cody.

Soon, I didn't care about hiding my feelings for Cody anymore. I was exhausted from feeling guilty all the time. I didn't want to be Jake's perfect care-taking girlfriend anymore; I clearly wasn't anyway.

That is, until I talked to Jake on the phone... which still was nearly every day. Hearing his voice made me melt into a puddle. I loved him. My heart ached for his circumstances. I wanted to give up everything to help him heal and get his life back. I listened to him vent about his clingy parents and moody nurses, making promises that I would get there as soon as I could to comfort him. In the moment, I truly wanted to. By the end of our calls, I convinced myself that he was who I needed to be with. I made silent vows to tell Cody we were done and make things right by Jake.

But that meant telling Jake the truth, and I couldn't bring myself to do it. He was already living the worst nightmare of his life; how could I confess what I did to him without making his life worse?

# Chapter 6

## December 2006:

## Colorado Confessions

During Jake's stay in Colorado, I visited him twice to sit by his side and return to my "real life" as his girlfriend. My first trip was booked immediately, and my stomach turned in anticipation. Frequent visions of him laying miserably in his hospital bed choked me up with guilt; I needed to return to his side and help him heal. *He's so depressed and angry at the world,* I thought. *He needs me to help him stay positive, to want to stay alive.*

And then I'd remember what I was doing to him behind his back. From there, a tape of self-loathing repeated through my head a little something like this: *I have to see Jake. Shit, I can't face Jake. I can't tell him what I'm doing; it will break his heart. I don't want to go. I have to stop what I'm doing. I don't want to stop what I'm doing. I want to stay here, hide, and confide in Cody.*

The frequent bouts of panic that accompanied these thoughts usually sent my heart racing at hyper-speed or stopped my breathing altogether. Either way, it felt like my entire body was about to spontaneously combust. Sick of fighting tears, the only escape was numbing myself. I diligently maintained any kind of buzz until the day of our flight.

I braced myself for the next week of sobriety… and traveling with Jake's family. I truly adored them, and I knew they loved me; at least, they loved the old me. *Do they know what a piece of shit I've become?* I didn't think I could handle it; I wasn't worthy of traveling at their sides to see their son. But I had to. So, I made sure I had plenty of my prescribed antidepressant and a handful of Xanax I got from a friend to bring with me.

Stepping into that hospital was a trip in itself. After so much had changed back home, it was like I had entered another dimension. I was Jake's girlfriend again, so kind and admired by many. My secret didn't exist here. Not yet at least. There was also a brighter sense of hope in the air, different than in Duluth.

Every other patient was in a wheelchair. Everyone shared a spinal cord injury to varying degrees. It was inspiring to learn their stories, returning me the forgotten feeling of hope. I found myself looking at Jake with fresh eyes and determination that he could still overcome this, and that I was meant to help him do it.

I quickly learned that Jake became friends with another young man the same age. They were born days apart, got hurt around the same time, and damaged the same part of their necks. Without a doubt, this friendship was Divine. Also, without a doubt, they loved to joke, tease, and make bets with one another.

Since they were both 19-year-olds with girlfriends coming to visit, they made the ultimate bet: who could have sex with their girlfriend first? I mean, this was a big one. Neither of them knew if their parts still worked. It was up to us girlfriends to help them find out.

Remember the bull in me? Who loves a good challenge? Of course, we were going to win this one. Even though I felt like a disgusting cheater, I needed to do this for Jake. And honestly, I needed to know if he still worked, too. If I was going to marry him, I had to find out if we could still have kids one day like we once planned.

Within thirty-six hours of my arrival to Colorado, Jake and I found the golden moment of privacy in his room. His parents had gone to lunch, his nurse just did her last check, and it was time to win the bet. I cautiously climbed on top of him, unsure if I could hurt him or if he could even feel it. We started kissing. I was nearly shaking from nerves of getting caught, and from the guilt of recognizing how different his kiss felt from Cody's. *But I have to do this. For him. For us. For winning the bet.*

I slipped my pants off, wrapped his blanket around me, and hopped on top. He was already hard. *Thank God, it works!* I thought to myself as I got to work. *Am I doing this right? Is this worth all the trouble?* I wondered. Jake's heavy breathing and the sweat on his brow seemed to say so.

"Can you feel this?" I finally asked. Without a word, Jake looked up at me, trying to catch his breath, and nodded "yes."

A moment later, we heard a noise, and I jumped off him and the bed to scramble my pants on. Hot and bothered, I sat down at my new perch just in time for another nurse to come in for a check-up. She was surprised to see how high Jake's heart rate was, but we played it cool and secretly celebrated our victory in winning the bet.

Part of me was proud of helping him win. Jake needed a win. But it felt completely wrong. And I didn't know how to make it right.

After exhausting internal battles of "should I?" and "shouldn't I?" I ultimately left Colorado exhausted by guilt and determined to stay faithful to Jake until his return home. But until then, I ran back to my constant escape from sobriety, and of course, I often ran into Cody. *Stay away, Krista*, I warned myself. *It's for the best.*

I mean, what was I thinking anyway? It was so difficult with Cody. My parents would hate it, the community would hate it, why would I keep putting myself through this, and put Cody through it, too?

Out of guilt, fear, and obligation, I pushed Cody away countless times. I did my best to numb my feelings for him, but the best high still came from being in his presence. I pretended that I didn't care, but secretly still longed for him. I had gotten used to our secret MySpace emails and missed getting them from him regularly. So every once in a while, I sent him one, acting like everything was fine and suggesting we hang out, just as friends, as if that would be no problem. He often reluctantly agreed, and we continued meeting with friends and at parties.

For a while, I thought this was actually going well. I could finally be faithful to Jake and spend time with Cody. Everyone wins, right? Almost.

If only it didn't take all I had to ignore the magnetism between Cody and me. Sometimes I failed, then rudely repelled him to compensate, yanking that poor boy around like a yo-yo. Naturally, it didn't take long to stir up a heated and heartbreaking argument. "I fucking fell in love with you!" he shouted at me one night. That was the first time he said "I love you" to my face, in a way I'll never forget. Though I stood in stunned silence, my heart screamed back, "I love you, too."

However, guilt had hardened my heart and kept Cody at bay. My words and Myspace messages grew cold, reinstating that I had to be with Jake and we could only be friends. Then, one day Cody's reply cracked my concrete heart.

Date: Dec 8, 2006
From: COdy
To: kris*

*Yeah i didnt make it to school today, its like 1:15 right now haha. I had such a fucked up dream, it was about everything, Like our friends went down to colorado to go see jake and i was with you, and jake was fine again, and me and him were talking in his hospital room about everything between me and you. I woke up crying, no matter how much i want something so god damn bad on this earth i will never get it. Im so sick of it. and it was just weird cause i never really have really vivid dreams like ones where i can actually make out the conversations after i woke. It was just messed up just like everything else in this world.*

*I dont know what to do about anything right now, what i want, how to go about this whole situation. I feel like i cant even hang out with you, cause the things you want me to be now is far to hard and hurts my feelings to much to just be friends, i've never looked at you as just a friend and i dont think i can after all this.*

*i hate drugs, i hate how they make people who they arnt and allow them to do things they normally wouldnt, I use them because its the only thing i can use to bandage all the fucked up shit in my life, and i dont want you to ever have to do that.*

*i dont know what to do, maybe we should just go back to how me and you use to be, never see or talk to each other again. my heart wont listen to what you want us to be now. I cant just not want to be with you. I dont want to leave you, oh god you dont know how much i wish everything was just fine. it makes me cry. I just dont know, fuck everything, fuck this place, fuck this world, fuck all these people in it. I just wanna be away from everything.*

My throat tightened reading Cody's words. Tears rolled quietly down my cheeks. I wished so badly to wash his pain away. I wanted to comfort him just as badly as he had wanted to comfort me. Jake and Cody were both in great pain and wanted me to be there for them. *But who did I really want to be there me?* Every time I asked myself that question, Cody came to mind first. *Fuck, that's not the right answer.*

My second trip to Colorado was quickly approaching. The question that plagued me until then was, *Will I tell Jake?*

On Christmas evening, my family embarked on the nineteen-hour journey to Colorado. As we drove further away from home and Cody, I dreaded the future that awaited me: confessing to Jake. By the time we arrived, my stomach was tied in knots, carefully planning my words that no one knew I needed to say.

I went through the first day in Colorado in silent agony, waiting for the right moment alone with Jake to finally come clean. By the third morning, I was ready to explode. So desperate to finally come clean, I didn't even realize the moment came on Cody's birthday.

As I confessed to Jake through sloppy tears, it felt like I didn't have to say who I cheated on him with; it was apparent. I suddenly realized how many connections the two boys had over the years. How many times Jake picked Cody up and drove him home in blizzards when he was walking miles down their country road. Jake knew of my brief history with Cody, but I never considered his.

Jake lay there, listening to my rambling apologies with silent tears rolling down his cheeks. "They should have left me in that fucking lake," he finally replied.

*This is all my fault,* I thought. *I'm the worst person ever.* My guilt reached an all-time high. Just as Jake first did years ago, I made promises that I wanted to but couldn't keep. *I get it now,* I realized. It killed me to hurt him so badly, I'd say and do anything to relieve his pain, and suddenly appreciated all his past failed attempts to alleviate mine.

With no words left to say, Jake and I both sobbed until we were interrupted by nurses.

The next day, after the most heartbreaking confession of my life, I had to talk to someone about it. Unfortunately, I couldn't think of anyone else to reach out to... but Cody.

Date: Dec 31, 2006

From: kris*

To: COdy

*hey, yesterday morning i ended up telling jake. i told him how i just fell apart and just wanted to be fucked up all the time.. i didn't care about anything.. and then i started hanging out with you and at the time we both just needed someone.. hooked up when we were all fucked up.. and then started seeing each other. i didn't go into any more details than that. but i tried explaining your situation a little bit too cause i dont want him to think that you would just jump on me like that knowing about him. we were both crying our eyes out and it turned into a breakdown of this whole accident.*

*he said "i hate this fucking chair. they should've left me in that fucking lake".. and thats when i lost it even more than i already did. i often think about what would've happened if he died that day.. it scares the shit out of me. i thank god every day that he's still alive cause idk what i'd have done if i lost him. hes a different person now and i'm still getting used to it but no matter what hes still jake. i love him and i have for the past almost 3 years.*

*i hate knowing that i hurt him... i hate knowing that i hurt you. this whole situation has been so fucked up and its just me fucking everyone over. i try not to feel that way cause this was never my plan.. but i still do cause i let everything happen.*

*last night i kept having dreams about you. i really need to get all the shit in my head straight but thats pretty hard to do right now. all i do know is that no matter what i still want us to be good friends..i really do care about you a lot.. and you worry me a lot! but idk.. i'm sure i'm making you really confused and i'm sorry idk what the hell i'm doing.. i never do. i gotta get going so i'll ttyl. i hope you had a good birthday!!! and have a good news years tonight too.. don't get toooooooo crazy haha*

    Cody didn't respond for days. Those days felt like years, as anxiety pulsed through my veins wondering if he read my message, how he reacted, and what he was doing. *Who else was he with?* I checked my messages daily, until his response finally arrived.

Jan 5, 2007

From: COdy

To: kris*

*I'm sorry, sorry everything had to come out like this. its unbelievable how much everything snowballed into this big mess of emotions and life touching decisions, i never expected any of it. i never regret a moment of it, i lost my faith in God a long time ago, but i thank him for every single moment and feeling he let me share with you, and even heartache.*

*i try to look at every experience as something that was meant to happen, to make us stronger or for whatever reason we might never know. But i know it had a purpose. I'd go back and do it a thousand times just so i could have those feelings again, Carefree, thats the best word to describe how you made my life when i was with you. I dont believe i could ever mistake what be had for a close friendship. I wish i could still be a close friend, but i cant be friends with someone i fell in love with so fast.*

*Jake comes back in 20 days, honestly how close can we ever be again when hes back here, you'll be with him all the time and ill just be the regret that should have never happened, and i cant be there for that. Being around you, just hearing your voice or even knowing your gonna read this makes my heart ache.*

*When i read this message, i cried, i cried hard, not just because it was all coming to an end, but because how strong i see your love can be, the love that drives you to go through all this, all of it since the accident, the love i will never get to feel. I felt the emotions we had, the passion, the feeling you gave me everytime i woke up. I just wanted that feeling to be so much greater, but i have to force myself to think with my head now, and not the heart like we did for so long.*

*Krista i wont ever forget the feelings i have for you, you've let me learn an experience i will hold in my head forever, and i thank you for that. I know in the end what we had will make me a stronger person. And i need as much aid to my strength as i can get. I'll miss you krista, every aspect i got to find about you. Everythings done for a reason in life. Cody.*

    Tears fell as my heart sank. Did I even have a heart anymore? I broke everyone's heart, including my own, and I couldn't see a possible way out of the mess I made.

After the truth of my affair with Cody came out, Jake and I knew our relationship would never be the same. *How can I fix this?* I wondered. *Do I have to? Do I want to?* These questions haunted me silently until I felt comfortable enough around my counselor, Suzanne, to confess my secrets. Suddenly, I had one adult in my life I could say anything to without fear of judgment or punishment. I finally stopped trying to skip our sessions and found myself looking forward to them.

I didn't think it was possible for an adult to truly see and listen to me, much less understand what I had to say or who I was. Every other adult tried to "fix" and correct me. Everyone else was worried about me. But not Suzanne. It was like she already knew my future and that I'd be okay. She made me feel like I was too strong, too important, and too smart to let these circumstances bring me down.

Suzanne encouraged me to listen to how I feel and let myself make decisions without worry of anyone else's reaction. She could see how much I loved Cody, and without meeting him, she spoke like she knew the unique and special human he was. With Suzanne, I didn't feel crazy or stupid for loving him either. I felt safe and free to admit it. When everyone else made me feel judged and worthless, Suzanne held me back up and helped me speak my truth.

And boy, did I need to speak my truth. By February, I couldn't believe I hadn't spontaneously combusted yet from all I was hiding inside. Jake was home, and I was ripping at the seams trying to juggle my two opposing lives. I couldn't fight my heart anymore; I had to admit that Cody had it. It was time to confess again and let Jake go.

I honestly can't remember what I said to make the final cut. But I do remember doing it through a lousy text, as I no longer had the courage to face Jake without dying a little more inside. Three years and a life-shattering accident ended with a text.

At last, my heart had won the battle against my head. I knew without a doubt that I wanted to be with Cody, and my feelings for him finally overcame the tremendous guilt that had held me back for the last five months. Finally free from the nightmarish love triangle from hell, I hoped for better days ahead. It couldn't get worse, right?

The day after my last text to Jake, I couldn't wait to meet Cody at his brother's apartment after school. Unable to wipe the grin from my face, I quietly stepped into the room to find Cody sitting at his computer, his back to the door. I crept up behind him, exhaled softly, and kissed his ear. He shuddered, just like he did six years earlier.

As he turned to kiss me, the energy between us surged. He stood up and hugged me. "I'm so happy to be with you and finally be able to call you mine," he said before another kiss. The feeling was more than mutual. I felt like a weight of ten thousand bricks fell off my shoulders. I suddenly felt free and bursting with so much love that I couldn't hold in my childish giggles. "Oh, hey," Cody said as we pulled away from a long embrace. "I got you something."

"What is it?" I asked curiously.

Cody turned back to his desk and pulled something out of a drawer. Reaching his hand out to me, he replied, "Here, this is for you." His palm opened to reveal a small glass pipe. Intricate swirls of blue, green, orange, and yellow wrapped around the long, thin piece.

"Oh wow!" I said in excitement. "Thank you! I haven't actually owned my own."

"I know," he replied with slight hesitation. "It made me think of you. Just don't let your mom find this one."

I laughed, taking the pipe into my hands, twirling it around in my fingers to look closer at its intricate craftsmanship. As I turned it over, I noticed the bubble protruding from the top had something in it. I looked closer. It was a bright little daisy.

"Oh my gosh, it has a daisy in it!" I exclaimed.

"I know," he smiled. "That's why I got it."

"It's perfect!" I exclaimed. "Thank you so much, baby. Better than the flower itself. I love it!"

"You're so welcome," he replied before giving me another hug. "Man, I'm just so happy to finally be with you."

I melted in his arms. My eyes closed in the comfort of his warmth. "Me too," I answered softly.

Although I knew the rest of the community, including my family, didn't approve of my relationship with Cody, I couldn't care less. The unstoppable flow of deep love and understanding was more than I had ever experienced, and I was willing to risk everything to have it. I mean, what else did I have to lose at this point?

All I had and needed was Cody. And now I could finally be with him without hiding, without guilt, and without fear of being seen. Now, Cody and I could be together forever, at last.

# Chapter 7

## March 2007:

## The Last Party

March 21st was just another long and tortuous day of school. I was antsy to get out and into Cody's arms. Except that day, not only did I have to last through the school day, but I also had to work for my dad in his electrical store after school until five. However, there was an extra excitement and nervousness about it this day; Cody would pick me up from work for the first time.

Knowing my dad wasn't thrilled with Cody's reputation and the trouble I had gotten into with him, I had no idea what my dad's reaction would be to Cody pulling into the parking lot. It didn't matter, though; I was clearly willing to go through anything to be with Cody.

At 5:00 p.m., Cody pulled up to the shop. My dad stood quietly as I headed to the front door. "Alright, Kris. Have fun, be safe," he finally said as I stepped outside. He watched in the window as I got into Cody's car, with concern and hope in his eyes. With one last look at my dad, we pulled out of the parking lot and toward Cody's brother's apartment.

We had talked for weeks about going back to Stargate, the dance club in Superior, Wisconsin. We knew Wednesday night was teen night, but by this time, we both had stumbled upon IDs of poor strangers who were twenty-one. Bonus, we could drink in the bar! We had pulled it off once before, and I couldn't wait to do it again, to escape from the real world and have a night of fun with the one I could finally call my boyfriend.

When we arrived at the apartment, Cody's brother, Chad, introduced us to the chinchilla he had gotten that day. Excited about his new pal, Chad hesitated to go to the club. Finally, he and Cody's friend, Alan, said they'd want to go if we could spend the night. However, I had to get back for school the next day and convinced everyone we could make it back and still have a good time.

A few hours later, the four of us headed off to Superior. The car was clouded with smoke the entire drive. We stopped along the way for alcohol that Cody bought with his fake ID, and after two hours of driving, we made it to Stargate. Terrified of not making it into the club with my ID, I practiced my name, birthday, and address the entire ride. At the door, I was questioned and nervously answered. The bouncer shrugged, laughed, stamped my hand, and let us in. I know he knew it was fake, and I thanked God that he let me in. I still wonder if he read the paper over the next few days…

Cody and I made our way to the bar to sit, drink, and talk. I remember ordering a Tequila Sunrise, the only "fancy" drink I knew. There, we talked about our future. We planned to enroll at our Community College in the fall and bounced around ideas of living together and proving the world wrong about our love affair.

After another drink and falling deeper in love with each other and our life plan, we headed to the crowded dance floor. Squeezing between the masses of other drunken teens, I'm not sure if we did more actual dancing or just swaying, hugging, and kissing. At one point, our electric energy turned up so high that we wandered over to the bathrooms with intentions to sneak into a stall to "be alone." However, the heavy traffic through both bathrooms left us without the guts to execute our risky plan. So, we returned to the bar for another drink and back to the dance floor.

For how excited I was to be there, unsettling energy increased throughout the evening. *Were my expectations too high?* I suddenly grew irritated with Cody and how he danced with me. *How sloppy drunk was he?* I suspected he had taken other drugs without telling me, and I was upset that he let himself get too wasted to be truly present with me. I wanted his undivided attention. I wanted him all over me. I wanted to take him to the bathroom. I wanted to have him all alone. *Why did I push to come to this crowded place again?*

By bar close, we stumbled out to the car, debating who would drive. Cody volunteered to take the driver's seat. I hopped into the front with him, and Alan and Chad climbed in behind us. I'm not sure how far we made it, but at one point, Cody admitted that he couldn't drive anymore and slowly pulled over. The possible options ran through my head. *Should we just stop for a while? Should I drive? I might be the soberest one in this car.* Just as I was about to open my mouth to speak, Alan piped in from the back, "I'm probably the most sober; I'll drive." *That's fine by me!* I thought. *I'll be able to sit in the back and snuggle with Cody.*

We quickly switched seats, with Alan driving, Chad in the passenger's seat, and Cody and me in the back. I settled in behind Chad, taking off my jacket and kicking off my shoes, snuggling up to Cody comfortably. We pulled back onto the road, and Cody leaned away from me to crack open another beer.

"Are you kidding me? Aren't you wasted enough?" I barked quietly, slapping his beer in hopes of knocking it out of his hands.

"What the fuck? Don't be a bitch," he barked back.

*A bitch?!* I thought. *Hell no.* I pushed away from him as far to my side of the seat as I could and buckled my seat belt, looking out the window with tears in my eyes. This was not how I wanted my night to end. I started running through all the nights of partying with him, culminating in him passing out, often pissing his pants, and completely blacking out. I still wanted all his attention on me and hated when he got too drunk to do so.

Isn't it ironic that I was the one needing to run from sobriety to justify being with him, yet I hated when *he* wasn't sober?

"I'm sorry, baby, I'm so sorry," he said sweetly as he put his beer down and crawled over to my side of the seat. "I didn't mean it. I'm so sorry. I love you so much, don't be mad at me." He wrapped his arms around me, and as his soft lips grazed my neck, I melted into a puddle in his arms. I turned to him with a smile and a kiss, and we cuddled closer, his arms wrapped around me and his head resting on my shoulder as we fell asleep for the rest of the ride.

I'm not sure what time it was. Somewhere around 4:00 a.m. Of a one-hundred-mile ride, we were about fifteen miles away from home. Sleeping soundly under Cody's warmth, a sudden jolt woke me up. All I could register was Chad directly in front of me, turning around in terror. We briefly locked eyes as he said, "Hold on!"

*Holy shit, we're about to crash!* The split-second moment of realization and surrender rushed through my bones.

Another sharp turn and jolt of the car, and I blacked out.

I woke up in the dark. It was freezing cold. I had no idea where I was. *Is this a dream?* I wondered. *I must be dreaming. Where the fuck am I, anyway?* I tried to move and immediately realized I couldn't; I felt paralyzing pain shoot through my body. *What the hell? Wake up, Krista! Wake up!* The cold wind blew through the trees and chilled me to the bone. This felt too real to be a dream, but *what the hell happened?*

Suddenly, I heard Chad's voice screaming hysterically in the distance, "Where the fuck is my brother?!" His cries echoed through the eerie silence of the night.

My next breath seemed to pierce my chest. *Holy shit, this is real.* "Help!" was all I could scream before sobs of tears burst out of me. *This isn't a dream.* I didn't know where I was. I was in so much pain I couldn't move, nor could I stop my body from shaking violently in the frigid cold. *Where is Cody?* I thought.

"Help! HELP!!" I cried in panic. I couldn't find the strength or words to say anything else.

"Krista, I'm coming!" Chad called out in response. I don't remember how long it took him to find me. The next thing I knew, he fell over me in tears. "Krista, Krista, are you okay?"

"No," I cried, again unable to find the strength to say any other words.

"It's okay. I promise. I'm going to get help. Just stay here; I promise I'll be back soon with help!" Chad said through trembling tears.

I must have blacked out again once he left. The next time my eyes opened, a circle of paramedics surrounded my head. I learned later that Chad ran to a house down the road, pounding on the door, covered in blood. The blessed couple that answered the door immediately called 911, and an ambulance was on its way.

I blinked my eyes in disbelief. *I'm still here,* I thought. *This isn't a dream.* Sound suddenly flooded my ears. The circle of strangers around my head repeated, "Krista, Krista, are you okay?" After staring blankly at them for a few moments, I finally remembered how to speak again.

"I don't know," was all I could say.

"You were in a car accident, Krista; we're taking you to the hospital. Is there anyone you want us to call?"

I had no idea. The first person I thought of was Cody, but I knew he was supposed to be with me. "I don't know. My parents?" I replied in agonizing pain.

They slowly gathered my parents' names and phone number from me and continued with questions about what happened. "Who was driving? Where were you sitting in the car? Do you remember anything that happened?"

I stumbled out all that I could remember. Cody and I were in the back seat, his brother in the passenger's, and Alan was driving.

"Is everyone else okay?" I asked between their questions.

"Yes. Chad and Alan were able to climb out of the car. We're transferring all of you to the local hospital."

"But where's Cody? Is Cody okay?" I asked.

"Cody is being taken care of, too. Both of you were thrown out of the vehicle and are in serious condition. You'll both be airlifted to Duluth."

*Holy shit,* I thought. *What's wrong with me? What's wrong with Cody? He's got to be okay.*

My body shook violently in pain as the paramedics continued to ask questions, and I struggled to spit out answers. Suddenly, I was in a vehicle with another circle of heads around me. I don't remember much of the ambulance ride to our small local hospital, other than my body shaking uncontrollably and continuously trying to break my knees free from the stretcher straps to bend them and relieve the excruciating pain in my back. The paramedics kept arguing that I needed to stay still until they could assess my injuries, that I couldn't move in case I had broken my back.

*Broken my back? Are you kidding me?* I had to be dreaming. I wiggled my legs again to make sure I wasn't paralyzed. Again, the paramedics warned and held my knees down straight; holy shit did that hurt. I didn't know what was wrong with me, but I had never felt so much pain.

The next thing I knew, I was in a bed in the local emergency room, and a nurse popped her head in through the curtains surrounding me.

"Your family is here to see you," she announced.

*Fuck,* I thought to myself as guilt overcame my physical pain. *They're going to be so mad.* My parents and sister slowly stepped through the curtains. Upon laying their eyes on me, we all burst into tears.

"I'm so sorry," was all I could say. I felt stupid and selfish for putting my family through this terrifying experience. I knew I lied to my mom the night before, claiming to spend the night at my girlfriend's house. They had no idea who I was with or where I was going, and at this point, no one knew what was happening.

My family wasn't mad. "We're just so glad you're okay," they said. Their words filled me with comfort and relief that they still loved me anyway. Even though I had fucked up. Again.

A few moments later, paramedics came back into the room. "Your helicopter is here. You're being airlifted to Duluth to assess your internal injuries better."

My family leaned over my bed to hug and kiss me as my mom promised to see me in Duluth. "You're going to be okay," she reassured me.

"Where is Cody?" I asked again while being transferred to another stretcher for the helicopter.

One paramedic replied, "He is getting airlifted, too. You both sustained serious injuries, but you're both in good hands."

"What happened to him? What are his injuries?" I asked. Nausea sank in my stomach as I waited for their answer. *He has to be okay,* I thought.

"We don't know yet," was the only response I received.

My memory of the helicopter ride is just as blurry as the ambulance ride. Both blend in a haze of extreme pain, cold, and confusion. All I know is that I continued to shake violently, attempting to free my legs from the stretcher straps, while asking if Cody was okay. And all I got in response were orders to stay still and that we'd be there soon.

*Why is everyone acting so weird when I ask about him?* My stomach turned. *He's got to be okay.*

Suddenly, I was in a new bed, in an actual hospital room this time. I was no longer wearing any of my clothes, all of them replaced with a hospital gown. Looking down at my arms and legs, my skin was covered in scratches and bruises. Grazing my tongue across my teeth, I was shocked to feel short and jagged edges.

"Oh my God! What happened to my teeth?!" I exclaimed out loud in panic. A nurse walked in the doorway as I spoke.

"You must have hit your mouth on something hard enough to crack your teeth," she replied. "You're actually very lucky you didn't completely lose any. Don't worry; they're easily fixed, and they're the least of your troubles right now."

I asked her for a mirror to see how they looked. She turned and pulled a handheld mirror out of a drawer before slowly handing it to me. I pulled the mirror to my face; I almost didn't know who was looking back at me. A girl straight from a horror movie was in the mirror, with scratches covering her face and a massive black and bloody eye. My eyeball was completely bloodshot, making my hazel eye look disturbingly green. My hair was a knotted mess, with dirt, rocks, and grass still stuck in it. I looked down my face and opened my mouth.

"Holy shit," was all I could say. I ran my tongue across my teeth as I stared at them, or lack of them. Every front tooth was chipped and broken at strange angles, and as I ran my tongue further back, I realized my back teeth were chipped, too. I was hideous. *What in the hell happened to me?*

But wait, *what happened to Cody?* I set my vanity down with the mirror and turned to the nurse. "Is Cody here? Is he okay? What happened to him?"

The nurse paused, clearly contemplating what she was going to say. Finally, she said, "Yes, he's here. He's hurt pretty badly. I don't know anything more right now, but I'll let his nurses know you are asking."

*He's got to be okay*, I thought to myself. *He can't not be okay. Why won't anyone tell me what's going on with him?*

A second nurse stepped into the room. "Krista, your mom just got here and would like to see you. Can I send her in?"

Thank God, someone I knew! "Yes, please send her in," I replied. Shortly after, my mom entered the room. Shock, concern, and sadness covered her face.

"I'm so sorry," was all I could say. "Thank you for coming."

"I'm just glad you're okay," she replied as she leaned over to kiss my forehead. "Oh my, we need to brush your hair."

"Do you know anything about how Cody is doing?" I asked her.

She paused for a moment. "I don't know, but I do know his mom is on her way. We'll all know more soon."

Nurses came in and out to check my vitals and ask more questions while my mom made the first attempts to brush the wild rat's nest on my head. Anxiety continued to burn through my blood as the shock settled in. *This shit is real. Cody's hurt badly. Why won't anyone tell me what's going on?*

Eventually, a nurse stopped in the doorway to announce that Cody's mom had arrived. My mom quickly stood up and told me she'd be right back. I felt a bomb of anxiety explode in my gut. *He's got to be okay.* A few minutes later, another new nurse slowly stepped in the door.

"Krista?" she asked. "Can I come in for a moment?"

I thought it was odd for a nurse even to ask; everyone seemed to come in and out without hesitation. "Yes," I replied nervously.

"Thank you," she said. "I have some news for you. It's about Cody."

My heart stopped. "Is he okay?" I asked one more time.

"Well," she replied, "he hit his head very hard on a tree when he was thrown out of the vehicle. He sustained severe head injuries. We did all that we could to keep him stable, but...."

*But?! But what?!* I screamed inside my mind.

"I'm so sorry, Krista," she continued, "but Cody didn't make it. He died peacefully shortly after arriving here in Duluth."

I froze. The world stopped. *This can't be happening,* I thought to myself. *This isn't real. I must be dreaming.* I stared blankly at the nurse, stunned silent, as tears streamed down my face.

"He's still in his hospital room. I wanted to check if you'd like to see him before they take him out. Would you like to see him?"

My heart began to beat again, now pounding through my ears. I looked up at the nurse in disbelief. "Yes," was all I could choke out of my mouth.

My mom stepped in. Looking at me, she started to cry. "I'm so sorry, Krista," she said. "We had to wait until his mom got here to tell you. She's here now, and she's in his room. Are you sure you want to go in there?"

"I have to!" I demanded through tears.

Two more nurses came in, unlocked the wheels of my hospital bed, and gathered my IVs. They slowly rolled my bed out of the room and down the hallway. I immediately recognized it.

*This is the same unit Jake was in,* I realized. The nurses led me up to the same doors that haunted me, with the words "Intensive Care Unit" over them. The doors automatically opened, and they pushed my bed forward.

I knew this unit of the hospital like the back of my hand. Jake spent what felt like an eternity here before and after his surgery. As my bed rolled further down the hall, I nearly vomited as it turned... right into the same room where Jake first laid after his accident.

My bed entered the doorway. There he was. Cody laid there so peacefully. With eyes closed, he looked like he was sound asleep. His mom sat at his side, running her fingers through his thick blond hair, with silent tears streaming down her face. She looked up at me with the saddest smile I've ever seen.

"He looks so beautiful, doesn't he?" she said.

"Yes, he does," I whispered.

The nurses turned my bed and pushed it alongside his. Though I could hardly move my own body, I forced myself to sit up and lean over the railing, sliding my hand under the sheet that covered Cody. I quickly found his hand and slipped my fingers between his. Still lukewarm, his fingers seemed to wrap around and hold mine.

*This can't be it,* I thought. *He's just sleeping. Cody, please open your eyes!* These thoughts repeated through my mind, though I couldn't find the strength to say any words. *Please, baby, open those eyes just one more time.*

"My baby," his mom repeated sadly from his other side, still running her fingers through his hair. "You'll always be my baby." The two of us sat in silence, tears rolling down our cheeks, and eyes looking over every inch of Cody's face, the love of both of our lives.

Soon after, the two nurses returned, telling us it was time to go. *Oh God, please no,* my mind screamed. *Cody, please just open those fucking beautiful blue eyes one more time!*

Tears flooded my face as I reluctantly released my hand from his and the nurses began to pull my bed from the room. Rolling through the doorway, I looked up and recognized the faces of Cody's close friend and his younger sister. For a moment, we all locked eyes, sharing the same shock and heartbreak.

My bed continued down the hallway and back to my room, but I think part of me died and stayed with Cody.

Though my diagnosis found a severely lacerated spleen and liver, chipped processes in my lower lumbar vertebrae, and a deep wound in my side from the seat belt buckle, I felt like they had forgotten something. The worst injury possible. My heart was broken.

The next day was busy with visitors. My heart continued crumbling away every time a new visitor walked in. Though I felt so broken, numb, and already cursed by my community, I was relieved to have anyone visit, support, and remind me that they still cared. I burst into tears when my best friends walked in. One was carrying a vase full of flowers; all were daisies.

"They were the only flower I thought you would want," she said through her tears. Every memory of daisies with Cody flashed through my mind like a flipbook.

"You're so right," was all I could reply.

After a few visits with my girlfriends and a morphine-heavy nap, A nurse notified me of another visitor coming.

"Who is it?" I asked. I heard shuffling down the hallway. A shadow appeared in the doorway as I recognized a familiar humming sound. An electric wheelchair rolled in. It was Jake.

I felt like my brain blew right out of my skull. I couldn't believe Jake had come to see me! He had every right to hate me and wish that I were the one dead. I immediately burst into the ugliest of tears, and he began to cry, too.

"Oh my God, Jake," I stammered. "I can't believe you're here. I'm so sorry. I can't believe this. I'm so sorry. Thank you for coming."

He rolled closer and settled at the side of my bed. "Of course. I had to come," he replied sweetly, carefully placing his shaky hand over the blanket on my feet. "You were here for me, and I had to be here for you."

A floodgate broke from my eyes. Suddenly, I felt a wave of relief wash over me. It felt as if all the pain from our past immediately dissolved into thin air. The old weights of anger, revenge, and guilt lifted from my hurting shoulders. There was nothing left to be angry about anymore. After we both faced near-death experiences, our petty dramas didn't matter anymore. They didn't even exist. The battle was finally over, and nobody won.

I don't know how long we sat there together. Mostly in silence, we just looked at one another with an undeniable understanding of mutual forgiveness, respect, and compassion. My tears continued to flow and wash away all the bullshit from our dramatic past, transforming into tears of joy that Jake still cared about me.

Though part of me died that day with Cody, from that moment on, I knew Jake would still hold a special place in my heart forever.

The next day, I saw a copy of *The Daily Globe*, my hometown's local newspaper. A gigantic picture consumed a quarter of the front page. It was Chad's car, dented on all sides and lying upside-down at the bottom of a ditch. Debris and pieces of the car were scattered across the hillside behind the vehicle.

"Holy shit," I said out loud. Immediately, I played that image of the car in my mind and attempted to rewind it. *How the hell did it go off the road?* I wondered. *How did Cody end up so far in the trees, but I was on the side of the road?* Thinking about it made my head and stomach hurt. It just didn't make sense. And every scenario ended with Cody crashing into a tree, a scene that would haunt my imagination for years to come.

I learned that the driver, Cody's good friend, Alan, fell asleep at the wheel with the rest of us. He failed to follow a slight left curve in the two-lane highway, and the car tumbled off to the right, rolling over and flipping end over end to its final stop at the bottom of a ditch. Cody and I had to have been thrown from the back window, the only missing window in the vehicle. Cody flew into the woods, and I was dumped off on the shoulder of the road.

*How the hell did this happen?* It boggled my mind every day. I couldn't figure out how to put the pieces together. Not that it mattered anyway. Even if I did figure out all the pieces, I could do nothing to put them back together and bring Cody back to life.

I also learned that Alan and Chad were able to crawl out of the car, both sustaining minor sprains and bruises. *What a miracle that the car didn't crush them both*, I thought to myself. Once Alan was discharged from the hospital, he immediately faced jail time, awaiting sentencing of up to ten felonies, including negligent homicide and injury by intoxicated use of a vehicle, underage drinking, marijuana possession, and blood alcohol content over the legal limit for each of Cody, Chad, and I. For days, the newspaper highlighted new articles about the accident and Alan's trial that made me sick. *It wasn't just his fault,* I thought. *It's my fault, too. If I didn't want to go that night, we'd all be okay.* The familiar beast of guilt returned to eat away at my insides.

Ironically, my insides were more than metaphorically torn from guilt and grief. My spleen and liver took a severe beating in my mysterious launch from the car that night. Just as ironically, I nearly broke my own back, yet somehow walked away with chips and cracks.

Well, slowly walked away. I was in the ICU for the next week as my spleen and liver healed and a back brace was made. I spent that week in a sleepy and morphine-dripped haze. If I wasn't sleeping, I was still in so much pain I could hardly walk or stand up straight.

The doctors told me that on a scale from 1-5, the damage to my spleen was between a 4 and 5. I hadn't heard this before, and sometimes still question its truth, but one doctor informed me that the spleen will regenerate itself once; if I were ever to damage it again, I'd have to get it removed, or it could kill me.

*Oh good,* I thought to myself. *I hope it kills me next time. And soon.*

# Chapter 8

## April 2007:

## Uncomfortably Numb

My body miraculously healed 100% without any surgery, but my heart was 100% broken over Cody's death.

In the hospital, I decided that I couldn't live without him. Cody was all I was living for, and it sounded much better to me to join him in the afterlife than to keep dragging my sorry ass through my miserable life situation. I quickly decided that if I were to make it a year after the accident, I would crash my car at the same accident site and hope for the worst.

Cody's death had made me all too curious to know what happens when you die. I wanted to know where he was and what the experience of death was like. I began fantasizing about it regularly without telling a soul; I couldn't admit that I could be suicidal to anyone, especially because I somehow became an "inspiration of strength" to so many people around me. I was embarrassed that I felt this way, but I couldn't fight the desire to die, and honestly, I was too tired to fight anything anymore.

The first two weeks after my discharge from the hospital were spent at home. I wasn't allowed to go back to school or go out with friends. With a supply of Morphine and permission to lay in bed and sleep my days away, I floated through these weeks like a dream. My life felt like a dream; recovering from internal injuries, Cody was dead; it didn't seem real, until my friends came to visit.

Just seeing the concerned looks on their faces as they walked into my room jolted me back to reality immediately. *Oh yeah, I'm covered in scars, half my teeth are missing, my eye is bruised and completely bloodshot,* I remembered. I was a hot mess for sure. My friends and I often cried, laughed, and sometimes locked my door and smoked pot out my bedroom window.

Some friends tried to dance around the subject and talk about happier things. Others dove right into it, asking details from the accident, leaving us all trying to make sense of how it unfolded. "How did the car crash?" they asked, striking visions of that dark, breezy night in my mind and making my stomach turn.

"Ugh, I don't exactly know," I replied. "I guess Alan fell asleep at the wheel and didn't make it around that curve in the highway. They said it rolled side over side, then end over end until it stopped upside down." Images of the front page of the paper haunted me. I could practically see the wheels still spinning through the snapshot.

"So, how did you and Cody get thrown out of the car?" my braver friends would continue to ask. Though it made me feel sick, I couldn't stop imagining the scene in my mind anyway and appreciated every opportunity to talk it out, as if I'd suddenly remember a missing piece of the puzzle.

"Out the back window," I explained. "I had my seatbelt on, and the seatbelt didn't break. I know Cody didn't have one on, but I can't figure out how the seatbelt let me go, too."

"That's so crazy!" my friends all said. A tingle ran up my spine every time I thought about it.

"They found me on the shoulder of the road, in the gravel," I continued. "Cody was thrown far into the trees. I don't know how, but it's like his body protected mine and took the harder hit. He might have literally saved my life...." My voice trailed off with my mind, imagining Cody's body laying over me and being thrown from the car first. Every time, my eyes welled with tears. *He didn't deserve this,* I'd think to myself. *I wish I died instead.*

At this point in the conversation, we were all usually in tears, my friends and I still stunned that such a tragedy could happen to us. From there, my friends would change the subject. Usually, updates on what was happening back at school or the latest weekend shenanigans. Then one day, my friend Kasye was bold enough to ask about me moving on.

"Could you see yourself dating anyone else?" Kasye asked while sitting with me on my bed one afternoon.

It had barely been two weeks since Cody died; I was stunned by her question. *How could I possibly want to be with anyone else?* I immediately reacted in horror. After all that I had been through to be with

Cody, I couldn't bear the thought of enduring any further relationship pain. He was the only one worth fighting for, and I lost the battle terribly. I didn't feel worthy of ever being loved again. I wanted to be angry at Kasye for even asking. *But come on, she's only asking an honest question,* I thought. *And I'm only eighteen; I can't really be alone forever.*

Still silent, I asked myself the question once more in my mind and was surprised by the answer. I paused for a moment and swallowed down the nauseating lump in my throat.

"You know what," I finally said. "As appalled as I am by this question, a bizarre thing popped in my head. Of course, I don't want to be with anybody besides Cody. But for some reason, Logan came to mind. I don't know why."

Until now, I thought nothing of Logan. He was just another friend in the grade below me. Well, I knew he had a crush on me years earlier. And we had kissed at a party while Jake and I briefly broke up the year before. But he and I together? I was too tangled in my webs with Jake and Cody; I never considered it. At least, apparently, not until now.

"That's really weird," I said to my friend in utter disgust of myself. "I can't believe anyone else came to mind."

"Not really. I could see you two together," Kasye responded thoughtfully.

I paused for another moment, brushed it off, and changed the subject back to Cody. Back to the greatest love and pain that I couldn't stop obsessing over. I wasn't ready to think about someone else. As much as I was missing the warm embrace of a hug, I didn't want anyone else. I just wanted Cody back. And if I couldn't have him, all I wanted was to sink into a dark hole and disappear from this Earth.

I got comfortable hiding in the safety and comfort of my own home during those two weeks and dreaded the thought of my first day back to school.

When the inevitable day arrived, I made my mom drop me off during the middle of first period so I wouldn't have to face the crowds of kids in the hallway before class. As I slowly approached the door, the coast looked clear; no one was down the hallway straight ahead. I cautiously stepped through the door. Suddenly, I saw someone come around the corner at the end of the hall.

*Oh shit!* I panicked, trying to swallow the lump in my throat. I suddenly felt like an idiot waddling like a stiff penguin in my full-torso back brace hiding under my baggy sweatshirt. *Who is that down there?*

As I stepped forward, I recognized who it was. *You've got to be kidding me,* I thought with dread. It was Logan. Surprise and sympathy washed over his face as he recognized me, too. His arms opened wide as he came closer.

"Krista, holy shit. I'm so glad you're okay," he exclaimed, wrapping his arms around my brace for a hug. "I'm so sorry about what happened."

"Oh shit, sorry. I'm wearing a back brace," was all I could sputter as I reactively pushed away and exposed the brace under my zip-up.

"Oh, I don't care, get in here!" he replied, hugging me tighter. I felt a wave of comfort wash away my embarrassment. I might have even felt a butterfly flutter in the pit of my anxious stomach. We chatted for another moment or two before I continued up the steps to face my worst fear: going back to school.

I already knew I couldn't stand people watching me, asking how I was, and giving their sympathy. Being in the spotlight of Jake's accident had practically killed me. But now? Cody really was dead. All because I wanted to party. And I sure as hell couldn't hide it; I'd been missing from school for weeks and still had scars and black eyes to show for it. *At least my teeth are fixed now,* was the only reassuring thought I could find. Still, I couldn't handle it. I couldn't focus. I couldn't think.

With Cody dead, I found myself racing even faster than before to the next substance that could numb my reality. I returned to autopilot through the motions of recovery, going back to school, and pretending I was "okay."

I didn't even realize at the time how far more intense my anxiety had become. I feared stepping foot anywhere in public that someone might recognize me and ask how I was doing. I could barely sit still for more than a few minutes, especially in the classroom. I could no longer hold in my tears before walking right out of class and out of the building. I was drowning in the unfathomable consequence of Cody's death.

I wasn't the only one drowning in consequences. Alan, the unfortunate one in the driver's seat that night, was sitting in jail awaiting his final sentence. I felt terrible for him. He didn't deserve this. I was just as guilty; he just happened to be driving. Through several confusing visits with my appointed lawyer, I was constantly questioned about the accident and eventually invited to his sentencing trial. If I wanted to, I could speak or write a letter to testify for or against him. My heart leaped at the opportunity to help him and wrote a letter immediately.

I eagerly attended the trial, nearly shaking with nerves; I hadn't seen Alan since before we crashed. I cried upon laying eyes on him. I could feel his grief was just as powerful as my own. I didn't end up speaking in open court, though my letter was reviewed by the jury. Alan ended up sitting in jail for another 467 days before being released on probation and able to rebuild a normal life.

Though standing up for Alan brought me some peace, the days carried on painfully, and I constantly longed for Cody and anything that belonged to him or reminded me of him. I wore his hoodies and even his cologne, melting in the familiar scent I loved so much. His mom started calling me often, which filled me with equal amounts of comfort and sadness. *She might be the only woman who misses him more than I do,* I thought to myself each time we spoke.

One day, she told me that, ironically, their two dogs happened to mate and that their sweet old black lab, Rosie, had just delivered two puppies.

"Oh, my goodness," I replied. "Can I please have one of the puppies?" Immediately, I knew I had to have one. *How is it possible that Cody's 12-year-old dog had puppies right after he died?* I thought. It couldn't just be a coincidence!

"Of course, I'll let you know when they're old enough," his mom replied sweetly.

The idea of bringing a new life into my world, especially one connected to Cody, gave me hope and something to look forward to. Yet, between brief glimmers of hope while thinking about these puppies, the rest of my days were long and depressing. What could possibly make me feel better at this point? Anything to make me numb.

*The Daisy Diaries* | 95

Once I was free to get out of the house with my friends again, I went straight back to partying. And what did you know, Logan was often there, too. I mean, he always was; I just didn't notice before. I was surprised and disgusted with myself to feel my heart flutter when I saw him across the room. He was already looking at me. My stomach turned in knots. Suddenly, I sensed a familiar magnetic force between us.

*Wait a minute,* I thought. *Cody is dead. How can I be feeling this?* Then, just as quickly, a sense of knowing came to me, like I was being directed to Logan. *Could Cody be leading me to him?* I wondered. *I know he wouldn't want me so sad and alone. He loved me so much. I know he wants me to be happy. He went through so much when he was alive to relieve my pain.* Tears automatically welled in my eyes. Embarrassed by the secret moment I was having in the middle of a party, I choked back those tears with the excruciating pain of missing Cody's physical presence. *I just want you back, Cody,* I thought to myself sadly.

Looking up, I caught eyes with Logan again. *Is Logan who you want me to be with now?* I asked Cody in my mind. I didn't wait for an answer. *It's too soon. Too much. I'm not ready,* I concluded. *But I'm so fucking lonely.*

The conversation in my head was too heavy to carry on, so I picked up my drink and took a huge gulp. The liquor burned from my throat down to my stomach. *That's better,* I thought, taking a big sigh of relief.

I looked up from my drink, catching glances with Logan one more time. As far as I knew, he was still dating someone anyway. *I don't need to think about this now,* I concluded to myself, taking another burning drink. I flashed a quick smile to Logan that acknowledged his attention and kept my distance. For a little while, at least.

The night before prom that year, I was drinking heavily, of course. Partly drinking my dread away for the next day, I was devastated over my broken plans with Cody and only slightly excited to honor him by going with his brother instead. Well, no. I mostly dreaded it. I didn't want to go with his brother; I just wanted to be with Cody. But his brother kindly offered, and my friends refused to let me skip my senior prom, so I felt obligated to go and be the only one alone at the end of the night.

As quickly as my mind sunk into misery over the following day, a noise caught my attention. I turned my head to look across the room and caught eyes with Logan. Again. My stomach turned, my heart fluttered, and I couldn't prevent a smile from spreading across my face. He bashfully smiled, too.

Logan and I talked and innocently flirted through the night within circles of our friends. Eventually, the numbers dwindled, but I wasn't ready to go home yet. I was never ready to go home yet. But it was time to leave the party, so the last few of us piled into my car and drove to a friend's apartment. There, everyone scattered and settled to sleep, leaving Logan and me sitting on the couch.

Looking into his dark brown eyes, I recognized a familiar feeling. Of longing, of being misunderstood, of so desperately wanting a connection, yet terrified of it at the same time. It felt so foreign, and so wrong, to be looking into someone else's eyes. Part of me wanted to crawl into my hole and return to sobbing out the unbearable grief of losing Cody. Yet, another part of me felt a similar comfort in Logan's new, brown eyes. *He seems as sad and lonely as I am,* I thought. *We must have been brought together for a reason. And gosh, is it nice not to be alone right now.*

Our conversation grew quiet. For a moment, we stared at one another as sparks seemed to fly around us, drawing us in like a magnet for a kiss. At first, it felt wrong. But a second later, I was consumed by this all-new sensation. I was desperate to feel anything good or comforting, and wow, it felt good to kiss someone again. Logan's lips were big and soft and felt just right in their own way. The heat continued to rise until the all-too-familiar shot of guilt struck me.

"Oh no!" I exclaimed, pressing myself away from him. "What about Teresa?"

"We're breaking up anyway," he attempted to reassure me. "I'll make it clear it's over tomorrow."

My gut knew that no matter how bad their relationship was or wasn't, he was going to feed me this line regardless. I mean, come on, he had me alone and all to himself for the first time after years of crushing on me. As a teenage boy with raging hormones, of course, he was going to take the opportunity! And what did I really care? Certainly not about myself. Did I know how to care about anything anymore? Instead, we continued fooling around and discussing our prom plans the following evening.

Oh, prom. The event of the year that always promised wild and illegal shenanigans of epic proportions. Teenage drinking, reckless partying, sex, and heartbreak, all wrapped into one night tied with ribbons of expensive prom dresses and rented tuxes.

Who knew that I would find myself in yet-again another love triangle at prom time? But this time, I was the other girl, not the girlfriend. As you know, Cody's brother stepped in to be my prom date. And Logan went to prom with his former girlfriend, who still believed they were dating. Little did she know about our rendezvous the night before, nor our plans for the after-party that evening.

Looking back, it makes me sick to think that I fell into such a backstabbing plot, especially considering my prom-trauma history. *How did I manifest another icky love triangle? And so quickly? What the hell is wrong with me?* I wondered. But my 18-year-old self was too blinded by denial and depression to take any responsible action. I couldn't see or consider anyone else's pain; mine alone was too much to bear. I numbed myself to the core and operated in survival mode, only thinking about what could possibly relieve any of my misery.

Instead of removing myself from the situation, I told myself that Logan and Teresa were destined to break up, whether or not I came into the picture. *I was led to him for a reason, right? I'm just helping them get through the inevitable, aren't I? This is for everyone's good,* I attempted to reassure myself. *Everything's going to work out just fine. And I'm not alone anymore.*

Although I thought I had found a new love in Logan, I wasn't ready to slow down the party. And through my relationship with him, I was still numbing the pain of losing Cody. I was accused of using Logan as "the replacement." To this day, I'm honestly not sure if I did or not. *Would we*

*have ever gotten together if Cody didn't die?* That was a question that would forever plague our relationship.

I did my best to ignore the accusations. *If I weren't meant to be with Logan, Cody would still be alive,* I concluded to myself. Just as much as I denied the accusations, I rejected the reality that I was still clinging to any bit of Cody left that I could find, including the puppies that were now ready for new homes.

Without mentioning it to my parents, I went to meet and pick up one of the puppies. I fell in love upon laying eyes on the sweet, black pup. I already knew what her name would be.

"You look like a Daisy," I said to her. We immediately locked eyes. There was something familiar about her eyes like we knew each other before. Perhaps she looked into my eyes with that same hope of being loved and taken care of as Cody did. So I brought her home and surprised my family, who ultimately couldn't resist her. Before we knew it, Daisy became the newest family member.

Though she would grow into a giant 100-pound German Shepherd/Lab mix, I carried that pup around with me everywhere like a lap dog. Everywhere I went, she was with me, and so was Logan. Suddenly, Daisy was like our "baby."

At least until the weekend evenings came, that was party time. Though I was excited by the new distraction of an adorable puppy, it wasn't enough to dull my pain. Nothing was, but I was still determined to drink, smoke, or snort anything that possibly could.

Though I was willing to do any drug offered to me, Logan refused to touch them. As you might imagine, that quickly became an issue. Although I loved the comfort of being with him and not being alone, I wasn't letting go of my numbing crutches.

One night at a party, someone flashed around a bag of cocaine and asked, "Who's in?"

*Hell yes!* I thought. I'd try anything. And little did I know just how much that would upset Logan. He didn't hold me back nor say a word for the next few days. I felt him start to pull back and distance himself, but then again, I was high as a kite the whole time anyway.

Logan ended up breaking up with me a few days later. He couldn't stand watching me get fucked up all the time. I couldn't blame him, but I was crushed. I mean, he was the one waiting for his chance for me! I was awesome, wasn't I? As he opened up about his personal pain from his parents' past drug use, my heart broke with guilt. I didn't even like the cocaine that much; I just didn't care about myself or my life enough to turn any drug down. If I had known how much it hurt him, I wouldn't have done it.

*Or would I have?* I guess we'll never know. We broke up, and I was alone again. And now that I didn't have anyone to care what I was doing, the partying continued even harder.

# Chapter 9

## July 2007:

### The Life-Saving Surprise

It was late July. I had barely made it through graduation and yet another heartbreak. Now free from high school, I could party even harder and headed to a rock festival with my friends for an entire weekend of camping and drunken shenanigans. However, I didn't feel like my usual self. My stomach felt full, and I had difficulty drinking as much as I wanted to. Even more strange, my cigarettes tasted terrible. By the festival's last days, I gave my nearly full pack to a friend; I couldn't smoke them anymore. *Weird*, is all I thought.

One morning, our group drove to a lake for my girlfriend and me to wash our hair. A few minutes after hopping back into the van and heading down the road, I felt queasy.

"Woah, I think I'm going to puke," I said. Immediately, my friends teased me about being the first one hungover enough to throw up as the van slowed down to a stop on the shoulder of the road. I leaned out the side door and threw up. Within seconds, I felt fine again. "Well, that was odd; I felt fine earlier." I shrugged it off, and so did my friends. We continued back to the festival, though I felt more tired, and man, cigarette smoke was starting to smell bad.

A few days later, it happened again. I was eating lunch at my mom's house, and within minutes of finishing my food, I suddenly felt sick and threw up in the bathroom. My mom was standing outside the bathroom door when I came out. "Were you drinking last night?!" she questioned.

"No, but this has happened a couple times before."

Light bulbs of shock lit up over our heads.

"Did you and Logan..." she exclaimed, not even able to finish the question we both already knew the answer to.

"Well…"

Both of us went silent.

"I need to get ready to go to the cottage," my mom finally declared. She packed and took off, leaving me to sit there and contemplate what was happening. I immediately called my best friend, Mel, and asked her to go pick up a few pregnancy tests and see if, in fact, my fate was leading me down another terrifying turn.

I peed nervously over the stick, with a knot in my stomach that told me I already knew what it would say. We sat the stick of destiny on the kitchen countertop. I couldn't look at it at all until it was time. My heartbeat raced. I wanted to puke again. After the longest two minutes of my life, Mel picked up the stick. A confused look washed over her face.

"What does it say?" I shrieked.

"Well, I'm not quite sure…." Mel replied. I snatched it out of her hands and looked down. Two lines. Two fucking lines. I was pregnant.

"It's fucking positive!!" I exclaimed in panic.

"Well, I thought both of the lines would be more defined or closer together, ya know?" Mel replied innocently.

"There are still two fucking lines on it, Mel!" I yelled. "What am I going to do?"

"Well, it's clearly meant to be," Mel calmly encouraged me. "You need this."

"How could I possibly *need* Logan's fucking baby?" I questioned.

*Wait a minute. When did we break up?* I suddenly thought, counting on my fingers. *Nine months from then will be… March… So, the baby will be due…*

"Holy shit!" I exclaimed in disbelief. "This baby will be here around the anniversary of the car accident."

A shockwave of tingles ran through my body. I didn't know what it was at the time, but some sort of power much greater than I filled me with a chill of hopeful fate. Mel was right; I did have to have this child.

"Shit," I said quietly.

"See, I told you!" she replied happily. "You're meant to have this baby."

I took a deep breath and swallowed down the truth of her words. "But I don't know what I'm doing," I finally responded. "And we just graduated! What about my new freedom? And getting a hippy van and driving down to Mexico?"

*And what about my grand plan to crash my car on the accident anniversary?* I thought to myself. Even Mel didn't know about that wild idea. No one could know, or they'd try to stop me from doing it.

"I guess God has another plan," Mel responded thoughtfully. "You'll be fine. Your motherly instincts will kick in at the right time. And shit, if my mom had me in high school, you'll be fine just out of it!"

"Oh, yeah. I guess this is better than still being in high school!" I agreed. "Ok, I can do this." I felt a strangely comforting sense deep within my core that made me feel protected. "Now… how the hell do I tell Logan and my parents?"

At least my mom already had time to process the situation after the scare of my spontaneous spew from lunch that day. As the person I tried most to keep my darkest secrets from, I was surprised to find that my mom was the only person I felt comfortable telling this time. She already knew. She already had to accept it. What I didn't want to do was say out loud that I was pregnant, and that Logan, my now ex-boyfriend who dumped me over my excessive drug use, was the father.

How could I tell Logan? He dumped me a few weeks earlier and was back with his ex. Thinking about it made my stomach turn. Ugh, I'm the "other girl." The "other girl," who got pregnant.

My biggest fear throughout my relationship with Jake was getting pregnant. Back then, we diligently used condoms, and I took birth control once I could get on it. The thought of getting pregnant at that age was utterly horrifying to me. Absolutely not an option. No way. We made sure it would never happen.

There was no doubt that I had gotten much more careless since Jake and I fell apart, and many of my encounters with Cody were under extreme intoxication, but even then, he and I were super careful, too. Nothing scared me more than getting pregnant.

Yet something changed in me since the car accident. Since I stopped giving a shit about myself and my life. Careless only mildly describes it. Completely reckless, I felt like I had nothing left to lose. *Who cares about me at this point anyway?* I sure didn't.

Apparently, my fear of pregnancy faded into the darkness along with everything else I once cared about. And for reasons far beyond my own comprehension, Logan ignited every one of my physical senses to a nearly uncontrollable state. While we were together, we couldn't keep our hands off each other.

For possibly the first time, I felt 100% confident in my skin around him. I knew he had a crush on me over the years, and perhaps because he was younger than me, I felt dominant and unusually motivated to teach him new things.

He later confessed that he was slightly intimidated by me, but I had always sensed that and used it to my advantage. In hindsight, I must admit that part of me wanted to play with him like a puppet; *do what I want, make me happy again, and worship the ground I walked on...* like Cody once did. And his reward for his obedience? Well, you know. Apparently making a baby.

But Logan's obedience only lasted as long as I could stay sober, which wasn't long at all. After that, he couldn't be intimidated by me anymore; he was disgusted by my excessive and reckless drug use. Well, now that I was pregnant, I guess I couldn't do drugs anymore.

Logan and I weren't talking, though; how was I supposed to tell him that I was pregnant? I ended up telling our friend Kasye, who promised to get a hold of him for me. To my surprise, he called within hours. I threw up in my mouth when I saw his name appear on my cell phone. *Oh shit, here it goes,* I thought to myself, swallowing my nausea.

"Hello?" I answered nervously.

"Hey, Kris," he said urgently. "Tell me what's going on. Are you pregnant?"

My eyes immediately welled up with tears. After a few seconds of catching my breath, I answered, "Yes."

"Holy shit," he responded. "I fucking knew it when Kasye told me I needed to get a hold of you right away. Fuck. What are we going to do?"

"I don't know," was all I could say, unable to hide my tears through the phone.

We agreed to meet in a couple days. With each of our best friends at our sides, we met to discuss our options: abortion, adoption, or keeping the baby. As I suspected, Logan was pro-abortion or adoption. "We're too fucking young to have a baby right now, Kris."

I agreed; the thought of having a baby terrified me. I knew I wasn't ready. Yet I couldn't ignore the tugging in my heart that told me I needed to do this.

After many days of discussing and fighting over our options, I reached a breaking point, yelling at Logan on the phone.

"I'd rather die than have your fucking baby," I shouted at him and hung up the phone, overwhelmed with rage. "I'm going to get an abortion and never deal with him again," I swore to myself.

I told my mom my new decision, who surprisingly took it well. "Whatever you decide, I support you," she consoled me. Being a devout Catholic woman, I couldn't believe she was willing to support my decision to get an abortion. It relieved me to know that she wouldn't disown or condemn me to hell for doing such a thing. *I'll figure out what I need to do next tomorrow,* I concluded.

I woke up the next morning with certainty in my heart and a heavy weight in my gut. *I can't get an abortion*, I realized. *I just know I must keep this baby. Logan can do whatever he wants; I'll do this by myself.*

I knew my final decision wouldn't go over well, especially since Logan was already back with his ex. But I couldn't deny the truth I felt inside me; I needed to have this baby. I knew Mel was right. I needed something to live for.

It was no surprise that my pregnancy at age eighteen wasn't celebrated. No one was excited about it; we were all terrified. I had no idea how to take care of a baby, nor did I really want to; I just knew I needed to. I felt trapped in my own life, even more than I already was, and I was angry about it. But I couldn't ignore my gut feeling that consistently said loud and clear, "You are meant to have this baby."

I had no idea why or how it could possibly help my current situation, but perhaps for the first time in my life, I stood firmly in faith. I had an unexplained sense of absoluteness that everything would work out. Like God was really here, supporting and helping me out. A feeling so comforting and foreign, it was like someone else put it inside me; I couldn't have created it myself.

Suddenly, there was so much to focus on: taking care of my pregnant body, preparing to bring a baby into the world, and registering for school at the community college. *How would I pick myself back up and do it all?* I had just spent the last year drowning in depression and drugs through reckless and suicidal behavior. But now I was pregnant; I *had* to be sober. I *needed* to be sober… and I needed a reason powerful enough to *want* to be sober.

Without a doubt, I believe that this baby was coming to be that reason. Long before I could feel them kick inside my belly, I felt the strongest bond forming between me and this new life I was creating. It's like we immediately signed an unsaid agreement between us: that they would come and give me a reason to keep living, and I'd love and take care of them with all that I had. Forming this bond with my unborn child is exactly what I needed to stop focusing on my dark hole of depression and turn around to face the light. I suddenly wasn't living for my sorry self anymore; I was living for another human life.

Looking back, I have all faith that Divine intervention helped my early transition into sobriety. The immediate responsibility for the health of this human kept my mind focused, and my body literally began rejecting the toxins I once depended on weeks before I knew I was pregnant.

By the second trimester, I got used to missing out on the parties and spending my evenings and weekends at home, often taking long showers or baths and going to sleep early. I wasn't the party girl anymore; I was an exhausted and pregnant new college student.

I started the first-year nursing program at my community college that fall; my mind was boggled over anatomy, physiology, and whatever random food I was craving at the time, likely cottage cheese. I also started a new job that summer at a women's clothing store in town, so my schedule quickly filled with classes and work shifts to keep my mind busy. And man, after that, all I wanted to do was sleep! I explored every option of crazy-shaped pregnancy pillows to help keep my precious sleep time as comfortable as possible as my belly grew to basketball size. Sleep, eat, school, repeat. Finally, I was back on a healthy routine.

Things were beginning to look up again for the first time in what felt like ages. I was especially surprised by the transformation in my relationship with my parents. Now that I was sober, we could communicate again. They had nothing else to worry about me now that I was already pregnant. Somehow, it felt like some of the pressure was relieved. The once-constant fear of "what could possibly happen next?"

had finally settled; there was nothing left to happen! Though the initial discovery of my pregnancy was a shock to us all, I quickly found myself comfortable in the presence of my parents again, no longer hiding my intoxication or drug paraphernalia.

I felt like part of me returned to life. Krista was back and going to school. My original, intelligent self was back in focus and ready for success. I needed a good job; I knew I would be on my own raising my baby, though I still held high hopes to make things magically work with Logan and my perfect family dream come true.

But something in my gut knew differently. *Depend on no one. Aim high. You can do this alone,* I heard.

And perhaps, the wild on and off rollercoaster relationship with Logan also spoke differently. Never knowing where I really stood with him, nor him with me, and most importantly, where he stood as a father to my child constantly stressed me out. Much of my pregnancy was spent in anxiety over our latest argument and fear of our future. Because of this, I tried to hide my pregnancy and avoided talking about it. I was embarrassed to have to explain who the father was. I was already traumatized by the nasty rumors that had relayed back to me about Jake, Cody, and the car accident. "Did you hear what she's doing? Can you believe what happened to her? Is she cursed?" I could hear the community whisper. *Am I cursed? What will they say about me now?* I often feared.

As the months carried on, and I first heard, saw, and felt the baby move inside me, our bond grew even stronger. That bond certainly didn't happen for Logan, though. He only joined one doctor's visit with me: the ultrasound that would predict the baby's sex. Until then, we were confident that we were having a boy. Honestly, I felt I needed a boy for Logan to have any genuine desire to be a father. However, the doctor saw otherwise.

"Congratulations, you're having a baby girl," he told us. I watched the excitement drain from Logan's face, though he pretended to be happy. Though I, too, was initially disappointed for Logan's and our potential future's sake, I ultimately felt even more connected to my baby girl.

This new connection with my baby girl was unlike anything I had experienced before. It fueled me with faith. I started embracing the journey to motherhood, letting my love for this unknown baby overpower my fear of judgment or rejection from Logan. Ultimately, it didn't matter what anyone else did or said to me; no matter what, I wasn't alone anymore.

This love and unwavering faith also fueled my curiosity to understand the meaning behind the complex events of life. *Why did Jake have to be paralyzed? Why did Cody have to die? Why, of all people, did I have to have Logan's baby?* These questions rattled through my mind daily. *How do all these broken pieces fit together? Who am I supposed to be with?*

I often brought these questions to Suzanne, who I was still seeing. By this point, I eagerly visited her every week. She had become my primary source of support, understanding, and clarity over the last year, and I found great comfort in her presence.

Suzanne always let me speak and listened without judgment or interruption, offering a safe space to open my mouth and heart. That alone meant the world to me. I was often interrupted in the fleeting moments I felt compelled to open up about anything to my mom. I know that she always meant well and wanted to give her best advice and support, but the frequent interruptions made me feel broken and stupid. Like I needed to be fixed for thinking the way I did. Though my dad was quiet and listened intently in each brief discussion we rarely had, I was too embarrassed to open up to him about my current problems. School or sports, sure. But the tangled webs with the boys I was having sex with? No way! I lived a parent's nightmare and could hardly look them in the eyes after all the stress I had put them through.

Suzanne's office became my safe haven, a place where I wasn't broken. The hours spent in her office offered far more relief and natural healing than any prescription or street drug I had ever taken. I didn't notice it yet, but I felt a little lighter and freer with each visit and release of my biggest worries and secrets. Suzanne always accepted and validated my craziest thoughts and offered encouraging advice. And now, with a baby on the way and unsure who I would end up raising the child with, I needed Suzanne's support and encouragement more than ever.

"You be nice to my Krista," she told me. "You've been through a lot, and you're way too hard on yourself. You don't know how brilliant and brave and inspiring you are, but I do. So you be good to my Krista."

*Wow, I guess I am really hard on myself,* I suddenly realized. Until then, I believed I deserved to be punished. I clearly did something wrong to deserve the tragic love triangles I manifested. Through the rumor mill, I had even heard someone name me "The Black Widow" for my involvement in Jake's and Cody's fateful accidents. And now, I was pregnant and tangled in another ugly triangle with Logan and Teresa.

I finally dared to ask out loud the question that plagued me for over a year.

"Am I cursed?"

Suzanne never hesitated.

"Absolutely not," she firmly declared. "Don't you say that. Those things would have happened to Jake and Cody whether or not you were involved. How lucky they were to have you around when they needed you. And now it's time to take care of you and your baby girl."

I released a loud sigh. "Yeah, this baby. That might not have a father. This is not how I wanted to have my first child," I replied sadly.

"You'd be surprised by how many kids I have here with separated parents," she reminded me once. "Many kids don't even know at least one parent, often both. Don't put such high expectations on yourself for having a "perfect" family. Trust that you are enough for this little girl and that the right person will come to your side, no matter who it is."

As Logan drifted away, I noticed Jake drifting back in. After absorbing the shock of my pregnancy, we started talking more often and rekindling a friendship. I suddenly couldn't imagine not having him in my life after sharing so many traumatic moments together. There was no one else on earth who witnessed all the same things that we did together, and now that the heart-breaking tension over Cody was dissolved entirely, I felt a new bond growing with him, too. I suddenly found it interesting that Logan was back together with his ex; *what if I'm meant to get back together with my ex, too?*

I spent more and more time with Jake, to the point that I started sleeping over at his house. The irony blew my mind every time. I couldn't believe that our parents were letting us have sleepovers. Well, what did it matter anymore now that I was pregnant? Paralyzed and pregnant, what a pair we made now. Though our old life seemed like another lifetime ago, it relieved me to feel his familiar presence again. I partially stepped back into my former role as caretaker, and we spent the evenings laying in his bed, watching movies, innocently cuddling and sometimes kissing, as if our romance had rewound. I often couldn't help but wonder, *If only we could have been more like this at the beginning of our relationship... Maybe that's why we're finally experiencing it now.*

I began to imagine a new future with a baby and Jake. *Could I really handle both?* I couldn't handle taking care of Jake the first time around, and now I had to add a baby to the mix. *Have I completely lost my mind?* I wondered. Well, if I did, I did a long time ago, so what did it matter? Jake loved me, he always had, and Logan chose his ex over me, so why wouldn't I want to love Jake back?

I decided to give it a shot and trust that the universe, or God, or something had my back and would guide me in the right direction. So, I continued exploring this new relationship with Jake, spending my time in his new accessible bedroom, talking for hours, playing games, music, and movies, and helping with his daily care routine.

Jake was one of the first people I told I was pregnant, but we hadn't talked much about it since. I was embarrassed that I got pregnant and dumped in such a short time. If I had only stayed with Jake, this wouldn't have happened. *Does he really want to take me back now?* As my belly grew, the inevitable was harder to avoid talking about. I constantly thought about my baby and how to deal with Logan; how could I not confide in Jake about it if we were going to be together? We eventually grew to share excitement for the baby, and Jake did his best to support me. But anytime I mentioned something offensive that Logan did or said to me, he'd get upset. "I wish I was still able to kick that kid's ass." My heart sank every time he said it. *I wish you were still able to, too.*

By wintertime, my belly got too large to walk Daisy anymore. My puppy quickly grew bigger and stronger and dragged whoever walked her across the icy winter roads. As I slowly lost my balance and view of my feet, my dad took over dog-walking duty. Daisy eventually transitioned into my parents' companion, and I solely focused on school and preparing for my baby.

I also grew more tired. Tired of being pregnant, tired of the daily routine with Jake, and tired of the sickness in my stomach over my volatile relationship with the father of my unborn child. As the baby came closer, I found myself growing closer to my child and drifting away from Jake, again. The reality of motherhood was looming over me now; my time was running out quickly. I had to put my priorities in order, and first on the list had to be my baby. Just weeks before the baby was due, I ended up softly breaking off the romance between Jake and I while lying in his bed one night.

"I just have to say," I nervously started as we both laid on his bed, staring at the stars on his ceiling. "I'm always going to love you with all of my heart, but with this baby coming, I have to give her all of my love for a while. I'm honestly too overwhelmed to think about juggling both our relationship and taking care of a baby at the same time. I just need to get used to being a mom."

"Oh," he responded softly. "I totally get it. I mean, I kind of figured anyway." He had a slight crack in his voice. "I'm always going to love you, too."

Just how many ways could I break one man's heart? I had lost count by this point. But we both knew that soon, once again, things would never be the same. Not after my baby arrived.

# Chapter 10

## March 2008:

## The Day Light Entered My World

One afternoon after work, I noticed that I kept getting a weird cramp in my stomach. Used to just "breathing it out," I ignored the pain, took a few deep breaths, and carried on about my evening. However, another hour or two later, I couldn't ignore the irritating pang that kept tying knots in my belly. I made a comment in passing to my mom about my stomach ache, and her energy immediately heightened, "You're having contractions!" she exclaimed. "How far apart are they?"

"I don't know," I replied. "I didn't know I was having them!"

"Start timing them," she instructed. "Why don't you go lay down, and I'll call the doctor. We'll bring you to the hospital when they get close."

I had no idea what I was in for. After another hour of contractions at home in my bedroom, we decided to head to the hospital. I laid up all night there, and though my contractions kept getting stronger, I wasn't making any progress. Every hour or so, a nurse or doctor would come in to check my cervix. *Holy shit*, I thought to myself every time while bracing myself through clenched teeth, *this hurts like hell! How the hell am I going to get a baby out of there? Good Lord, help me!*

Until now, I felt overly confident in my ability to give birth. My mom had easy pregnancies and deliveries with my sister and me, so I assumed I would have a similar experience. I didn't pre-sign for an epidural ahead of time, but by hour twenty of labor and contractions, I was ready to kill someone I was in so much pain.

"Oh my God," I exclaimed through gritted teeth, my face spotted with beads of sweat. "When is this going to be over?" Then, while laying on my side with a death grip on the hospital bed railing and my mom's hand, a poor woman was forced to inject a late-notice epidural into the spine of my crazed and sweaty, impregnated body. A few moments later, I felt sudden relief.

"Oh, wow," I exclaimed with a loud sigh. "That's so much better. And I'm exhausted. I'm so ready for a nap!" However, the baby had other plans. As soon as I finally got comfortable, two nurses came in, and one said, "Okay, great news! You're ready to deliver!"

In came the party for my delivery. Logan stood at my bedside, my mom on the other side, plus my friend Kasye, then my sister, and even my dad. *Just make sure Dad stays back in the corner,* I thought. Two nurses held my feet as the doctor started cracking jokes to my about-to-be-born baby.

"Come on out, baby," he coaxed, "I'll give you a pony if you do!" After what felt like forever trying to push but unable to feel how hard, cheers of awe and excitement filled the room. "It's a girl!" the doctor exclaimed as he placed her on my lap.

As soon as I laid eyes on her, tears burst from my eyes. I couldn't contain the overwhelming rush of longing, connection, and unconditional love for this baby. I had been waiting for so long to know what she looked like. This baby that lived hidden inside me for the last nine months. That I could feel every kick and wiggle, yet not know her face.

And here she was, right in front of me. I was suddenly a mom. And I was suddenly in so much love.

Logan stood by the side of the bed with a white-knuckle grip on its rail. Looking at him, a nurse asked, "Would you like to cut the cord, Dad?" He looked around the room with surprise, as if she might have been asking someone else. I looked up at him with an amused smile, "Yeah, go for it, Dad."

"Uh, okay," he replied nervously, releasing his grip. I couldn't see much of the action, but the group cheered after he cut it.

As quickly as she was put on my lap, the nurses took her away to be weighed and cleaned up. I laid there in a daze, feet still in stirrups as the doctor finished his business that I really didn't want to know about. "Just fix it up down there and don't tell me about it," I cringed, though still numb from the epidural.

Oohs and ahhs filled the room as Logan and my family took turns around the baby girl, letting her wrap her tiny hand around their fingers. Then the nurses took her away for what felt like ages to do her fingerprints and get her dressed. When they finally brought my baby bundle back in, she was swaddled in a white blanket, wearing a white and pink striped hat.

My heart overflowed as she settled into my arms. *Oh my God. This is my baby.* It felt so surreal and peaceful. Almost like how I once felt in Cody's presence, but this went even deeper. I created this human, and now no soul could be closer than her and I.

"I love you so much," was all I could say to her. Her little eyelids lifted, and her dark eyes looked up at me. I felt like our souls recognized each other in agreement to our partnership in this lifetime.

Though Logan was there to witness her birth, and I secretly hoped that he would have a change of heart (and, well, his entire nature) and become the father and partner I dreamed of having, I knew deep down that it was going to be just her and I. I looked in her eyes and silently vowed, *I'll never leave you. He might leave us, but there's nothing in the world that will ever take me away from you.*

My new love remained nameless for the rest of the afternoon. The entire time I was pregnant, I read through many baby name books but struggled to find one I really felt good about. I threw around names like Haley and Jaden, but Logan was not a fan. On the evening of her birth, a group of us were gathered in my hospital room, including Logan, my sister, parents, and Logan's best friend. With the baby sleeping soundly in my arms, we all tossed names around the room, none of which Logan and I both got excited about.

"Alright, here it is," Logan's best friend chimed in. "Krista, Jr." The room burst into laughter. We were clearly running out of ideas.

"I still really like Jaden," I said.

"No way," Logan argued, "it reminds me of a character I don't like."

"Are you serious? You're going to reject an awesome name because of a stupid cartoon character?" I argued in laughter.

"What about Jaelyn?" my sister suggested.

The room went quiet. Logan and I looked at each other as smiles grew on our faces.

"Jaelyn," I repeated.

"Jaelyn, I like that," Logan said.

"Jaelyn Rae Lindquist. Jaelyn Lindquist," I repeated, along with everyone else in the room.

"Jaelyn Rae it is," we finally agreed.

The next day was full of visitors, mostly mine and Logan's closest friends. It was like a high school party in my hospital room; teenagers were wandering in with excitement to see little Jaelyn. "Oh my God, I can't believe you have a baby! She's so precious!" they all said.

I still couldn't believe I had a baby either. As our classmates left, Logan went outside with his buddies. Just a few moments later, there was another knock on the door.

"Helloooo," called a familiar voice I immediately recognized. It was Jake's mom.

A wheelchair whizzed through the door, and there was Jake, with a big smile on his face. As he stopped, the buzz continued. Another wheelchair pulled up alongside him. It was his friend from the Colorado hospital, who happened to be visiting at that time.

"I believe congratulations are in order," Jake exclaimed.

"Oh my goodness! I'm so glad you're here! And it's so good to see you, too, Andy!" I replied. "Here she is."

I leaned forward with Jaelyn in my arms as everyone ooohed and ahhed.

"Want to hold her?" I asked Jake with a smile.

"Um, I'm not sure I know how to, but we can try!" he replied. I slowly placed Jaelyn in his lap as his mom snapped pictures for us.

Looking at Jake, my mind wandered into fantasy land. *This is crazy. I used to think I'd have his babies. What if this were his baby? Oh my God, I'm sure he'd be a much better father than Logan.* I looked up at his face. He was already looking at mine. We locked eyes for a moment, and I felt like he might have been sharing the same questions in his own mind. A little guilt stirred in my stomach. *I can't believe what's happened since we were together. Cody's dead. Now I just had some short-lived fling's baby. And right now, I really wish this baby were Jake's. I wonder if we could get back together. Could I take care of them both?*

My mind continued racing through the thousands of possible alternative realities. Until someone's cough dropped me back into the room. *This is what was meant to be for some reason. Maybe Jake can't have kids. Perhaps this could work. I love him so much for showing up and still caring about me. I want him to permanently be in Jaelyn's life somehow. I want Jake to be her godfather.*

After two nights in the hospital, it was finally time to take Jaelyn home. I first woke up in the wee hours from my hospital bed. The sound of silence filled the dark room before a gust of wind hit the window outside. A memory flashed into my mind: the cold wind blowing through the trees in the darkness, exactly one year earlier.

Just like it was happening again, I could see the dark sky and trees overhead from my vantage point lying on the highway's gravel shoulder. My body tensed and shivered with chills as I pulled my blanket up to my chin. Like a movie in my mind on fast forward, spotty memories of hearing Chad's frantic screams, him laying over me in tears, and the circle of paramedics around my head played before me. Then I envisioned something I had never actually experienced first-hand. It was Cody, flying out the back car window before me and slowing down my trajectory. Glimpses of him flying through the air and into the trees filled my imagination, before zooming over to my "softer" landing on the road.

A lump filled my throat. My eyes welled up. *I miss you so much*, I thought about Cody. *I can't believe it's been a whole year without you. And look at me now. I'm a mom. Because of you.* Tears rolled down my cheeks. *Thank you so much for saving my life... but I wish so much that this baby was yours. Why the hell am I here with Logan? He doesn't see me the way you did... and I don't think he ever will.*

The tears continued to flow while I sulked for a few more moments in the tingling pang of loneliness that swirled through my veins. My heart burned while I pictured Cody looking at me in my mind. Hugging me. The electricity between us stopping the world around us and making me feel like everything was okay. And then my eyes opened, dropping me back into the hospital bed. Back to reality. Back to the dark room, where I laid alone, while my baby was swaddled in the nursery down the hall. I took a deep breath in. *Everything happens for a reason*, I reminded myself. I said a quick prayer for Cody, Alan, Chad, and Cody's mom and slowly dozed back to sleep.

When I woke again, I couldn't wait for the nurses to bring my baby back to me. She was so perfect. So innocent. So mine. Every time I took her back into my arms, a flood of emotions poured like nothing I'd ever felt before. Now that I had Jaelyn, I had something to live for. I had made this perfect tiny human, and if I could do that, then I could do anything.

With her in my arms, nothing else I had before was good enough anymore. I immediately wanted to give her so much love and the best life I possibly could. But how could I do that? Not working as a nurse, which is what I was already in school for. Looking down at my sweet little babe asleep on my chest, I knew that I needed to challenge myself in a different way. Nursing was too personal to me; just being in a hospital to have my baby gave me chills from the past. I'd make a mess of a nurse, an emotional wreck. As much as I wanted to help others in pain, I now had to give all my care to my baby. And now, I had the motivation to rise above my painful past for this little girl.

For a second, my mind flashed back to high school chemistry when my teacher first told me I should be a Chemical Engineer. *Yes,* I thought. *I'm going to be an engineer.* I smiled. *But for right now, I'm going to enjoy taking Jaelyn home.*

Logan came back to the hospital later that morning for the big event. We awkwardly changed Jaelyn's diaper together and put her in the car seat. It felt unreal going through the motions with Logan and my family, but every time I looked at Jaelyn's face, it felt like I had been waiting all my life for her to appear.

That night, I laid in bed staring at the baby girl in the bassinet next to me. My heart overflowed with love. Suddenly, a memory came to me. On this day, I planned to kill myself. I once wanted to escape this life and join Cody on the other side. I imagined driving out to the car accident site in my little red SUV. I could see it flying off the road, tumbling its way to the bottom of the ditch. My heart skipped.

*I don't want to die anymore.*

Suddenly, I dropped back into my body, pulled by an anchor of love for my baby. I looked at her, sleeping so peacefully, as my eyes welled up with tears. "Thank you so much for choosing me now," I whispered to her. "You saved my life." I rolled to my back and pulled the comforter up to my chin, taking a deep breath in.

As I exhaled, I knew: *my work's not done here yet.*

As much as motherhood filled me with unfathomable love for my new baby girl, I still had no idea what I was doing. I was secretly thankful to still live at my parents' house with their help, even though I had awaited my entire life to break out of that house once I graduated. Instead, I was a new and clueless mom, figuring it out one diaper, breastfeeding, and puke-covered shirt at a time.

As for Logan, he was still finishing his senior year of high school. He came over a few times a week after track practice, where we gave Jaelyn baths together, played with her, and ogled at my large, hard boobs at feeding time. "Wow, your tits are huge, Kris," he teased. To an 18-year-old boy, of course, this was fascinating. And who am I kidding? To an 18-year-old girl, the sudden transformation was just as fascinating.

I had always wanted kids; I just never considered it possible to do so this early. I thought I'd have more time to prepare and know what I was in for. But I guess I never learned that way in my life; I had a habit of learning through experience, and all too often, mistakes.

I also always thought that I would get married before having a baby. Shit, I thought I'd be married to Jake right now and having his kids. Even though the door with Jake was still open, I couldn't get over my obsession to make my "real" family work with Jaelyn's father. I was scared that being with Jake would be too hard, and apparently believed struggling with Logan was somehow easier. So I kept Jake in the friend zone, even accepting the idea of him being with someone else, and continued to struggle.

Even though red flags waved all over my relationship with Logan, I believed I could make it work. *I'm meant to show him what a loving and stable family is like,* I thought. *We'll just stay together, go to college, get good jobs, and live happily ever after. No more bad things need to happen anymore!* Oh, the future in my head was so bright and rose-colored. Yet reality continued to paint a much darker and more complicated picture.

Though he ultimately broke up with Teresa, and we started a new on-again, off-again pattern, Logan still seemed distant and vague in discussing our future. I knew he was overwhelmed and scared; he was far from ready to be a dad. As I learned more of his traumatizing childhood, my compassion and determination to show him real love grew. Plus, there was still a powerful physical connection between us; it *had* to be love. I trusted that although things were complicated, everything would work out.

Just as much as we couldn't answer the questions about our future, we seemed to be hung up on one major question from our past: *If Cody didn't die, would we still be together?*

This question usually came up in heated discussions over where our relationship was going. As I put more pressure on Logan to get on my page and create the life I was dreaming about, he threw this question at me more often. And every time he asked the question, his eyes pierced me with his fear and uncertainty. Guilt and my own uncertainty struck me every time. I was afraid to ask myself the question. I couldn't let myself face the truth and quickly stopped him in his tracks.

"We were brought together this way for a reason," I tried to reassure him as much as myself. "If I were meant to be with Cody, he wouldn't be dead. And if I weren't meant to be with you, I wouldn't have gotten pregnant with your baby."

My words were comforting, temporarily. They often led to yet another steamy make-up session, and we'd be on again for a time, but that question would forever haunt us. Especially every time we looked into Jaelyn's eyes.

While I was pregnant, I constantly imagined what my baby would look like. Realizing that Logan and I had almost identical coloring, brown eyes, and brown hair, I always pictured a dark-haired, dark-eyed baby. However, as Jaelyn got older, her dark eyes lightened up until they became a bright, vibrant blue. So bright blue, they were mesmerizing.

One day while Jaelyn was sitting on my lap, we locked eyes for a long moment. I felt myself get drawn into those eyes, discovering all the complex swirls of white weaving through the deep blue for the first time. These eyes seemed to pull me in deeper than the ocean, and I was suddenly struck with a memory.

In my mind, I was suddenly sitting face to face with Cody in his bedroom, staring and sinking deeply into his bright blue eyes, mesmerized by the complex maze of white swirls…

*Oh. My. God. Jaelyn has Cody's eyes.* I realized. The eyes I once desperately longed to open one more time as I said goodbye to Cody's dead body. Suddenly, they were staring right back at me within my baby girl.

*No way, could she really be Cody's baby?* My mind automatically wondered. *Of course, no, she can't.* We did a paternity test. She was born a year after the car accident. Plus, I hardly survived that crash; there's no way that a baby would have survived that with me. *What does this mean?* I ultimately concluded that I was given the greatest gift in those beautiful eyes.

There was no way I could say these things to Logan, though I wondered if the same thought ever crossed his mind. *Nah, he's a guy. He probably doesn't even know what color eyes Cody had.* To him, I kept it to our basic seventh-grade science; with brown eyes, we both carried the blue-eyed gene. Both of our siblings and one parent also had blue eyes, so it really wasn't that much of a surprise. To this day, I don't know if he's ever seen Cody in Jaelyn's eyes as I have. I was always too afraid to ask at risk of digging up the painful question again.

*If Cody weren't dead, would we still be together?*

I guess we'll never find out.

# Chapter 11

## September 2008:

## Growing Pains

Though Jaelyn's birth literally saved my life, the transition into motherhood was a painful one. Like a young kid having a growth spurt, I felt like the changes happening to my body, in my mind, and in my unbelievable life situation were moving far faster than I could process.

Without a doubt, I believe that Jaelyn entered this world to save me and bring meaning back to my life. She gave me a reason to be sober and care about myself again. And based on the state I was in when I got pregnant, I have faith that Divine intervention helped my early transition into sobriety.

After Jaelyn was born, breastfeeding was no question; it was something I had to do because my body was designed to do it. But, of course, that meant I had to stay clean. Luckily, the instant focus on a newborn was enough to distract me from wanting to numb my emotions, at least temporarily. My attention on Jaelyn let me store my pain away and ignore it. Without constantly dwelling on my past mistakes, it was much easier to find more happiness and optimism. Jaelyn truly brought light back into my world.

Even my relationship with my parents significantly improved. Jaelyn magically brought us all back together, always spreading her adorably contagious smile. Who could be upset with the sweetest, happiest chunky baby around? Though I still butted heads with my mom regularly over parenting, we communicated and worked together as a team for what felt like the first time. And my dad's heart completely melted for Jaelyn. That little baby wrapped him around her tiny finger, and watching them together made me want to cry. *Thank God I can share my amazing dad with her,* I thought.

Jaelyn even brought me closer to my older sister, Monica. Since we entered our teen years, we drifted apart. I was the wild, outspoken party girl, while she was the quiet, well-behaved firstborn. But now, I was grown up and more responsible. Plus, I wasn't dating Jake, her classmate, anymore, resolving the years of unspoken awkwardness between us. Now, we had an adorable baby girl to adore and play with. Not to mention, Jaelyn's gorgeous blue eyes made her resemble my sister more than me. Jaelyn won over Monica just as quickly as the rest of us, and "Auntie Mony" would surely win over Jaelyn's love and adoration just as much. For the first time, my family truly felt close.

Except my new little family wasn't as strong. I still didn't know where I stood with Logan, nor where he stood as Jaelyn's father. Young and scared of raising a child, and still so confused about our feelings for one another, we constantly created conflicting tension and passion.

No one seemed to get under my skin quite like he did, and by this point, we learned all too well the right words to dig deep. It made me sick. Plus, I was jealous of his increased drinking and the freedom he had that I didn't.

Getting pregnant with Jaelyn halted my reckless party streak that had run fast and hard since I was fifteen. Now, knowing that all my friends, including Logan, could party as they pleased, I was envious. I still wanted to party, too. I wanted freedom. But I felt like an animal in a cage, confined by schedules. School, work, my parents' availability to babysit. Not to mention taking care of a baby. And I still really had no clue what I was doing. Overwhelmed? To say the least. And what was the only thing I knew to relieve my anxiety? Drugs.

I wanted to lean back into my old numbing crutches. But I was breastfeeding; smoking wasn't an option. Instead, I scheduled pumping and dumping around weekend outings just to drink and feel included with my friends. I begged my parents to babysit on weekends so I could live part of a "normal" 19-year-old life. I wanted to be free, but I had to be responsible. I felt tethered to Jaelyn, and it often made me feel trapped from living how I wanted to, but clearly, what I wanted was far from what I needed.

Jaelyn was about six or seven months old when we stopped breastfeeding for good. By that point, I was juggling babysitters and daycare schedules with my college classes and a new job waitressing at a local restaurant. I had pumped so much to fill bottles for babysitters and my weekend drinking relief that, by that time, my boobs felt like they just couldn't do it anymore.

Perhaps I manifested it. The old party girl in me wanted an escape from the dramatically frustrating relationship with her baby daddy, and she didn't want her body to be responsible for anyone else anymore. I thanked God that I could breastfeed as long as I did, and we slowly transitioned from the last of stored breastmilk to formula and baby foods.

I bought a pack of cigarettes within days of my last attempt at breastfeeding Jaelyn. I couldn't stand my own anxiety over Logan anymore and wanted a fix, just like he always had as a long-time smoker. That first puff of freedom was the best thing I had ever tasted. I finally had my own body back and could do whatever I wanted to make it feel better. Though it wasn't all to numb my pain and guilt this time, it was to keep myself going. I needed to keep up with my baby, school, and work... all by myself. And I wanted something to help me do it all.

It didn't take long to return to taking Adderall to get through my busy days and smoking pot to calm my busy mind at night. At first, it worked brilliantly. I had more energy and focus when I needed it, and I had relief to help me sleep at night.

*I wish I could get these prescribed!* I thought to myself. *They seem to do more than my antidepressant does.* As soon as breastfeeding was over, my doctor wrote me yet another new prescription; this one would also help with my back pain from the car accident and carrying a nine-pound baby. At first, it made me feel more tired and moody, the exact opposite of what I needed. Again. *What is this synthetic concoction, anyway? What is it doing for me?* Part of me wondered how much the trials of antidepressants over the last two years had really helped. Each one came with a torrential week or two of emotional chaos before settling a dull numbness in the background of my experience.

What surprised me more was what seemed to be helping me the most. For the first time, I recognized that I was using cannabis in a healthy way. Yes, I was using it, but I wasn't abusing it. Instead of smoking as much as I could, I took a puff or two on my couch after getting Jaelyn sound asleep. Immediately, I felt relief from my busy day and mustered up the motivation for homework. I became more interested in my assignments. I dove into books filled with calculus and physics equations, fascinated by and excited to solve them.

Though I spent most evenings alone on my couch doing homework, Logan was livid once he learned I returned to smoking pot. "Pot is for deadbeats," he'd say, glaring into my eyes like I was the lowest scum of the earth.

"How is smoking a bowl by myself, while our child is safely sound asleep, not to mention after I took care of her by myself all day, worse than your frequent drinking?" I argued.

"It's not the same, Kris," he'd bark back. "You know that. Pot is fucking illegal."

*Ugh, I know it's illegal,* I thought to myself. Fear of Logan holding it against me in court nauseated me. I couldn't fathom the thought of losing my daughter over a drug conviction. *But it helps calm my mind and get me into my really confusing homework. How is this mood-swinging antidepressant legal?* I wondered. *I feel way better about smoking a plant than swallowing a laboratory-made pill.* I knew well the extreme swing of emotions pharmaceutical drugs could induce, but for me, a hit of cannabis only produced calm and creative focus.

"But it's illegal," I kept hearing Logan's voice berate me in my mind.

The conflict was so exhausting, I found the only conclusion was to quit smoking pot altogether. *I'll have to find another way to calm my mind,* I thought. And my anger. By this point, just hearing Logan's name made my stomach churn. I needed a release and continued leaning on my parents to babysit on weekends so I could escape for a few hours of freedom. For those few hours, I was untethered. I was included again, and more often than not, encountering Logan in a baby and responsibility-free zone.

Any given party with Logan around was like a box of chocolates; you just never knew what you were going to get. One night, we could be all over each other and disappear to make up all over again. And the next, we'd stir up jealousy with other people or start a fight, and very often, both.

The more tangled our messy relationship, the more alcohol consumed, amplifying the drama. Once, in a drunken fit, I punched him in the face repeatedly. Luckily, he never hit me back. But his silent stabs seemed to hurt much worse. All too familiar scenes unfolded as Logan disappeared with other girls. It was like reliving my party days with Jake, except adding a baby and a lot more fighting. And how was I used to responding? With retaliation.

The same old blur of happiness, cheating, breaking up, seeing other people, and making up again is still a murky puddle in my memory. *How did I manifest this situation again?* I wondered. Could I have really been cursed? Or was I addicted to the painful drama? *Holy shit, this needs to stop.*

I tried to break the cycle and found a new crowd of friends from the community college to spend my free time with. In that group, I met a genuinely kind and honest guy who piqued my interest. He was refreshingly calm. How naturally we came together shocked me.

We dated for a few months, and I lavished in the comfort of this new man's stability; I knew he wasn't going anywhere. He seemed crazy about me, almost like Cody was, and it blew me away that he was okay with me having a baby. He even admired who I was, regardless of my bizarre recent past. It was so simple. And easy. Almost too easy. It seemed too good to be true, so I believed it was. *What's the catch? When is something going to go wrong?* I suddenly started questioning.

Perhaps I really was addicted to the drama and pain of my past relationships. Maybe I wasn't ready to accept that I couldn't make a stable connection with the father of my child. As I got closer to this new man, I found myself wanting to run away.

On the same night that he mustered up the courage to tell me he loved me, I broke up with him. Instead of accepting the healthy love of an honest and loyal man, I instead slipped right back into the toxic drama cycle with Logan. On again, off again. He loves me. He loves me not.

The painful battle with Logan commenced once again. Every time we "ended it," he bounced between other girls, and I did the same with other guys, entertaining meaningless flings, even with some of our mutual friends. To this day, I don't know if I did it more out of genuine interest for the other men or to rub in Logan's face what he was missing out on. Every weekend seemed to include a heated argument with Logan before either we stormed away or snuck off together. More jealousy. More pain. More making up "just one more time."

The next spring, I felt it was time to get out of my parents' house. So, Jaelyn and I moved into a cute little two-bedroom apartment in town. Though my parents' house was less than ten minutes away, it was official: Jaelyn and I were on our own.

That's also when my first baby, Daisy, officially became my parents' dog. Since we couldn't have her in the apartment, and I was an overwhelmed single mom in college, my parents kept her. Perhaps they needed her, too, since their baby and grandbaby were leaving them as empty nesters. Daisy and my dad had grown a strong bond by then anyway; it felt right that they stayed together.

Now that Jaelyn was a year old and I had a year of motherhood under my belt, I felt ready to be on our own. And wow, I was ready for more privacy and autonomy in my parenting. As you can imagine, becoming a parent while living with your parents has pretty clear pros and cons. The support and ease of built-in babysitters were monumental, although I was more than ready to find my way as a parent without the constant commentary of my mom.

Though I knew my mom meant well, I still felt uncomfortable confiding in her with my deepest concerns. For that, I retreated to Suzanne's office. I still made regular visits, now taking baby Jaelyn with me. In her office, I could gather my thoughts and find clarity in what I needed and wanted to do. She always filled me with confidence and motivation to move forward and trust the process of life.

"Go with grace and ease," Suzanne always said. She wrote those words on a blank piece of paper that I would stick to my bathroom mirror for the next few years. It became my mantra. When things felt too complicated, Suzanne's voice came to mind, *Go with grace and ease.*

Go with grace and ease. Suzanne always made it sound so easy and sustainable. But maintaining grace and ease while being a new mom, college student, and waitress constantly stressed about her baby daddy drama outside of Suzanne's office was much harder. I couldn't run away from it all and do drugs to avoid my challenges anymore. I had to parent and coordinate schedules with childcare; hiding was no longer an option.

Luckily, thanks to a nearby daycare and the kind heart of Jake's mom, daytime babysitting worked out amazingly well. In the evenings, my parents babysat as I waitressed part-time at a popular family restaurant on the main street of Hurley, Wisconsin: a tiny town claimed to fame by its vast line of bars and strip clubs on Main Street.

Once I finally turned twenty-one, the bars became all too tempting after work on the weekends. I often asked my parents to keep Jaelyn at their house for the evening, and I'd go all out after my work shift. As if my shenanigans weren't reckless enough at underage parties, being free to stumble down an entire street packed with bars took my heartbreaking game with Logan to a new level. More times than I'd like to admit, I woke up so hungover that my parents would have to take care of Jaelyn for me until I got myself together, or Logan came over to help. *Wow, I really can't drink like I used to*, I began to notice.

I couldn't see that I was running myself ragged. Early mornings fueled by coffee and Adderall got me through the motions of daycare and school. I thought I was amazingly productive as my days became races from one thing to the next. But my anxiety kept climbing. My thoughts obsessed over baby, school, work, and Logan, while my body sped through the motions on autopilot.

Besides my increasingly debilitating hangovers, I suddenly started contracting unusual illnesses and injuries. I visited the ER about four or five times within a year, each visit concluding another unbelievable diagnosis. Bronchitis. Ginormous kidney stones. A new herniated disc. And every time, my parents came to the rescue. As if I hadn't put them through enough by this point, mom always came running to my medical rescue, and dad always followed with his select words of comforting support.

"This, too, shall pass," he'd say quietly. "Don't give up. You're going to be okay."

Just as quickly as those illnesses came, they disappeared, and I jumped right back into my new race of life. Back to school, to work, and to navigating motherhood.

Though my body was screaming that it wasn't healthy from the inside, on the outside, I appeared to have my act together, and looked great! Breastfeeding did wonders for losing baby weight for me, and by this point, my busy schedule and Adderall use kept the weight coming off. For the most part, I felt great and focused. I found excitement in the challenges of figuring out motherhood and engineering school. Until I burned myself out with too much running during the week and too much drinking on the weekends.

It became obvious that I couldn't party like my reckless teenage self did, but I didn't want to stop. Logan didn't have to stop, and I wasn't ready to give up on showing him what a great family and opportunity he had with Jaelyn and I. So, I kept going out on the weekends, either to vent my frustrations to my friends, or to find him and pretend we were meant to be. On again, off again, our relationship remained undefinable.

# Chapter 12

## August 2010:

## The Fork in the Road

By summer's end, I had reached the inevitable point in college: it was time to transfer to a bigger school to finish my degree. That meant that Jaelyn and I had to move away.

"I'm so proud of you, honey!" Suzanne exclaimed as we discussed my plans to get my bachelor's degree in chemical engineering. Not that she was surprised. Now my counselor and confidant for four years, it was like she knew I had this in me the entire time.

"Just remember," she said. "Go with grace and ease."

Jaelyn and I were headed to Michigan Technological University in Houghton, MI, about one hundred miles away from home, where my dad attended college. But first, I had to get myself to class! I was moving away from my parents and babysitters; I had to figure out a new full-time daycare plan. Not to mention an appropriate place for my baby and me to live. In the nick of time, I got an on-campus apartment in family housing and confirmation that Jaelyn made it into the university's daycare. The pieces lined up so quickly, the transition from my hometown apartment to college was a whirlwind of change. I felt so ready to leave everything behind and start fresh, though that meant leaving behind my friends, my old party life, and Logan.

"You're the one choosing to leave," he reminded me, as if I were abandoning him forever and taking his child away. We argued for some time about our options to stay together, and neither of us wanted to budge. He didn't want to leave our hometown, and I didn't want to stay. I couldn't pass up this opportunity to get a degree that would lead to a great job and life for Jaelyn. I couldn't risk throwing that away in hopes that Logan and I would actually last this time.

"I have to do this for Jaelyn," was my final answer.

"Just remember you chose this," he bitterly responded.

I guess that answered it; by leaving our hometown to go to college, I was leaving my relationship with Logan behind, too. He didn't seem willing to entertain any kind of long-distance relationship, and I wasn't sure I wanted to either. Even though it felt so close to finally working out, it was over. Again.

Though another small town within the secluded Upper Peninsula of Michigan, moving to Houghton was like entering a new world. It looked a lot the same but felt completely different. I didn't know where anything was. I didn't know anyone and felt totally out of place. But just like every other uncomfortable experience, I kept moving forward and moved into our newest apartment on campus.

Near the end of moving day, I got Jaelyn down for a nap and sat outside on the sidewalk. I watched older graduate students pass by, many with their spouses, babies, and even live-in parents. *Am I really supposed to be here?* I wondered. I looked down and immediately noticed one big daisy growing through the sidewalk cracks. A rush of chills and warmth washed over me. Suddenly, I could hear Cody's comforting voice in my mind say, "Yes, you've got this, Krista."

I took in a deep breath. Love and gratitude filled me. *You're right, baby,* I thought to myself. *I do have this!*

I sure needed that little sign from Cody and quickly grew to appreciate every daisy that crossed my path. Noticing that first daisy suddenly opened my eyes to Cody's presence all around me. Until then, I thought all I had left of Cody were the fleeting dreams that left me depressed for days upon waking. But now, I found hope in the possibility that he was still here. I could feel his love when I saw these signs: the daisies, birds flying by, coins on the ground, and familiar songs on the radio. I needed his signs. I needed all the encouragement and support I could get.

Suddenly, I was beyond overwhelmed with harder classes, trying to make new friends, adjusting to Jaelyn's preschool, and juggling our schedules. I had hours of homework to do after Jaelyn's bedtime and didn't even notice how quickly my old drinking habits fell away. I didn't have my parents across town to babysit anymore, I didn't have any close friends to lure me to the bars, nor did I have hook-ups for Adderall or cannabis. The temptations disappeared. Perhaps from this new experience of sobriety and intimidation of my new environment, I felt a clear, new purpose: to survive engineering school as a completely independent parent.

Being in a new town and going to college as the only mom among classmates, I often felt out of place. The odd one out. Always. I was a year or two older than most classmates, and the parents I met at Jaelyn's daycare were mostly university staff and graduate students, often at least ten years older than me. *Where the hell do I belong here?* I wondered.

Within weeks of my first day of classes, recognizing this lack of belonging made me miss home. I missed my friends and family. I missed Suzanne's office. I missed the comfort of my familiar environment. I missed the fun. So, I started making the short two-hour drive home to escape my intimidating new life on most weekends.

During most home visits, I made sure to see Suzanne, who continued standing firm as a primary pillar of support. Now, Jaelyn was a toddler and very familiar with her office, often spending our sessions playing with toys, coloring, or molding clay while Suzanne and I talked out my latest concerns. I'd leave her office with renewed optimism... that slowly faded as I returned to my hometown for the rest of the weekend.

I thought I left my wild old ways behind, but I still craved an escape from my stress and kept coming back to them. I'd go back home and party with old friends... and every few visits, I'd run into Logan, and get pulled right back into our addictive ways. Part of me still wanted us to work out, for him to wake up and realize how much he had with Jaelyn and me. *We could go to school, get good jobs, and live a happy life together with our little family. How could he not see that?*

That's what my family did. And their families. Being married to your childrens' father was all I knew, and then "til death do us part." But what I knew was very, very different from what Logan knew. Hindsight is always 20/20, isn't it? I learned so much more about him after our relationship than during it. He had a very guarded heart, and bless it, he still does. But back before I knew the details of his painful childhood history, my stubborn nature was determined to make him just "get it" and get on my page.

We continued our ping-pong love affair on the weekends in my hometown, and occasionally he came to Jaelyn's and my apartment in Houghton for a week or two.

I first thought this was a brilliant idea, to get away from our hometown and the tempting bars and be alone with our family in Houghton. This was exactly what I hoped for, and he was finally open to it.

But by Wednesday or Thursday of every week he visited, I felt drained, like I was the only one doing any work. I brought Jaelyn to daycare, went to school all day until my brain hurt, picked her up, and came home to Logan, who had nothing to do but wait for our return from another busy day. He was our stranded visitor, unable to work, without a vehicle, and with zero connections to the area.

Once we got home from school and daycare, I felt like I had to be in control. By all means, Logan certainly helped with changing diapers, feeding, bath time, and all the other necessary motions, but I still felt like the leader. I had to ask or tell him what to do, and it was starting to feel like I was taking care of two kids. *Is this really easier than taking care of Jake?* I couldn't help but wonder.

Perhaps part of me enjoyed that sense of control. Since middle school, I knew I had the upper hand with Logan. He always was the cute younger kid with a crush on me. And honestly, a lot of my attraction to him was fueled by that intimidation and sense of dominance.

Looking back, I realized I tried to control him with that power, which clearly proved ineffective. Neither of us could be controlled, and we certainly couldn't control one another. We both had a natural resistance to authority, and even though we had an irresistible connection that sparked our passionate reunions, we just couldn't get past our hard outer shells. Our armor was too thick, our past pain was too deep, and we were too young and immature to understand how to handle our situations.

As my birthday approached the following spring, Logan had been with us in Houghton for nearly two weeks. By that point, I was so sick and tired of him lingering like a leech without purpose, I couldn't stand it anymore. I felt like I was running miles around him. Every day, my schoolwork got more complicated, my stress level rose, and I still had to come home and direct him through the evening. I suddenly felt irritated by his presence, laying in disgust next to him at night wondering, *Why isn't this what I wanted?*

I knew he was only there to please me and help with Jaelyn, but now that we were finally practically living together, I realized something was missing in our connection. Sure, we had the physical attraction down, our body parts were practically magnetic to one another, but I needed to feel something more. My mind and soul were yearning for something deeper, to feel seen and understood without words. I was constantly explaining myself and what I wanted to Logan, yet it always came across like a foreign language to him. And his language was foreign to me, too.

Lying there in bed, I realized that Logan and I truly had nothing beyond a physical relationship for the first time in three years. We never were on the same level, and we weren't on the same level now. I had been forcing him to "catch up" with me and move on, but the more I forced, the harder he dug his heels into his own familiar ways.

Staring blankly at the ceiling with Logan sound asleep at my side, I felt torn between two worlds: my new one in college and old one back home. I wanted so badly for Logan to move on with me into this new world, but I could feel in my heart that that would never happen. I couldn't force him to be who I wanted him to be. *Who did I want him to be anyway?* A still-living version of Cody, the first person to have seen into my soul and love every depth of it.

*This is crazy*, I realized. *I can't expect Logan to see me like Cody. If he can't see it on his own now, he never will. I can't blame him for that.* I needed Jaelyn, but neither of us needed to suffer through this relationship.

I rolled over to my side, and following my movement, Logan rolled over behind me, wrapping his arm around my waist. I took a deep breath in and out to release the sickening knot in my stomach. *Everything's going to work out just fine*, I assured myself. *With grace and ease, I go.* I closed my eyes, repeating those words in my mind until I dozed off to sleep.

The next day was my birthday, and a Friday, so we drove home for the weekend. I remained reticent through the drive, contemplating my options. *Do I suck it up and stay together? This is what I've been fighting so hard for, isn't it? But what if life would actually be easier, and happier, on my own?* Thoughts battled back and forth until, towards the end of our drive, I felt word vomit rise from my stomach and shoot out of my mouth.

"I can't do this anymore," I blurted.

"What?" Logan asked in surprise. "What can't you do anymore?"

"This," I replied. "With you. I can't do this with you anymore."

"Do what?" he asked, his volume and anger rising.

"Play 'house' with you," I said. "And take care of everything. I know you don't have anything to do there, but it drives me crazy that I get Jaelyn to daycare, go to school all day, and come home to you like a deer in the headlights waiting for me to lead the show at home, too. I need you to do something. Take the lead. On anything. I'm exhausted."

His breath was heavy. "Krista, I don't know what the fuck to do there. I can't work, I don't know anyone, I can't drive; what do you expect me to do? I came because you wanted me to."

"I know," sighed. "But now that we've actually lived together, something doesn't feel right. I need more than you can give, and I can't make you miserable anymore trying to make me happy."

"What the hell does that mean, Kris?" he asked in frustration. "I'm finally doing everything you ask me to, no questions asked. What else do you want me to do? I'll do it."

"That's the thing," I replied. "I don't think you can."

"What?" he questioned. "What do you mean, Kris? How would you know that I can't?"

"It's hard to explain," I sighed again. "I know we have great physical chemistry…."

He smiled and laughed, "Hell yeah, we do. Like nothing I've ever felt before." I cringed as he looked into my eyes.

"But we don't have more than that," I said. "I need a deeper connection. We just don't have that, and I don't think we ever will."

"Come on, Kris," he argued, staring more intensely. "You know we have a connection like nobody else. Why else do you think we have a kid together? It was meant to be. We're meant to be."

"I thought that, too," I said softly. "But if we had a real connection, it wouldn't be this hard to be together. You didn't even want to be with me through my pregnancy and when Jae was first born. Do you know how hard it was to go through that alone? And feel used by you while you stayed with Teresa and fooled around with me on the side? If we had a real connection, that wouldn't have happened. That or all the other girls you've been with since. Too much damage has been done."

"Teresa was a mistake," he rebutted. "You know that, Kris. I've said I'm sorry a thousand times. I'm not gonna say it the rest of my life if you won't let it go. And talk about being with other people. What about all the other guys? You took your stabs at me, too."

"I know I did," I admitted. "I did all that to get back at you. I know it was stupid and didn't work. I'm sorry for that, too, but again, it just proves that too much damage has been done. We're going in different directions. Maybe we're becoming different people."

"I can't believe it," Logan said. "I'm finally doing everything you fucking wanted, and you don't want it anymore? Are you sure you really want to do this?"

Stoplights flashed ahead as we rolled into our hometown. I paused for a moment. *Fuck, what if I make a mistake?* I thought. *Just say what feels right in your heart,* I heard someone else say in my mind.

"I'm sorry, Logan," I responded softly. "I'm sure."

We rolled up to his house, I parked the car, and we sat for a moment in silence. "Fine," he eventually replied bitterly. "If that's what you really want. Just know I did everything I possibly could to make you happy. This is your choice. Not mine. Remember that."

He glared into my eyes for another moment before turning back to Jaelyn sleeping in her car seat. "Tell her Daddy loves her when she wakes up, please."

"I will," I replied. "Again, I'm sorry."

He nodded in silence, gathered his bags from the backseat, and walked away from the car. I sat there and watched him, feeling guilty for the relief that came as he walked away. His energy was gone. I was free.

"Alright, Jaelyn," I said quietly, looking back at my sleeping babe. "It's just you and me, girl."

Back at school, I was nearing the end of my first year. My days were overwhelming but stimulating, and I felt like a weight came off my shoulders since letting Logan go. Though I returned to smoking cigarettes after I stopped breastfeeding Jaelyn, I was surprised to suddenly lose the desire to smoke. I wasn't around Logan anymore, nor talking to him often, and didn't feel as much of the stress that drove me back to smoking in the first place. I quit cold turkey, happily leaving that old habit behind with the rest of my past.

I also started coming out of my shell and making new friends with classmates. I even made friends with Jaelyn's preschool mates' parents. It felt so refreshing to surround myself with this new and mature crowd. Instead of drinking and smoking in bars, I met lab groups for homework and parents for playdates. My entire world was changing, and my old world began to fade away.

It was still stressful, though. I drove away from campus between classes many days just to cry before my next class. School was so hard. *Am I smart enough to do this?* I questioned. *I'm the only one with a kid; how will I survive?* Though my bad habits fell away, I felt exhausted and drained by my new ones. *Did I take on too much? What else could I do instead? Go back to Ironwood?* The thought made me shudder. *No, I'm here for a reason; I've got to keep going.*

This breakdown and personal pep talk often occurred daily, and only in my car; I couldn't bear the thought of breaking down in front of anyone else. I had to stay strong. *Suck it up, Krista,* I thought. *It's not that bad; just keep going, no matter what. Go with grace and ease.* I drove around until my tears dried or until I ran out of time to get to my next class, whichever came first. Then, taking a few deep breaths, and sometimes a puff of cannabis from back home, I pulled myself back together, gathered my books, and walked back to class with a happy smile on my face.

Some days, I went back to class still holding tears and overwhelming anxiety. And other days, I felt a rush of love flow into my heart that filled me with reassurance that I was on the right path. I didn't know where it was coming from, but it was something much greater than myself. On those days, I drove back to school with a smile, grateful to be alive and able to have this experience, and told myself:

*I can do this. I trust the process. I go with grace and ease.*

# Chapter 13

## May 2012:

## The Visits

A couple of months later, I officially survived my first year at Michigan Tech. I couldn't wait to get home, take a break, and see my old friends. And honestly, I couldn't wait for a drink at a familiar bar.

Shortly upon my return, I received a text from Logan. "What are you doing, Kris?" it read.

My heart jumped with alarm and excitement. I quickly caved to the temptation for a drink, escape, and attention and found myself sitting in a dark bar with him. We laughed and poured more glasses until my vision turned rose-colored. *Maybe we can make this work,* I thought in drunken brilliance.

One thing led to another, and we were at his place, "making up" for the one-millionth time. That is, until his roommate and my good friend, Kasye, came home. After seeing my car in the driveway, she stormed up to the bedroom, yelling at Logan to tell me the truth.

Apparently, he had been with another girl, who cheated on her boyfriend with him, and she was pregnant, unsure who the father was. As this twisted secret came out, my blood boiled. Shocked and still naked, I pushed Logan away from me and started yelling. A dramatic fight broke out while we scrambled to put clothes on and stormed downstairs.

My memory of this moment has no words. All I see is a mute screenplay of us screaming at each other and me hitting him until, at one point, he wrapped his hand around my throat and pressed me against a kitchen countertop.

"Do it," I snarled at him. "Choke me. Show me how much of a man you are." We glared intensely into each other's eyes for a moment before Logan softly released his hand and backed up.

"I'm sorry, Kris," he said. "I wouldn't choke you. You know I'd never hurt you."

Suddenly, the other girl pulled into the driveway. Apparently, Kasye called her over to confirm her side of the story. It didn't matter; I couldn't even hear her words. My brain was spinning too fast inside my skull. *Enough!* I thought. *I can't handle this Jerry Springer show!*

Overwhelmed by anger and exhaustion, all I could say was, "I've got to get the hell out of here," before walking away. I got into my car, started the engine, and let the floodgates burst from my eyes. I started driving forward and wondered, *where the hell am I going?* Suddenly, a great idea came to mind. I turned left on the highway, past the turn to my parents' house, and continued driving out of town. I was heading to the car accident site, about fifteen miles away on US 2. I felt sickly excited that I was finally going to experience what I fantasized about for years now, but as I got closer to the site, I felt an intense presence in my car with me.

"Krista, go home."

*Who the hell was that?* I thought to myself. *Am I going crazy?* Suddenly, out of the corner of my eye, I saw someone sitting in the passenger's seat. It looked like Cody, sitting hunched over in my small SUV with hands on his knees. My heart skipped as I looked to my right; no one was there. *You're losing your mind, Krista. There's no way Cody's here.*

"Krista, go home."

*Okay, that sounded just like Cody's voice.* I still convinced myself that I made it up. Of course, I was thinking about Cody; I was on my way to crash my car where he died four years earlier.

As I looked further ahead on the road, a glowing shape of a person next to me reappeared in my peripheral vision. The presence emanated overwhelming energy. Loving energy. It felt like Cody was right next to me, and it felt so good, I burst into tears.

"Krista, go home."

I looked again to my right. No one.

"Ah, Cody!" I exclaimed out loud, tears now streaming down my face. "Why the hell did you leave me here like this? To deal with this asshole and raise a baby by myself? Why can't you be here instead?" I continued to sob, tears clouding my vision of the dark road ahead of me.

"Krista, go home."

*The Daisy Diaries* | 137

This voice did not sound like my own inside my head. I kept looking over to my right in desperation of catching eyes with Cody, but he wasn't there. Yet every time I looked forward again, I could see his warm presence in the corner of my eye. Tears poured like waterfalls. My heart sank down to my belly as I got closer to the accident site. *Okay, it's just up here,* I thought. *I should speed up.*

"Krista, go home."

I couldn't deny that Cody was with me. And I couldn't not listen to him. "Ah, fuck!" I screamed as I slowed down and pulled over on the side of the highway. Still sobbing, I stepped out of the car and walked a few steps down the hill where a car once tumbled and rolled to its fatal stop. Just like four years earlier, it was dead silent, except for the eerie wind blowing through the trees. Pieces of the crash flashed through my mind. I let out a few blood-curdling screams into the silence of the night. They echoed, just like Chad's did that night.

"Krista, go home."

I stood there, my body jerking with each sob, as I kept hearing Cody's soft, loving words.

"Krista, go home."

After screaming and crying out all I had left in me, I took a deep breath in and suddenly felt a wave of calm. I let out a loud sigh, looking up to the clear starry sky. After a few moments in silent stillness, I walked back to my car, got in, and drove home.

The next morning, I woke up a different person. I was finally ready to leave Logan and all my past behind. I packed up and took Jaelyn back to Houghton, determined to finish school, create a new life, and never look back.

It was easy to keep my mind occupied as a student and single working mom. Every day, I raced against the clock to keep up with my school, work, and Jaelyn's daycare schedules. Being focused on doing something allowed me to ignore my shameful collection of grief and guilt. I learned to hide it well and painted a brilliant mask of optimism everywhere I went. I quickly became a "fake it till you make it" master, on the outside at least.

Yet on the inside, I was terribly critical of myself. I didn't even notice how habitually harsh my self-judgment became since I was a teen. *I shouldn't have done that. I should have done this. I must do better.* These thoughts shadowed me. They beat me for every mistake. And with every mistake came a flashback from the past.

Out of nowhere, scenes from the car accident flooded my mind. The jolt that woke me up, the desperate look on Chad's face, the eerie dark silence that found me on the cold, hard ground. My imagination tried to make sense of how the car tumbled and threw Cody and me out in opposite directions. I obsessively wondered how Cody's body might have protected mine, how the seat belt let me loose, how the hell I broke so many of my teeth. And then the "woulda, coulda, shouldas" began.

My mind rewound a few hours to the moment Cody pulled over the car. *I should have said we need to stop. I should have offered to drive. I should have said or done something different.* Rewinding several more hours in my mind, *I should have never suggested we even go to that stupid club.*

Then debilitating guilt took over. My chest caved in each time I thought of Cody's mother; I was responsible for her baby's death. *I was so stupid and selfish,* I told myself.

Once I returned to the present moment, I concluded that I couldn't make a critical mistake like that again. *I should do better. I will do better.* At the time, I thought this just made me a perfectionist. That was a good thing, wasn't it? I set high standards for myself. I was proving how smart and capable I could be despite my past. I couldn't see that my inner critic was actually punishing me and running away from my pain.

The harder I was on myself, the more stress I collected. I clearly needed a break, so a friend offered to babysit for me to attend an evening yoga class. At first, I felt guilty leaving Jaelyn and making someone sit at my house. Many days, I didn't want to go. But my friend kept showing up and encouraging me to take "me time." Within a few weeks, I fell in love with that hour.

I experienced my first glimpse of freedom and enlightenment in that class. While the instructor guided us through sun salutations, reminding us to match one breath with one movement, something suddenly clicked. My breath and body finally synced together. I felt like I was floating somewhere in between as I moved through an effortless dance on my yoga mat. *Wow, I get it!* I thought, feeling deeply connected to something more powerful than myself for the second time in my life, since finding out I was pregnant with Jaelyn.

That class inspired my commitment to a daily yoga practice. The quiet time allowed me to breathe, get in sync with my body, and set intentions for the day. It became my morning prayer that connected me to God and reassured me that I was on the right path.

Wait, a connection to God? After abandoning the Catholic church as a teen, I never thought I had or would feel a connection to God. Ever. And on the yoga mat? Is that allowed? I almost couldn't believe I tapped into a spiritual connection on my yoga mat. I mean, I knew yoga came from spiritual practice, but I didn't join yoga for that. I joined to relieve my sore and exhausted body. The spontaneously spiritual spark seemed to happen by accident.

How it happened didn't matter. Something clicked, like a switch was turned on that had been off my entire life. *Why didn't I know about this before?* I wondered. My yoga practice became my fuel to keep marching forward, show up to each daunting class, and push through mind-boggling homework every night.

Though this new routine connected me with flashes of bliss on my mat, the rest of my waking hours were still full of stress. *Something is missing,* I thought to myself. *What am I lacking to feel relaxed and at peace? How do I make my mind quiet when I'm not in yoga class?*

I started exploring further into natural stress remedies. Everything but meditation that is; my mind was too busy for that. Instead, I burned candles and incense and made regular dates with my bathtub and Epsom salt. I diffused essential oils and started reading about the healing properties of crystals and precious stones. But what really brought my mind both excitement and ease was reading about psychics and communicating with the "other side."

Since Cody died, I grew desperate to know what happened to him. *Was his spirit still here? Did he actually appear in my dreams or in my car that night?* I started reading about after-death experiences and communicating with the "other side" and stumbled upon the website of a local Medium right in my college town.

Immediately intrigued, I eagerly read through her page, describing how she channeled Spirit messages and helped people communicate with their dead loved ones. I made a no-brainer decision before I was done. I knew I had to meet and speak with this woman; I had to communicate with Cody! So I picked up the phone and scheduled an appointment for the very next week.

The morning of, I woke up full of excitement. *I'm going to talk to Cody today!* I could hardly focus on school or work; I was busy counting the seconds until my appointment that afternoon. My mind raced with questions. *What will this be like? How are we going to do it? Will it be weird?*

A warm familiarity settled in as I pulled up to the big olive-green bungalow. My eyes were immediately drawn to a yellow pot of daisies sitting on the wooden deck railing. My hair stood on end. The charming house reminded me of the home of my dear friend, whose earthy mom so beautifully decorated it into a hippy's happy place that I absolutely loved. *I wonder what it looks like in here!*

Heart pounding, I rang the doorbell to be greeted by a joyful woman who not only owned a house just like my friend's mom, but she kind of looked like her, too. I don't know if it was her physical resemblance or familiar soul, but I immediately felt like I had known her before. Looking into her joyful blue eyes, round and soft face, and light hair shining in the sun, I felt like I was visiting an old friend. A mentor. Maybe a guru.

"You must be Krista," she said with a beaming smile. "I'm Sherry. Come on in."

I stepped through the entrance to find the sun beaming through huge picture windows on every wall. Warm yellow, orange, and green walls wrapped around each room, decorated with cozy, oversized furniture and Native American artwork. Bizarrely like my friend's house back home, I quickly fell in love with everything in this place.

"Oh, my goodness, your house is beautiful!" I exclaimed to Sherry. "I love absolutely everything about it. This is exactly how I would want my own home to look!"

She thanked me and offered to give me a quick tour before starting our session. I graciously accepted, gushing over every new painting, furniture piece, and knick knack I laid my eyes on.

"Well, I sense we must have a lot in common," Sherry smiled. "When is your birthday?"

"April 21st," I said.

"No kidding!" she laughed. "That's my birthday, too."

"Wow!" I exclaimed. "That's really interesting. No wonder you were the Medium I was meant to see!"

*The Daisy Diaries* | 141

"Oh, just a minute," she said, suddenly turning away to her stereo in the corner of the room. She turned on native drumming music and turned the volume up. "I just need a little something to distract your visitor," she smiled. "He's very excited to see you."

My heart skipped a beat. *Oh my God. He's here.* I suddenly couldn't wait to get started.

Sherry poured me a glass of water, and we made our way to the living room. She guided me to sit on a big brown leather sofa that squeaked as I sunk into its cushions. She sat across from me in an oversized chair and pulled out a pair of gold rim sunglasses with yellow shades.

"You might find that every Medium works differently," she said. "Personally, I find it necessary to wear sunglasses. Since Spirit isn't used to this human body and seeing through our human eyes, they find it much too bright once they get in here. I try to keep my eyes closed, but the sunglasses help me stay focused."

"Oh, okay," I nodded. *Wow, what is about to happen here?* I wondered.

She slipped the sunglasses on in silence, sitting up straight and placing her palms on her knees. I could see her closed eyes through the yellow glasses, and they looked like they were darting around under her eyelids. Her shoulders suddenly lifted and rolled back as a shudder appeared to rush through her body.

Sherry wriggled in her seat some more before sitting erect again, palms gripped to her knees, opening her mouth with a smile.

"Your guide is here. She's been with you for quite some time," Sherry said with a low tone in her voice. "I can hear her rattling off her name quickly. It's long and a mouthful. Something like Josephine Satchel Serena."

I reached for the notebook and pen sitting next to me and began scribbling notes.

"Protect yourself from dangerous men," Sherry continued. "Wrap them with white light."

"Oh, geez," I responded nervously. *What a way to get started*, I thought. "What kind of dangerous men?"

"Don't worry, you are safe," she said. "There will be many. Just wrap them with white light when you recognize them."

She continued, changing the subject. "You and your daughter are very close. You will be lifelong partners. She'll even live very close to you."

A warm relief flushed through my chest. *Oh, thank goodness that she'll still like me at that point, and so much to live near me!* I kept scribbling notes.

"Protect yourself from her father. He'll be in and out of your lives," Sherry, or Josephina, or someone continued. "He will be forever changed by your example. Inspired. He will choose sobriety many times... but won't succeed permanently."

Slightly disappointed, I wasn't surprised by these words. *Good thing I'm done with him,* I validated to myself. I knew I had made the right choice.

"You are intimidating to men," she said.

I laughed. "Am I?"

"Yes," she answered. "Many adore you, but few believe you could need them. It's the dangerous men that dare to pursue you. Just wrap them in white light." She turned her head toward me.

"You'll find a sober man to marry. He's exceedingly strong and will want to protect you." She smiled. "You have more children around the bend."

Another wave of warm relief came. *Oh good! I won't be alone for long,* I thought.

"You miss your young lover, though," she said softly, shooting a pang of grief into my gut. "You loved him very much. You still do. You're still not sure if you're allowed to love someone else."

Tears welled in my eyes as a lump closed my throat.

"Don't worry," she consoled me. "You will be happy. It will be clear. You'll have a dream about him in five years. But you'd like to talk to him now, wouldn't you?"

My heart jumped and kicked the lump in my throat. "Yes, I do," I choked out with a sobby smile.

Sherry cleared her throat and began wriggling in her seat again. Rolling her head back and forth, side to side, around in circles with her shoulders. Finally, she coughed, widened her stance, and resettled her hands on her lap. Her posture shifted, which I immediately recognized as the posture I saw in the passenger seat of my car the night I drove to the accident site.

A nearly visible wave of energy shifted over her. She smiled with a low, masculine giggle.

"How ya doing?" she asked in a voice even lower than before. It was apparent that this wasn't Sherry or Josephina anymore. The tears rolled out of my eyes as I felt overwhelmed by Cody's all-too-familiar presence.

"I knew I'd make you cry," he said with a whimper. "I love you so much. You walked on water to me."

My heart burst with love and longing, tears dripping on my notepad while I wrote down his words. He continued to tell me about his death experience.

"They told me that you'd be okay," he said before describing his "passing over" like landing at an airport and having papers checked, though it was a "light, colorful, and glorious party like New Year's Eve." He told me he felt no pain; he wasn't afraid. Everyone was there to help him adjust.

He described a lady with black hair and a frumpy dress who asked if he wanted to say goodbye to me. "I didn't want to say goodbye," he said. "I thought that that's when the hurt would come."

My heart sank. I pictured myself saying goodbye to his dead body in the hospital. *That is when the hurt came*, I thought.

"I got to die with Krista," he continued. "It was the best way to die." I let out a soft laugh through my tears. I couldn't believe what I was hearing.

"Were you there when I said goodbye in the hospital?" I asked.

"Like a snapshot," he replied, "Like a cropped photo, I saw you hovering near me." Chills ran down my spine, imagining his spirit watching that moment.

"We'll have alone time when you cross over," Cody assured me. "Until then, just send me love emotionally, not physically. You'll find out; it's way better than physical satisfaction." I scribbled notes like my life depended on it.

I paused for a moment. "Can I ask another question?"

"Of course, baby," he replied with a big smile.

*Baby, he used to call me that,* I thought. Suddenly, a flashback of him laying on top of me and kissing my neck appeared in my mind, "I love you, baby," he said. My heart melted as chills tingled up and down my spine.

I shook my head of the daydream and looked down nervously at my notes. "Were you there when I went to crash my car at the accident site?" I finally asked.

Without hesitation, he responded, "Absolutely. I told you to go home. My teachers knew you would listen to me. Your number isn't up yet."

I shuddered in mild shock at his response. "I can't believe that was real," I unintentionally thought out loud.

"You did hear me," he confirmed, still smiling. "I'm glad you listened." Still stunned, I sat and stared at Sherry's yellow shades in silence. After a short pause, he giggled and said, "Remember that time I poked your ear with a needle?"

Immediately, I pictured myself sitting in my friend's kitchen, holding a roll of paper towel behind my ear, waiting for Cody to pierce it with a safety pin. I let out a chuckle. *I forgot about that,* I thought. "So random for you to mention that!" I finally said.

"I was so scared to hurt you," he replied.

"I know," I said with a teary smile, remembering how long it took him to build up the nerve to pierce my ear.

"Our love was perfect, perfect, perfect," he continued. "I can revisit you after your future marriage, that lucky bastard. Another man is coming for you, and he will be more than me," Cody continued. I felt a conflicting knot in my gut. I knew I needed to move on and be with someone else, but it felt wrong and unbelievable for anyone to measure up to Cody in my eyes.

"He's older, big, with a squared-off jaw," Cody described. "You'll walk right into a scene and have a perfect love affair. He's a kid lover and wants Jaelyn's acceptance." My heart melted a little bit more.

"He'll make you feel safe. He's big and stable and has resources, like a degree or a house. I know you will be so happy," Cody smiled.

I didn't know what to say. The words were equally comforting and painful. Cody seemed to recognize my sadness and guilt as he spoke.

"Don't worry, my crossover was so easy," Cody said. "I never felt cheated of my adulthood. Now, I just want to be big and loving and out of your way." I looked up from my note writing and smiled sadly.

"Your love is like a waterfall when you send it," he continued. "And my love is like a cloud floating over you. I can float in when you need me and drift away when you don't."

"Go for a car ride," he added with a smile. "I'll ask my teachers if I can join you."

I smiled, too. "Okay!" I replied in excitement.

"I'm so proud of you," Cody said. "Just look at you. I'm beaming. That's my smart girl. And your beautiful daughter."

I tripped over what felt like two timelines crossing over, talking to Cody about Jaelyn. *I can't believe he knows her.*

"You could show her my picture," he said. "I can be mommy's friend that she loved very much. Give her a big hug from me."

"Many people ask if she's yours," I said quietly.

"Wait, is she mine?" Cody replied. "Oh..." his voice trailed off into a few moments of silence.

My heart sank again. *I wish she was yours*, I thought.

Clearing his throat, he continued. "Dream. Don't obsess over seeing me. My guides wouldn't let me visit for quite a while because they said it would keep you from life. Balance right-now time. Accept the good, let go of what you're finished with. Be here right now."

*Wow, dreaming of him did keep me from life for a while*, I admitted to myself. *I think I wanted to stay in the past where his memory belonged.*

"You're right," I replied. "It's time for me to live right now." He paused for a moment while I wrote notes. Then he took a deep breath in and let out a loud sigh.

"My teachers tell me it's time to go now," he said. "I love you so much. I just want to hug you and be as close to you as possible."

I felt nauseous hearing that he had to leave me. I had missed him so much over the last five years; I wasn't ready to say goodbye again after what felt like only five minutes. I still had so many questions to ask him. With tears welling in my eyes, all I could say to respond was, "I love you so much, too."

After that mind-blowing experience, I knew without a doubt that I had to go back for another session. I didn't care what it cost; now that I learned how to communicate directly with Cody, I would do anything to do it again. So before I left Sherry's house, we booked another session for two weeks later. As I stepped outside and walked to my car, I felt a significant shift within me.

*This is real,* I thought to myself. *We can really communicate with the other side.* A blanket of comfort wrapped around me. Suddenly, I felt protected and safe. I looked up and around with a smile as I realized, *I was just reunited with Cody and my Spirit Guides.* I didn't know I had so many angels watching over and guiding me! And I didn't think I actually could communicate with them.

*I guess I'm not on my own after all,* I concluded as I sat in my car and started the engine. The radio turned on, and I quickly recognized the lyrics to "I Will Wait" by Mumford and Sons. My eyes automatically refilled with tears as a powerful sense of Cody's loving presence wrapped around me.

"Thank you for waiting for me," I said out loud to Cody through my happy tears. "I miss you so much. I can't wait to see you again."

I couldn't help but notice more unusual things happening in the two weeks before my next visit with Sherry. Suddenly, every song on the radio was singing to me from Cody. I started noticing even more coins on the ground and birds, butterflies, and dragonflies flying by. *Those are my signs from Cody and my Spirit Guides,* I reminded myself, *and they've been here the whole time.*

Once my next visit arrived, I could hardly wait to leave campus again. My mind was preoccupied all day, wondering what I would hear from Cody that day. This time, I came prepared with questions and extra notebook paper. I was ready to capture every detail!

When I arrived at Sherry's house, the pot of daisies greeted me again. Sherry directed me back to the couch and asked me to lay down. "You're going to do what I do someday," she said with a beaming smile. "I think you're ready to try this."

"Try what?" I asked with hesitation.

"Shamanic journeying," she replied. "It's a form of astral travel, an out-of-body experience for your soul to freely explore the other side and visit your guides on your own."

"Wow," I responded. "That sounds awesome! Are you sure I can do this? How am I even supposed to do it?"

"I've been told it's in your cards," she said. "And how lucky for you, so young. I didn't learn how to do this until I was in my 40s, but you will

*The Daisy Diaries* | 147

learn these skills at a very young age so that the rest of your life can be dedicated to spiritual work."

"Really?" I asked with excitement coated in doubt. *But I'm in engineering school*, I thought. *That's quite the opposite of this spiritual mediumship shamanic journeying out-of-body craziness that I hardly understand. Can she really be right about this?*

"Yes, really!" she exclaimed. "I'm so excited for you! Here, you just lay back, relax, and let the music take you."

"Um, okay," I replied. "Take me where?"

She laughed and played Native American drumming music with a hefty, steady beat. "The rhythm will help match your vibration and allow your spirit to lift from your body. If you feel yourself lifting above or falling below your body, that's great! Just let it happen," she directed me.

"Well," I replied with curious confusion. "Let's see what happens." I closed my eyes.

I laid there awkwardly for what felt like an hour. *Um, is anything happening? Am I supposed to be dreaming? What else am I supposed to do?* My thoughts continued racing as I tried desperately to relax and let my soul lift out of my body or fall in whatever direction it was supposed to. *Is she sure about this? I don't think I can do it!*

I wasn't sure if I should speak. I mean, I was apparently supposed to be out of my body at this point. Though I did feel like I could jump out of my own skin from anxiety and discomfort alone, I was definitely still intact in one piece.

*Okay, just breathe, focus, and relax,* I reminded myself. *Just let it happen. Let your body float away.* For half a second, I felt a glimpse of the lifting sensation Sherry mentioned. *Holy shit, I'm doing it!* I thought. Then back down, I fell onto the couch. *Shoot, I ruined it. Okay, stop thinking and do it again.*

Breathing in and out, trying my best to relax, this time, I felt myself sinking deeper into the couch. Sinking. Lower. *Yes, do it!* I thought. Immediately, my consciousness zipped me back up. *Damnit, I did it again.* In pure frustration, I couldn't hold my silence any longer.

"Hey, Sherry?" I asked. "So, what am I supposed to be doing here? Should I like fall asleep and be dreaming?" I could tell she could feel my discomfort. I also felt a slight sense of disappointment.

"No, you'll certainly stay awake while journeying," she replied. "I thought you would flow right into it, but maybe it's a little early yet."

"Oh, wow, yeah, I have no idea what I'm trying to do here," I confessed. "Can we try it again later?"

"No problem, my dear," she lovingly replied. "Your visitor is excited to speak with you anyway."

*What a relief!* I thought as I practically jumped upright on the couch. *I can't wait to talk to Cody!* Sherry grabbed her sunglasses and took a seat in the big chair across from me. After a few moments of deep breathing and wiggling in her seat, she suddenly sat up straight, widened her stance, then leaned back into the chair. A smile spread across her face as she turned her head towards me.

"This is exactly what the doctor ordered," she said. "Pay attention to the life forms and guide forms before you. There are messages from animals for you. Crows and birds remind you that the world is full of messages." She continued, "Friendly messages from Spirit sending their love. They love to thrill us. They fall down laughing with joy when you recognize their signs."

"Your message for today is this," she suddenly said loudly and firmly. "You're on a great path. You have many good fortunes to come. Accept and deserve them. Your troubling early years are over."

*Wow, I thought, thank goodness!* I leaned back into the couch, soaking in the comforting words. *This must be my Spirit Guide talking to me.*

"This is your warning," Josephina continued. "Don't dismiss the gifts you receive. Believe that you are deserving. Don't feel guilty; instead, let delight manifest.

"You'll have many goodies in this lifetime, like a house, car, pool," she said. "Be deserving of them and your stable financial success. Material things will come easily to you. Stress-free years are ahead for you. Indulge in spiritual retreats."

"Just follow the joyful path and accept good news," she continued. "You are a teacher. You are hardwired in this lifetime for spiritual activity."

My reality as an overwhelmed engineering student struck me. *What the heck would I teach? I certainly can't teach what I'm learning now. And engineering is on the opposite side of the spectrum from spiritual activity.* But hearing these words still felt good. Something within me resonated with the tone of "spiritual activity" alone.

"Your visitor is ready for you," she said. I immediately perked up and forgot all about my engineer versus spiritual teacher dilemma. I couldn't wait to hear what Cody had to say. I sat upright in anticipation, watching

*The Daisy Diaries* | 149

Sherry wiggle around again, as if someone was literally trying to get into her body like a suit.

"Jesus Christ it's hard to get in here," she exclaimed with a deep chuckle. She shook her shoulders and rested her hands on her knees as they opened wider and more relaxed.

"Hi, beautiful," Cody said with a smile.

Again, I immediately teared up and stammered, "Hi there."

"Try this journeying! Just feel this," he said. "Just be in it. Relax! Stop analyzing and anticipating. Just be in the moment!"

"Okay," I replied quietly. "I'll keep trying!" *Damn, now I have to do it again,* I joked to myself.

"I'm learning how to move at light speed," he said. "When you call, I can shoot myself to you like The Flash. I can drop in and drop out and answer you occasionally."

"That's amazing," I responded in awe. I told him that I had brought questions this time. "Can I ask you?"

"Of course, baby," he replied with a big smile.

*Baby,* my mind melted into daydreams again. I shook my head and looked down nervously at my sheet of questions. "So, what do you think about me being in chemical engineering school?" I asked.

"I'm shining. So proud of you," he replied, smiling even wider and wiggling more upright in the chair. "We're connected. I knew you would do this."

Old MySpace messages from him ran across my mind's eye that reprimanded me for quitting physics and calculus our senior year. *He did know,* I thought.

"What about Jaelyn?" I asked. "Is her soul connected to yours?"

"All of us are everywhere," he replied. "We're all one. Jaelyn knows me. She has access to the spirit world. She's very close to me in spirit life. Yes, her blue eyes. We came from the same 'pod of beings.' The same soul family. We're on the same mission."

Stunned, I couldn't say anything. Changing the subject, I asked if there was anything he wanted to tell his mom.

"A lot of stupid things I did," he replied. "And a lot of stupid things I didn't do because of her."

"I visited her during her dreams," he continued. "Held her hand and said thank you. I want to say thank you, thank you, thank you, times one thousand. She never failed me. Tell her I love her and appreciate her. I'll try to keep sending love to her, but she is resisting. She feels jagged, heartbroken, and cheated. She's angry, and it's hard to console her. But she always understood everything. She was a great mom."

I scribbled notes as fast as I could before asking, "What about your brother and sister and anyone else? Do you want me to tell them anything?"

"They're still very angry," he replied. "It's very hard for me to get near them. The noise around them is so loud and staticky. It hurts like hell. But dark dream time quiets the snowy static. They can ask me to come into their dreams."

I nodded and scribbled down his instructions before asking my next question. "Are you at the cemetery or accident site when I visit?"

After a brief pause, Cody spoke.

"Counselors help people in grief. The Universe meets you there with angels, spirits, comforters, and guides. The cemetery is a mega comfort den. Sometimes I am there; my teachers show me how to pop in. Just call, and I'll be there."

"Interesting," I mumbled, scribbling on my notepad until my hand cramped.

"You're going to do great things," he said, changing the subject. "Forms of happiness compress your training for life abilities. Stay delighted. Experience receiving things. I love you so much."

Those visits with Sherry forever opened new doors for me, giving me permission to believe in the experiences with Spirit I was finally noticing. They gave me permission to communicate directly with Spirit myself. Suddenly, I felt more deeply connected to God, a higher power, the Universe, in a way far more profound than anything I ever felt from a church pew, even my yoga mat. Contacting my guardian angels was no longer a fantasy; it was real. And I wanted to do it more often.

But that meant I had to stop reliving and running from my past. I had to practice being in the present moment, even off my yoga mat. I had to learn how to meditate.

Since sitting made my old back injury hurt, meditation as I knew it was a frustrating experience. So, I started listening to ten-minute meditation recordings before falling asleep or getting up in the morning, trying my best to stay focused and breathe. I figured I was already set up to relax while lying in bed, so my chances of success had to be greater.

I tried listening to different voices and music styles until I found a couple that really felt good for me. I knew them when I heard them; the sound vibrations seemed to resonate in my soul. Most of the time, they made me fall asleep. But hey, at least that meant I was really relaxed. Every other time, my mind still raced and ignored the soothing guided words. On those days, all I could do to distract my mind was count my breath. At least if I was counting, I couldn't think about anything else.

Every now and then, after counting long enough to pause my thoughts, I'd feel myself float or sink a little bit. *Ooh! Am I going out of body?* I noticed in excitement before losing the moment.

Other times, Cody's presence would flood over me, welling tears in my eyes immediately before blanketing me in warm love. Sometimes, I felt inklings to call a friend, go somewhere, or look something up, and every once in a while, I heard things like "keep going, you're on the right path."

Whoever's voice I was hearing sounded familiar and felt like it was calling me home. Though I had no idea where this path was taking me, I was determined to keep going and find out.

# Chapter 14

## August 2013:

## Waking Up

Though I was diving deep into spirituality, I was still avoiding the pain from my past. Guilt silently followed me like a dark shadow, and instead of turning to face and shed light on it, I kept running away from it. I thought that was all I needed to do, trusting that the more I did to improve my outer world, the better I would eventually feel on the inside, too.

I literally began running more often, finding refuge in the gym, and quickly developing a new addiction to exercise. My short cruises between classes weren't enough to calm my busy mind. So, I squeezed more gym time between classes, not even noticing how obsessed I was becoming with working out, nor how thin I was getting. On the outside, I thought I looked more toned and fit than ever. But on the inside? That was another story.

It felt like forever since I had truly felt good on the inside. No one would know that, though; I was a professional at faking happiness now. I was a strong, intelligent, and independent single mom going to engineering school; I really had to be confident in myself to do that, right? But really, motivation came from an obligation to prove myself. To whom? To everyone. I was so ashamed of the bizarre tragedies of my past; I was convinced that I had to prove to the world that I wasn't the cursed and wild mess that the rumors in my small hometown once told. Even though cannabis still seemed to be the only drug that truly helped, I battled internally over its legal complications and my personal shame for my drug-abusing past.

By this point, I had been on antidepressants for seven years. Over those years, I tried a handful of different medications, slowly increasing doses to maximize their effectiveness in reducing my anxiety and sudden drops into doom and depression. I'd been taking them for so long, I didn't know any different, nor could I notice that I was speeding on autopilot. Antidepressants dulled my anxiety enough to stay focused on what was ahead of me. I didn't have to feel my pain, especially if I didn't look back. So, I kept running forward.

Then one day at the Shopko pharmacy, the pharmacist pulled out my prescription and muttered, "Ah, yes," to herself after reading a written note on the bottle. She looked up at me, over her rectangular glasses that slid down her nose. "So, do you know why you're taking this dosage?"

Confused, I answered, "Um, because my doctor prescribed it?"

"Hm," she hummed. "Well, you're prescribed twice the maximum dose we'd recommend, and we normally try to wean our patients off it within a year. It looks like you've been on it for three."

"Holy shit," I exclaimed out loud. "I had no idea." *And that's only this specific medication... how long have I been on antidepressants altogether?* I suddenly wondered, counting to seven on my fingers. *Wow, that's a long time.*

"I'd recommend slowly weaning off of it," she advised. "Very slowly, though. You need to be careful with this stuff."

"Oh, wow, okay," I replied. "How do I do that?"

"Talk to your doctor and have them start reducing your prescription," she answered, then continued explaining her recommendations on how to do so. Well, that meant it was time to find a new doctor in our new town. So I searched online and made the earliest appointment possible.

We planned to wean me off over the next month, and it went great. I didn't notice any significant symptoms as we slowly reduced my dosage every week. I felt empowered and proud of myself for finally letting go of my crutch and my body's dependency on synthetic chemicals. It inspired me so much, I decided to stop taking birth control, too. *My own life is my birth control right now*, I thought. Since Logan and I last broke up and I poured all my energy into school, Jaelyn, and running away from my grief, I had no interest in men nor the libido to attract one.

I felt fresh, clear, and determined to return my body to a healthy and independent state, and you know, conquer yet another challenge. Then, one day, I forgot to take my antidepressant. *Oh well*, I thought. *I'm almost done anyway, might as well stop right now.* That night, I woke up dripping in sweat. My sheets were completely soaked, like someone dumped a bucket of water over me. *Oh my God, what's wrong with me?* I was so wet, I had to get a towel to dry off and lay on the bed beneath me.

I couldn't believe how sweaty I was. Then I noticed a tingle at the base of my skull. It buzzed and pulsed into my brain and down my neck. *Why do I feel so strange?* I wondered.

For the next week, this sweat soak repeated every night. By night three, I was tired of rewashing my sheets and started sleeping over towels on my couch. The tingling in my skull was constant by that point, making me wonder what the hell kind of chemical dependency my brain had developed in seven years. *Do I give in and go back to a low dose?* I wondered. *No. I'm almost there; I can get through this.*

The sweaty symptoms finally subsided within another few days. I was starting to feel like myself again, except for one thing. I started noticing more pimples forming on my cheeks. Throughout my life, I was blessed with clear skin. Sure, I got the occasional pimple here and there, but I never suffered anything remotely close to acne until now. Over the next few months, acne took over my face, spreading across my cheeks and jawline.

Each day, I woke up horrified to see more pimples developing. Those suckers were painful, too. Some got so large, they itched to be popped and break out of my skin. My friends and I immediately concluded that it must be from quitting my antidepressant and birth control simultaneously, and they reassured me that it would clear up. Yet my already high stress level only rose with my frustration. Day by day, my skin looked worse. *At least I have make-up to cover it,* I reassured myself. *And at least I'm skinny, too.*

I had already lost weight after having Jaelyn, and my new obsessive fitness routine continued shaving every last bit of fat off my body. *I'm just super healthy,* I told myself. In reality, I was a volcano of stress that was slowly erupting through the pimples on my face. *But my body still looks fantastic; I'm in the best shape of my life,* and that's what I thought really mattered.

It took me many months before I noticed, but as I continued shrinking in size, my period disappeared with me. *I'm just super athletic now,* I reassured myself. *And talk about convenience, no period.* Plus, my sudden explosion of acne was enough to keep me occupied in search of the right natural remedies for my body anyway.

I became paranoid about every bit of food I put into my mouth after I learned that sugar, wheat, and dairy could be causing my acne or making it worse. This didn't go over well back home. I started bringing my own food on visits and ranting about how bad the white sugar, flour, and corn-

*The Daisy Diaries* | 155

syrup-filled foods were that comprised my mom's pantry. I got tense and anxious at every gathering, wondering if there'd be anything I could eat and if anyone would ask why I wasn't eating the "best" things. I became anal about shopping all-organic, meal prepping, and resisting carbs and dairy at all costs. While striving for perfect health, I wondered why my body still felt so tired and stressed.

*What am I doing wrong?* My inner critic tormented me, judging my every move for its potential effect on my skin and appearance. Still, on the outside, I mastered and maintained my "fake it till you make it" happy face. My skin might have damaged my outer confidence, but my body was in peak physical shape, and I let that inflate my ego enough to make up for it.

My friends could clearly see how much more stressed I was and encouraged me to get out and join them at the bars on the weekends. I needed to get a babysitter and release my tension, they advised. I had found a couple of younger students to babysit for me during evening tests and school events, but I couldn't imagine paying them just for me to go out and drink.

"Oh, come on, Krista," my friends told me. "You deserve a break. You need to get out; it's good for you!"

Eventually, my stress level reached the point that I agreed with their logic. I started going out occasionally, quickly becoming the intriguing "new girl" that was never out before. Suddenly, I felt afraid of the attention, awkwardly closing up around the boys approaching me. *Come on, lighten up, Krista,* I told myself. *Be confident. Fake it till you make it.*

So, I faked it until I started having fun flaunting about the bars with my girlfriends a couple times a month. One night, sitting at a high-top by the bar with my two girlfriends, I noticed a tall and attractive guy looking at me from the bar and whispering to his group of friends.

*Wow, he's hot,* I thought to myself, blushing and turning back to my girls. I tried my hardest not to look back, but I could feel his eyes from across the bar. *Oh my God, is he really interested in me?* I wondered, getting more excited.

My friends quickly noticed where I kept looking. "Yeah, girl," they encouraged me. "Go flirt with him! You need to get out there!"

I didn't have to go far; within the next minute or two of making eyes with him, he came wandering over and leaned his elbow on the table in front of me. He smiled and said, "Hi, I'm James. What's your name?"

I was smitten. I introduced myself and my friends and made eyes at him over small talk. A minute later, he looked down at my nearly empty glass and asked, "Can I buy you a drink?"

My girlfriends smiled as I slipped out of my seat and settled next to James at the bar. We got to sharing our backstories and flirting while sipping our drinks, and the night flew by without notice. When my friends were ready to leave, he said, "You're more than welcome to stay here with me." I was tempted but couldn't miss my guaranteed ride home to my daughter. Not to mention I was on the babysitter's clock!

"I wish I could, but I've got to go," I replied. "Maybe we can do this again."

"I really hope we can," he said coyly. "Can I get your number?"

I recited my number as a friend started tugging on my arm. We said goodbye, and I turned away to go home and daydream about this gorgeous new man I had attracted. *I'm so glad I went out!* I thought to myself.

James texted me the next night, asking if I could go out again. I didn't have a babysitter, and though embarrassed, I admitted my single mom status. "Oh, that's okay, I totally get it," he reassured me. We continued texting through the week, making plans for the following weekend, my excitement escalating every day. James said he'd take me out for dinner and meet up with friends for drinks after. But when that evening came, he had a sudden change of plans, claiming he got stuck at a family party and couldn't make it for dinner. Though he promised he would still meet for drinks after.

Disappointment stirred in my stomach. *Is he for real?* I wondered. I decided to give him the benefit of the doubt and meet him at the bar later anyway. In the meantime, I still had a babysitter coming, so I got dressed up and went out with a girlfriend. I was extremely thirsty at the bar, trying to quench my anxiety over whether James would show up or not. By the time he did, I was half in the bag and thrilled to see him. We picked up where we left off, flirting, smiling, touching, and sipping down the drinks. Toward the end of the night, he leaned in and smiled, "Ready to get out of here?"

My friend sat on my other side, with a male friend of hers on her side, who glared at me, shaking his head like he was silently saying, "No, don't do it!" I turned back to James, excitedly contemplating my options. I knew what he wanted. Is that what I wanted, too? It had been such a long time, and come on, the guy was gorgeous. *Why not let me have a little fun? I deserve it, right?*

"Where do you want to go?" I asked.

"Can we go to your place?" he asked, rubbing his hand on my knee. A chill ran down my spine.

"Well, I have to relieve my babysitter anyway, so as long as my daughter is sleeping…." I trailed off, getting distracted by the devil and the angel fighting on my shoulders.

"Awesome," he replied quickly. "I just need to go to the bathroom. I'll be right back." He leaned in and kissed me on the cheek, pulling away with a smile and locking bedroom eyes with me before turning toward the bathroom. More chills ticked me. *Oh, man, how can I resist?*

"Don't do it," a voice nearby said. I turned to my friend and her friend, who continued, "He's a player. I'm sorry, but he's totally using you. I've seen him do this a thousand times."

"Oh, come on," my friend interjected. "You don't know that for sure. Girl, you do what you want to do."

I got the warning, but did I listen? I took the last gulp of my drink as James came up behind me, wrapping his arms around my waist and whispering in my ear, "Are you ready to go?" I let him take my hand and lead me out of the bar. We walked to my apartment, tiptoed up the stairs, and slowly opened the door. My babysitter was sitting in the living room. She looked surprised by my visitor and could undoubtedly tell I was intoxicated. She gave me a brief report of the evening, thanked me for the cash, and slipped out the door.

I gave James the short tour of our tiny apartment before we put in a movie and settled on the couch. We sipped on new beverages as the sofa seemed to suck me in deeper and closer to James. First, he slipped his arm around me, and before I knew it, we were spooning. My heart pounded, but it felt so good to be in someone's arms again. *Wow, I've missed this,* I thought.

"You're so beautiful," he whispered in my ear, sending chills down my spine. *Yes, keep telling me all the things I want to hear!* Suddenly, he ran his hand along my side and kissed my neck. *Oh, good Lord, help me,* I thought. *It's been so long!* James was on top of me before I knew it. I have no recollection of what movie we watched.

Many minutes, or hours, later, I was exhausted and had an active 5-year-old to wake up to in the morning. We sorted through clothes in the dim light of the TV before I led James to my front door.

"I had an amazing time tonight," he said as he leaned down to kiss me. "I'll give you a call tomorrow." He quietly slipped out the door, and I tiptoed into my bedroom. Exhausted, smitten by this new romance, and satisfied, I dozed off imagining what it might be like to be with this guy.

He started coming over to my apartment after Jaelyn's bedtime every few days or so to continue our rendezvous. I told my closest friends all about him, and they excitedly cheered me on for snagging such a hottie. "He's got a badass chemical engineer woman, what a lucky man!" they told me.

However, he apparently didn't feel the same. Over the next few weeks, his texts came fewer and further between, and he suddenly had many changes in plans. Eventually, his texts stopped altogether. I never did go on that dinner date.

A few days after realizing I'd never hear from him again, it suddenly hit me: that was a "dangerous man." An attractive and seductive one who easily faked interest in me and lured me as his latest flavor of the month. *Come on, Krista, you were even warned about that! How did I not see it coming?* For a moment, I went down a spiral of criticism. "I was supposed to wrap him in white light," I suddenly remembered out loud. "I wonder if I still can. I guess it doesn't hurt to try." I closed my eyes, visualizing him and surrounding him with white light. "God," I prayed out loud. "Please wrap him in white healing light and protect me from other dangerous men."

I breathed in compassion for myself and my mistakes. I forgave myself for getting swept up in the excitement of being 'wanted.' I was still seeking approval from others, and being picked by the hot jock in the bar was definite proof of my approval status, wasn't it? *How shallow,* I realized. I immediately saw a playback reel of all my former relationships and flings in my mind. *Wow, every single one of my exes and flings were "pretty boys,"* I concluded. All very dangerously good-looking, and they all knew it, too.

A sickening chill ran down my spine. *Yuck, I let myself get used,* I thought to myself in disgust. *This guy didn't care about getting to know me; he just wanted a piece of ass. He only looked at my body. He couldn't look deep into my eyes.*

Cody always looked into my eyes. And something about his gaze made me feel truly seen, that he was really looking into my soul. *I refuse to settle for anything less anymore,* I promised to myself. *No more pretty boys. I want the real thing. Someone who can and wants to see my soul. I already know what it feels like, and I won't settle until I feel it again.*

At that moment, I raised my guards all the way up. Swearing off all men, my focus shifted to gaining approval and validation from other places. I worked harder, dedicating myself fully to nothing else but being a mom to Jaelyn, finishing school, and making some money working on campus. I almost didn't notice that James disappeared from my life just as quickly as he came into it, and I no longer felt the icky guilt that it left me with. *Maybe the white light still worked,* I wondered. *And perhaps I just need to stay busy to keep my mind focused and out of trouble.*

Not that I needed to fill my schedule or brain with anything more. The single mom/student/employee lifestyle was more than enough. Plus, my confidence and trust in life had just been shaken by my hot jock encounters. Just as quickly as I first discovered inner peace from my yoga practice, I lost touch with it again. Stress continued to rise as I moved through the busy motions of my daily routines.

Within weeks, I couldn't stand the silent unease within me; I had to satisfy a craving to understand myself and the world more. I needed to find a way to stop beating myself up for my past and worrying about what I needed to do in the future. So I did a quick internet search for enlightening self-help books and stumbled upon *The Power of Now* by Eckhart Tolle. I immediately ordered it and dove into reading.

That book was my first introduction to the concept that "I am not my thoughts." *Those critical, judgmental, shaming thoughts are not mine? What a relief!* I didn't realize it was possible to separate myself from my thoughts before. I found great comfort in reading about the ego and higher self; the concept seemed to wake me up. It felt like I had dreamed my entire life that I was controlled by my mind, and I just woke up to the reality of my soul being separate and more powerful than my thoughts.

Though this definition of ego, as the unwanted controller of the "monkey mind," was a completely new concept, I resonated deeply with it. *Of course, I'm not my thoughts. Of course, I'm not actually this ego, and I don't have to identify with all its mean and painful judgment anymore.* Just like that, I felt a weight fall from my shoulders.

Eckhart's description of ego and the pain-body, or the "collector of emotions triggered by our experiences," struck me like an obvious truth I couldn't believe I forgot. The concept of the pain-body made sense to me; it felt familiar. Reading about it introduced me to my shadow self, to the source of my pain and suffering that had collected over my entire life. Being introduced to it as its own entity, separate from my true self, allowed me to detach from it for the first time. *Wow!* I didn't realize how heavy and clingy my pain-body was. In releasing its heavy weight, I felt lighter and could feel the life in my body like never before.

I started doing Eckhart's body awareness exercises woven through its chapters. For the first time, I connected my breath, body, and soul, even while off the yoga mat. I almost couldn't believe the intense high and bliss that could come from just breathing. This new reality was so magical, it had to be shared. I started buying used copies of the book and sharing them with friends. I was so excited about it; the book even came up in conversation with my dad during a visit back home.

"That sounds really interesting," he said with eyebrows lifted in curiosity.

"Really?" I replied in surprise. "I have a few copies with me. Do you want to have one?"

"Sure," he said with a smile. "I'm excited to check it out."

I had stopped speaking to either of my parents about anything religious or remotely spiritual many years earlier. I couldn't believe I could open this new spiritual side of myself to my dad, but it was awesome. My mom had always controlled the religious talk and beliefs of the household, maintaining the strict Catholic rules as her own family had done. I guess I never knew my dad's spiritual beliefs. He was always quiet and let my mom run the show. It was refreshing to connect with him on a new level and realize how open-minded he was. *Perhaps I do have more qualities from my parents than I realized,* I thought.

Reading *The Power of Now* was like discovering a new and better drug. It took a lot of practice, but every fleeting glimpse of bliss and presence in the moment was an ultimate high like no other. I looked forward to bedtime when I could get cozy and practice breathing into each area of my body. I could feel the energy pulsing through my veins, tissues, skin, and all around me.

In those moments, I felt in tune with a higher power, completely safe and supported by it. I often fell asleep in this state of bliss and woke up feeling healed and more energized for the day ahead. A fresh excitement filled me for my challenging and interesting classes, making new friendships, and enjoying the beautiful new place we lived in.

Soon, life was brighter and filled me with new zest that I hadn't felt since Jaelyn was born. My growing bond with my breath, body, and spirit replenished the energy I had drained and depleted over the last several years. I found ease in trusting the Universe and looked forward to the little surprises each day brought.

The positive shift in my energy didn't go unnoticed. I was radiating confidence and a new love for myself and catching more eyes with cute boys around campus and town than I ever noticed before. What I didn't realize, though, was that it was also attracting men that I didn't want attention from, including my friend's boyfriend.

I met him first through a mutual friend, and as we became friends, I was introduced to his girlfriend. I quickly grew close to them; they were the only other parents I knew my age and had kids my daughter's age, too. It was a huge relief to know I wasn't the only young parent around, and I found a lot of comfort in bringing Jaelyn to their house in the evenings to cook meals together while the kids played. It was the perfect way for all of us to decompress. At their house, I was comfortable being my unfiltered self. After long days of intimidating classes, surrounded by insanely smart humans who all seemed to be competing for the smartest human award, I often couldn't wait to get to their house. There, There, I could relax, sip on wine, and laugh my cares away. Our kids got along exceptionally well, and so did we. For we adults, though, apparently too well.

After a month or two of spending much of our free time with their family, I felt deeply understood and respected. They both expressed admiration for what I was doing with my life as a single mom, and they cheered me on more than anyone. I felt smart and confident; it was easy to express my truth to them, which was more difficult to do under the high expectations of my new college environment. It felt so good to feel understood by someone, especially a man. I felt safe in that friendship; knowing he was in a relationship let me take down my guard. Of course, he wasn't interested in me; maybe that's how he was able to understand and appreciate who I was, not just what I looked like. That's the noble story I told myself, at least.

On the car accident anniversary that spring, unlike the previous years, I decided I wouldn't stay home and feel sorry for myself. My friend (and temporary roommate) and I got a babysitter for our kids, and we went out to the bars.

I felt deserving of drinking my grief away that night and did it quickly. Soon I was buzzed up, feeling good, and suddenly inspired to find myself a new man. I wasn't going to lay in bed crying about Cody this year. I knew it was time to move on, and with another vodka cranberry in hand,

I was going to move on that night. A few boys approached me through the evening, but none sparked my genuine interest, and I drank away disappointment with my grief. *Ugh, is there anybody out there even comparable to Cody?* I wondered.

Sitting at the bar, I zoned out and stared at the liquor behind the bar. My mind imagined Cody with that look on his face when he got lost in my eyes. He could see right through to my soul and loved every aspect of it. I took another drink, Cody's image still painted across my mind. And then, his clothes came off, exposing his tall and muscular body. A tingle ran up my spine, and bam, I was turned on like a light switch. I looked up and around the bar, automatically scanning the room for an attractive man. Still, no one caught my attention. Disappointed again, I was ready to give up, go home, and return to sulking in my sorrow, wishing Cody were still here.

My roommate saw the shift in my mood and became determined to cheer me up. "Here, have another drink!" she said. "Let's go dance!" I shrugged in agreement, took the free drink in hand, and we made our way to the back patio to dance with the crowd and DJ. A few songs later, I paused to check my phone for messages from my babysitter. She had sent a text that Jaelyn was sleeping, and I had also received one from my friend's boyfriend. "Hey, how's it going?" it read.

We had been good friends for a while now, so it wasn't unusual to get a text here and there from him. Unsure and unsuspecting of what he wanted, I wrote back that I was out at the bar for much-needed drinks, and we chatted small talk. I thought nothing of it beyond having someone to text and feed my attention between dances, drinks, and disappointing encounters with uninteresting boys.

Soon, the evening blurred. By bar close, my roommate and I were hammered, and luckily able to walk to our house from the bar. We stumbled there and relieved our babysitter. My roommate went straight to her room, though I remained awake and unsettled in an emotional cocktail of grief and loneliness. He was still texting about being bored and unable to sleep, and one more text and bad decision later, he was knocking quietly on my front door.

As soon as he entered the house behind me and I turned around, he reached for my waist and pulled me in for a kiss. Stupidly surprised, I froze. *What is wrong with me?* I suddenly realized. *Why did I let him come here?* But someone was kissing me. Someone who understood me and knew who I was, unlike the jocks I had grown so sick of attracting in the gym and bars. Being kissed by someone I thought respected me filled me with familiar comfort. I hadn't felt anything close to that since Cody last kissed me. In a way, it was like kissing Cody, wasn't it?

"I've been waiting to do this for so long," he said. *Cody once said that, too*, I thought, lost in my own drunken fantasy. I let myself get carried away in the moment, blinded in ecstasy by the physical contact I had been craving for so long. Then, reality hit me, and I pushed him away from me. "Holy shit," I whispered in panic. "We can't be doing this. You need to go."

He pulled away in surprise, "Oh, woah, I'm sorry. Don't worry. Nobody needs to know." A bomb dropped in my stomach, exploding all-too-familiar plumes of disgust and guilt. *Another dirty secret,* I thought to myself as flashbacks of the nightmare love affair with Jake and Cody ran through my mind. *I'm the other girl again.* I swallowed down the lump in my throat as Logan and Teresa also flashed into my vision. *Except this time, I just destroyed a real relationship, with kids. What kind of whore am I?*

He gathered his things and promised to lock the door on his way out. As I heard his slow, quiet footsteps go down the stairs, I crawled into my bed, pulling the covers over my head, and sank heavily into self-loathing. *What the hell is wrong with me?* I thought to myself. *How the fuck could I do that to someone, especially a close friend of mine? This is exactly what Jake and my friends did to me. I never thought I could do that to somebody else. Am I that desperately lonely, or really just a piece of shit?*

I laid there berating myself until eventually, my exhaustion overcame my nauseous guilt, and I dozed off to sleep. That night, I had a vivid dream. I was at my family's cottage in northern Wisconsin for a big party. The house and yard were filled with people, and amongst the crowd, I spotted Cody. Immediately flooded with excitement and love, we ran to one another, embracing arms in a tight hug. "I'm so happy to see you," I said, my voice cracking as tears welled in my eyes. "I missed you so much."

"I missed you, too, baby," he replied, hugging me tighter. I leaned back just enough to look at his face.

"I need to take a mental picture of this moment," I said before kissing him on the lips. "I know we don't have much time," I added, with all-knowing that I was dreaming and he was only visiting for a short time. We hugged again, and my brain scrambled to capture and remember every sight and sensation. *I can't forget this moment*, I told myself.

Then, my mom walked up to us through the crowd. "Are you ready to meet everyone?" she asked Cody. I was shocked. *My mother, who once put great effort into keeping me away from Cody, now wants him to meet everyone?* This really is a dream! With a nervous smile, Cody leaned in and replied, "Yes."

Suddenly, I woke up, feeling startled, disappointed to be awake, and sickly longing for Cody. Just as suddenly, a subtle understanding struck of why I fell weak the night before. Then, a spontaneous thought came to me, *the dangerous men will keep manifesting until you detach from the physical.* I swallowed down another lump in my throat. It was true. Another dangerous man snuck in under my radar, and for months, I had no idea. But this time, I felt just as dangerous.

I closed my eyes for a moment, visualizing my white light. *God, please wrap him in light, help him respect his woman, heal his relationship, and protect me from dangerous men and situations,* I prayed silently. In that moment, I could no longer deny my need to stop living in the past, be aware of the dangerous men around me and my own dangerous behavior, and do what Cody said way back through the Medium. It was time to detach from my physical attraction to Cody and focus on the spiritual connection. "Write it down," I heard in my mind. I picked up my pen and old journal from my bedside table and scribbled down what I could remember of my dream.


Mar. 23, 2014

*Dreamt of Cody last night. Found him in a crowd of friends and family at the cottage playground. We held each other on a tire swing, hugged, and kissed. Embraced the moment we knew was only temporary. Mom came up and asked if he was ready to meet the family. He leaned in and awkwardly said yes. I forgot how shy he could be. My heart still overflows with love for him. May it soon overflow with love for my living life partner.*

- Kris

Within a few days, the truth of my rendezvous came out to my friend, and honestly, I was relieved to be caught. It wasn't pretty, but I couldn't bear to carry the guilt of betrayal like I had done in the past, even if it meant ruining two good friendships that I had leaned and depended on so much over the last couple of years. Much to my surprise and relief, she forgave me, and we tried to still hang out like nothing had happened. But we all knew that it would never be the same. And I knew that no matter how much I apologized or how easily she had forgiven me, I was never going to be free from the guilt I created for myself. I started meeting her alone with our kids and avoided seeing her boyfriend, unable to ignore the truth in my gut that I needed to remove myself from the situation altogether. As the end of my final school year was quickly approaching, I got busier and busier with final reports, resume building, job applications, and interviews, making it easier for our two families to slowly drift apart. By summertime, Jaelyn and I would move to our next new home, removing me from the dangerous situation for good.

My immediate future suddenly became my biggest concern. Where the hell am I going to work when I graduate? Anxiety filled my chest. *Okay, slow down, Krista,* I told myself. *Focus on finishing school first. You've almost made it! Let yourself celebrate this accomplishment and trust that the right job will come at precisely the right time. Go with grace and ease.*

It really was time to celebrate, and my family agreed. We decided to take a family vacation during my last spring break and celebrate Jaelyn's sixth birthday. We went to Disney World, unintentionally staying at the same resort we had first stayed at exactly twenty years earlier. We all had a great time together; I couldn't remember the last time I had that much fun with my family. And one thing to especially celebrate was my growing relationship with my dad. He and I really bonded on that trip. Now that I was a mom and discovered that my only available time for true peace and quiet was before Jaelyn woke up, I finally woke up early and joined my dad for his morning walks. We explored the paths around the resort, enjoying the foliage and flowers, birds and lizards, and the warm and humid morning breeze. I couldn't help but notice and count every daisy along our path. *Cody must be happy for us, too,* I thought with a comforting smile.

We talked about my college experience and how proud he was of me for getting through it. We laughed over how fun it was to explore that campus and town together. We even chatted about *The Power of Now* and how he brought the book on the trip to read. "It's very interesting," he commented. "I've never read anything like it. It's really a whole new way of thinking, isn't it?"

"It sure is," I said with excitement. "It rocked my world! If only the whole world could read it and detach from their own ego-driven and fear-based thoughts. Imagine how different the world could be."

He chuckled softly. "I know. But at least we can start with us." I smiled. *How cool that I can talk to my dad about spiritual stuff?* I thought. I could never talk to my mom about these things, not unless they followed the Catholic rules. But my dad was more open than I had ever known. So, I opened myself up to him. I shared my dreams and fears for the future, and he listened quietly, responding with an occasional "hmm" and "mmhmm," saving his select few words for the best moments. Finally, he often said, "Just remember, work hard, play hard. Work hard and always do your best, but don't forget to stop and play just as much."

I laughed. "You always have the best advice."

We bonded over the rest of our trip and the following weeks leading to my graduation. When that day arrived, the bliss and family connection of our Disney World trip was blown out of the water; graduation day took the cake. I was beyond proud to finally earn that degree and to have my family watch it be handed to me, especially my dad. I was proud to graduate from the same school he attended and adored. After all the mistakes and trouble from my past, it felt incredible to do something he could finally be proud of. I hoped he could feel relief from worrying about me in the past and confident that I learned something from him and could make it in the world.

With his help, I certainly did feel confident. He was always there to help and give the answers I needed. Especially as I noticed the tendencies of my girlfriends to lean heavily on their relationships, I found pride in my independence. "Whatever I can't figure out myself; all I have to do is call my dad," I told them. "He'll always either tell me how to do it or come help me do it." I suddenly realized how lucky I was to live so independently but with such stable support from my dad and family. *I really do have it all.*

As graduation came and went, my anxiety about the future skyrocketed. *I should have gotten a job by now,* I believed. *What's wrong with me that I can't find the right job?* I started spending more time on my yoga mat to calm my anxiety and boost my confidence in my future success. I also stumbled upon the Netflix documentary, *The Secret,* and was immediately drawn to watch it. A documentary about the Law of Attraction blew me away with its simple concept that what we think about is what we attract. It all resonated with me deeply. I suddenly realized, *Oh my goodness, what have my negative thoughts and worries been attracting? I need to focus positively to manifest the career and future that I want!*

The next day, I bought myself a pretty new journal and dedicated it to my positive affirmations. I started writing down exactly what I wanted in my dream career, home, relationship with Jaelyn, and relationship with a future partner while imagining the picture-perfect scenes of my ideal life. I wrote in that journal almost every day, getting more and more detailed on the specifics of my manifestation.

4-29-14

*I have a great job as a Research & Development Engineer. We live in an adorable and cozy home, with lots of windows and open space. We live close to Jaelyn's amazing school, and we both adapt well to the community. Dance classes for both of us are nearby.*

*I have a genuine, loving, honest, hardworking, family-oriented, adventurous, smart, and handsome partner. He's a carpenter or at least loves building things, and even fishing, and teaching me how to. Music lover. Honest. Loyal. Trusting. Tall. Has kids of his own for me to love and grow close to Jaelyn.*

-Kris

A few weeks after graduation, I decided to keep my on-campus job and stay in Houghton for the summer. *I'll relax and enjoy one more summer before we go!* I told myself. Though as soon as I relaxed, a job offer appeared. It was for a wire and cable manufacturer in western Wisconsin. *Far enough, but not too far from family,* I thought. *This place just might be perfect for us!* A few calls and interviews later, I was searching for a new home in Wisconsin. Just like arrangements in Houghton lined up perfectly at the last minute, everything fell into place as we transitioned to another new life. An adorably cozy townhome appeared, right next to Jaelyn's elementary school. We moved to Wisconsin on Father's Day weekend, following my dad's truck and trailer full of our belongings. My dad and I, alone, moved and unpacked all of our furniture together, and he, Jaelyn, and I celebrated a memorable weekend exploring the area. We had so much fun, I almost forgot how nervous I was to start my first day of work in the real world on Monday.

Of course, my first days and weeks of work were intimidating. I felt like I was drinking from a firehose of information every day, trying to absorb the ins and outs of making cable, not to mention remembering the names of all my new coworkers. Though looking back, I settled into the corporate world quite well. I had finally made it: I had a high-paying job, was quickly earning the respect of my coworkers, and before I knew it, I was climbing higher and higher.

I finally felt like I had reached success. I thought I had finally proved myself. *I'm a successful engineer now, in Research & Development, too! I manifested it! I'm living the dream now, aren't I?* Though the accomplishments I had made on paper by this point were quite impressive, I was still hiding and denying a rising stress level inside me. "fake it till you make it," I reminded myself. "The more I think about and pretend to be happy, the happier I'll eventually be."

Instead, I focused on "external perfection" of appearance, health, and career. In other words, I focused on what I now consider "false healing," or busy-ness. I was still masking my acne with make-up, styling my thinning, short hair, and self-consciously squeezing into tiny sizes of the best name-brands of work clothing. *How did I appear so happy and healthy on the outside? Why didn't I feel it on the inside?* Every time I asked myself this question, my heart knew the answer. *Because I'm so damn lonely.*

My heart still ached for Cody. I longed for that deep, spiritual connection. I longed to be held in someone's arms again, someone who truly understood and cared about me. I regularly laid in bed at night thinking about him, and he still often appeared in my dreams.

And now that I was living in a new town, I didn't know anyone once again, reminding me just how lonely I was. Feeling sorry for myself, I spiraled down a hole of anger. I was angry that Cody was taken from me. Angry that I had attracted so many assholes since. Angry at myself for being weak and entertaining dangerous men who couldn't see me like Cody had. But once I hit the bottom of my angry pit, I remembered,

*Focus on what you DO want.* So, I pulled out my journal and continued writing down my prayers and affirmations.

July 10, 2014

*God, please help me dig deep and see myself for who I really am. Please help me let my light shine. Please guide me to my life partner that is genuine, honest, kind, and hard-working. May he love my soul above all else, teach me knew things, and learn and grow with me through life. May he love Jaelyn and even have kids of his own for me to love, too. I am worthy of being loved. I love myself and my ability to create a beautiful life!*

– Kris

# Chapter 15

## July 2014:

## The Real Awakening

One month into my engineering career, I slowly started to feel comfortable in my new home, new town, Jaelyn's new school, and of course, my new workplace.

I was finally understanding what the hell wire and cable was all about, beginning to make friends with my coworkers, and felt my invisible shield of protection slowly dissolving. But now, my days were even busier than in college. No more breaks between classes, so that meant I had to squeeze in my gym time before or after work. And yes, this was a must; I was addicted to the gym and the precious "me time" it gave me to run away from the stress I pretended I didn't have.

Our days were longer, our nights shorter, and I quickly found myself out of touch with my old friends and loved ones. Including my parents. I know they meant well, but they could be so annoying with their constant calls and checking in to make sure I was okay.

One night, I felt particularly exhausted while going through the motions of dinner, homework, bathing, and bedtime with Jaelyn. Somewhere between the bathing battle and bedtime, I saw my silent phone light up with a call.

'Mom & Dad' it read.

*Ugh. I'm busy.* I thought. *Not right now. I'll call them back tomorrow.*

I rushed through the rest of our evening routine and could hardly wait for my head to hit the pillow. I was so tired and determined to get the most of my few hours of rest before getting up early and starting the next day's race.

Just as I was closing my eyes, my silent phone lit up again on my bedside table. Irritated, I leaned forward to see who was calling: an unknown number from my hometown. *Who the hell is messing with me at this hour?* I turned my phone face down and went back to sleep.

In the dead of night, somewhere around 2:00 am, my precious rest was rudely disrupted; I was startled awake by my doorbell ringing.

DING DONG.

*Holy shit! What is that?!* Living in our new home for just one month, I hadn't heard my doorbell ring before.

DING DONG. DING DONG.

*Oh my God!* I panicked. *What if it's some rapist serial killer who saw it's only Jaelyn and I living here and is waiting to attack me at the door?!*

DING DONG.

*Holy shit! What do I do?!*

I stumbled out of bed in the darkness and reached for the baseball bat my dad gave me as an extra weapon of protection when I first moved out of his house. I crept up to the door slowly, trying to get a glimpse of the intruder waiting outside. It was a cop.

*What the hell?!* I thought. *Am I in trouble? What could I have possibly done?* Shaking, I answered the door, holding the baseball bat behind my back.

"Hello, I'm so sorry to wake you. Are you Krista Lindquist?" the officer asked.

"Um, yes, I am," I replied, my voice trembling.

"I don't know what happened, but I was sent here to deliver a message to you to call the Grand View Hospital in Ironwood, Michigan."

"What? What happened?!" I squeaked.

"Do you need a phone to call?" the officer asked.

"Oh, um, no. I'll get my phone," I quietly replied before stumbling back to my room.

I picked it up to realize I had six missed calls from a few different unknown numbers. *Oh my God, whatever happened, they've been trying to contact me!* My heart pounded in fear as I walked back to the front door, where the poor clueless officer stood waiting for me. "Here's the number you need to call," he said.

My arm felt like it was moving through thick molasses to lift the phone to my ear. I didn't know who I was calling, and I wasn't sure if I wanted to. *Ring... Ring...*

"Hello, Grand View Hospital, how can I direct your call?" a woman's kind voice answered.

"Um, this is Krista Lindquist? I was told to call the hospital, but I don't know why?" I asked, my voice still trembling.

"Oh, yes, okay. Hello, Krista. I am so sorry to disturb you this late; we've been trying to find you all night," she replied.

My eyes automatically welled with tears. "What's going on?" I asked and braced myself.

"It's your father, Brian," she replied.

*What? My dad?* I thought in shock. *What could have happened?*

"There's no easy way to tell you this," she continued. "But your father had a heart attack tonight. He was rushed here as quickly as possible, but there was nothing we could do. He passed away peacefully. I'm so sorry."

Yet another atomic bomb of shock dropped in my stomach. With my back against a wall, I sank down to the floor.

"Oh my God," was all I could say, now sobbing with my head between my knees. The police officer continued to stand in my doorway, watching me while I melted into a puddle on the floor.

A shocking blow buzzed through my body, then a tingling numbness set in. This was too familiar. The pain of death, of losing my hero. This time, losing the most important man I *ever* had in my life.

*This can't be happening. I can't do this again.*

For a moment, all time stood still. I couldn't feel my body. It was like I completely stepped out of my own skin to dodge the familiar pangs of shock running through it.

"Your family wanted to make sure you were notified right away. But, it wasn't easy finding you. Your mom went into shock and couldn't remember where you lived," the woman explained.

I just kept sobbing into the phone.

"Your mom is still pretty shaken up right now, but your sister Monica is here," she continued. "Would you like to speak with her?"

"Okay," I squeaked out between sobs.

"Okay, hold on just one moment, please," she responded.

Still sitting on the floor, I leaned my head on the wall in an attempt to stop my brain from spinning. After a few moments of shuffling noises over the phone, I heard my sister clear her throat and say, "Hey," her voice trailing off, its sound provoking more tears.

"Hey," I responded softly. "This is crazy. I can't believe it."

"I know," she replied sadly. "I know. Me neither. Mom's pretty out of it right now. She's okay, I think, just shocked."

*The Daisy Diaries* | 173

"I'm shocked, too," I said. "I can't imagine what kind of state she's in right now. Was she with him when it happened?"

"Yeah, I think so," she answered with a loud sigh. "At least, she found him. Ugh. I can't imagine. I mean, I saw him, too, and really wish I didn't. But I didn't find him like that. I just can't believe he's gone."

"Oh my God," I shuttered. "I can't believe it either. I'm so sorry. I don't know what to do with myself. I don't know how I'm going to tell Jaelyn this. But I'll be there as soon as I can."

"I don't know either, just be safe and take your time getting here," she said. Both of us took a deep breath in, letting out long, confused sighs. We were exhausted and shocked; there was nothing to say. Just breathe, and let reality set in.

"Okay," I finally responded. "I'll keep you posted as we make our way there. Tell mom I love her and give her a big hug from us. We love you, too. I'll see you soon."

The next few days were a muddy blur as we drudged through the motions of funeral and burial arrangements, writing his obituary, and reassigning his assets. I felt numb the entire time. It was as if I was floating through each scene, my consciousness refusing to fully participate in reality and confirm its truth. Handling my father's death? I had never thought about it before. I wasn't supposed to deal with these things for many decades yet. How was this happening?

I didn't even get to call him back. *I wish I would have just answered the damn phone,* I thought to myself with regret. *I missed my chance to have my last words with him. How selfish of me to have let my moodiness stop me from answering his call.* With a deep inhale, I shook my head of the thought. *This is happening for a reason,* I reminded myself, struggling to find comfort in the words.

But why now? We didn't even get a warning. Why did this one heart attack have to kill him? My dad didn't have any major health conditions and never had a heart attack before, but this was his last. As much as my mind wanted to curse the injustice, I ultimately had to accept it as my new reality and trust that God would get me through this, too.

After his death, my mother was left owner of his electrical contracting business and quickly uncovered how much work he had been doing on his own. The bidding, blueprints, purchasing, payroll, taxes, not to mention overseeing and troubleshooting job sites; his staff was stunned by his sudden absence.

How did one human complete all this work and still take care of his family and home? How could he always keep his cool and never complain? Anyone who ever had the pleasure of knowing my father would likely describe him as a man of few words, easy-going, and hardworking. No one could guess how much weight sat on his shoulders.

Not in my life as his daughter did I see a true glimpse of how hard he worked. He was just the best dad in my eyes. Always eager to listen, take his family on vacations, and be there when we needed it. He made it look so easy, I assumed that it was.

I see now that he held his stress inside. Never complained, very rarely lost his temper (and trust me, as a teen I gave him countless opportunities to lose it!), and always got things done. Where did his stress go? Buried underneath his quiet and calm demeanor.

Over time, he did develop high blood pressure and cholesterol, common conditions in our bloodline and today's working world. Managed by typical medications and evening beers to unwind from long work days, his heart was silently working hard to its last beat.

Heart disease is the leading cause of death globally, and stress is a leading cause of heart disease. Yet stress is worn as a badge of honor in our culture. I finally had to admit that I actually found pride in my own stress; it was what made me a strong and independent single mom. I couldn't imagine accomplishing anything without the high-level stress I was used to. It took my own father's death to recognize this bizarre reality and start questioning, *Why the hell do we live this way?*

My dad dying was a massive cosmic slap in the face to prioritize relieving my own stress. For me, that meant more yoga and exercise. More endorphins, less stress. Got it! I booked gym and yoga time on my work calendar to help break up my long days and allow me to head home with Jaelyn right after work. Many days, this worked great. I was young, eating healthy, steadily building physical strength, and had plenty of energy to run and balance my ambitious daily schedule. I even became diligent in my eight hours of sleep, though it grew even easier to fall asleep from pure burnout. Over time, it finally caught up with me.

"Slow down," I could feel something telling me in my gut. I couldn't deny it was true. I really was tired of running around and doing it all. I knew I didn't need to do it all every day, but why couldn't I make myself stop? *Is there something wrong with me?* Well, obviously. I still wasn't getting a period, and no medical doctor could find a physical diagnosis from any bloodwork, scan, or ultrasound I had done. I always felt mild anxiety in the background, no matter how good of a mood I was in. It was as if I was perpetually stuck in defense mode, the fight-or-flight state. I was shocked by bizarre tragedies enough times to cultivate some serious paranoia. *When will the next trauma strike?*

As I continued reading more about alternative healing and the law of attraction, I was naturally guided to look deeper into the energy of things, especially ourselves. A Google search quickly led me to the body's energy centers and the primary seven, or the seven chakras, and how Reiki energy healing is used to clear and open them. I was fascinated by the chakras and the meanings, colors, and physical, mental, and emotional connections with each one. It all made sense to me, and I couldn't believe I had never heard of such concepts of human energy before. *Why wasn't this taught in school?* Understanding the nature of my emotions and energy would have been so helpful to my mental health back in high school! The more I researched, the more it made sense to me; no wonder I couldn't find physical cures for my body; it must be energetic blocks causing my acne and lack of period.

I decided to explore Reiki energy healing. Divinely enough, in mentioning it to my fellow soul sister and coworker, she recommended a local Reiki Master that her family raved about. Immediately, I looked up the Reiki Master and called for an appointment. I was surprised to learn that she did home visits. *How convenient,* I thought. I had no idea what to expect, but at least I could find out in the comfort of my own home. On the evening of our first session, I felt incredibly anxious getting through the after-school routine with Jaelyn, wondering what the Reiki session would be like and what Jaelyn would think of it. *Am I completely crazy?* I asked myself. Well, even if I was, I had nothing to lose. I had to give it a shot.

The doorbell rang, and we both ran to answer it. A short, young, and kind-looking woman was at the door with gorgeous golden curls and flawless skin. She glowed from the inside out. Her dark shirt had a big, bright daisy on it. I opened the door, and she said with a smile, "Hi, I'm Melissa. You must be Krista! And Jaelyn," she added, leaning in to see Jaelyn hiding behind me.

"Yes, hi Melissa!" I replied with a relieved sigh. "Come on in. Can I help you carry anything?" She picked up the bulky massage table at her side with both hands and leaned it against her leg as she waddled it forward. "No worries, I do this all the time. Just tell me where to get set up." I led her into the house, giving her a brief tour on our walk to the back sun porch.

"I thought it'd be nice to do it in here with all the windows and fresh air," I said with a smile. Melissa nodded in agreement, beaming.

"Yes, this is perfect," she declared, unfolding her massage table in the middle of the room. She slipped the large bag from her shoulder and set it on the floor, pulling out a pillow and blanket and setting them on top of the table. She reached back into the bag and pulled out an abalone shell, a feather, and a bundle of sage. Grabbing a lighter from her pocket, she lit the sage bundle, set it on the shell, and began wafting the smoke with the feather. Melissa walked toward me with the burning sage and said, "I'm just clearing your energy fields before we get started." I stood up straight and still. *Yes, please clean up all my energy!* I thought.

After circling around me a few times and wafting the smoke up and down my body, she went around each corner of the room, and then around herself. She put the sage shell down on a small table and said, "I just need to grab a few things, and we'll get started. Go ahead and lay down on the table. Get as comfortable as you can." I awkwardly climbed on top, settling in the best that I could. I closed my eyes and noticed how fast my breathing was. I tried to slow it down before Melissa came back. *Just relax, Krista,* I thought to myself. *This is what you need to finally heal!*

As I felt my heavy heartbeat start to slow down, I heard Melissa shuffle back into the room. She was sifting through another bag; it sounded like tumbling rocks. I opened my eyes. She had a handful of crystals that she started placing one by one on the table around my body. "These will help ground you and heal your energy," she said. I closed my eyes again, taking another deep breath in.

"I'll take all the healing energy I can get," I replied quietly with a smile growing across my face.

"So, you've never had Reiki done on you before?" she asked. I shook my head no. "Okay, so I'll be quiet at times, and other times, I'll ask questions and deliver messages for you that the angels give me. Sometimes, I'll tell you what I see, if I see anything. But even if I don't speak, know that you are receiving healing energy. I usually won't actually touch your body unless I feel you really need deep energy there, but you will probably feel the warmth of my hands hovering over you as I work my way down your energy centers."

Overwhelmed, confused, but wide open to anything that could bring me relief, I nodded my head again, keeping my eyes closed. A few moments later, ambient spa music started playing. Melissa turned back to the table, rubbing her hands together before hovering them over the top of my head. *Ooh, it does feel warm,* I thought as a warm tingle swirled down my spine. I immediately felt safe and protected. My body quickly relaxed into a wet noodle on the massage table. Suddenly, Melissa chuckled and startled me.

"Wow, you're not at all where you're going to be," she laughed out loud. "You're in a completely different environment right now, but don't worry, it'll change when it's ready to. You need to write. You're a teacher."

"What?" I exclaimed in disbelief. "Write what? And what the hell would I teach?"

"About the spiritual path," she answered quickly. "I can see the world come out of your head and a cross emerging from it. You have angel wings covering your eyes." With eyes still closed, I scrunched my nose. *What the hell is she talking about?* I wondered.

She continued. "Use your heart and not your head to influence others. Be aware of your tone, too. But don't worry. You're preparing for all of it now and will know when the time is right."

"Okay," I said, still in disbelief. *Hmmm,* I thought. *Is this for real?* Melissa was hovering her warm hands over my left arm and hand now. Suddenly, I felt a bit of pressure on my right hand. My finger twitched. I stretched my hand, rolled my wrist, and rested it back down on the table.

"Did you feel that?" she asked. I could hear the smile in her voice. "Your dad is here. He's holding your right hand." My heart skipped a beat.

"Oh my God," I said quietly. "I did feel that."

"He says 'let it go,'" she continued. "I can hear him singing it, actually. Like that one song. What's that Beatles song?"

"Let It Be?" I asked.

"Yes," she said. "That's the one! I can hear him singing that tune but saying let it go instead. Let go of your past, of losing him, of being hard on yourself. Let it go and let it be." A saddening comfort warmed my chest. *I'm working on letting it go,* I thought. A tear fell from my left eye and down the side of my face. Eyes still closed, I pulled my hand out from the blanket to dry my cheek. I took a deep breath and slid my hand back under.

"Jaelyn can see angels," Melissa continued, changing the subject.

"Wow, really?" I asked. "That's crazy, but it really doesn't surprise me."

"Yes, she's a very old soul," Melissa said. I laughed in agreement. "She's very in touch with the spiritual world. It's important to support her in this. Let her explore. Don't try to influence her to believe specific things."

I laughed again. "Oh, how I wish my own mother did that for me," I joked. Melissa's hands were over my waist and hips at this point.

"Your other half is within your radar now," she said. My attention immediately heightened as excitement shot through my body. *Yes!* I thought. *Now, this is what I'm talking about. Thank God he's finally nearby.* Melissa continued, "He will challenge and irritate you. Friends first, lust last!"

"Perfect," I said with a chuckle. "Now, where is he?"

"Let it go, love yourself, and he will appear," she replied mysteriously. She continued scanning further down my body to my legs. "You absorb your mom's energy like a magnet," she said, holding back a chuckle. "Protect your energy, and don't let hers bother you. It's not yours."

I swallowed a lump in my throat. *Ugh, my mom,* I thought. *Things had gotten so heavy and stressful since my dad died; just thinking about being near her makes me cringe sometimes.*

"Appreciate your mom's love and how she shows it," Melissa continued. "Accept it as it is. Accept that it's not how you wanted it, but that's the best way she knows how. Say it how it is to her, without judgment or tone. It is possible to be yourself and express your truth around her."

"Damn," was all I could say in response. I knew Melissa was right, and I couldn't believe how obvious it was for her to see. As she settled down by my feet, it felt like our session was ending. After a few moments of silence, she opened her mouth with eyes still closed.

"Compare yourself only to yourself, not to anyone else," she advised. "Acknowledge progress, not perfection." I felt like I needed to be taking notes as she rattled off more brilliant words of wisdom that fit me perfectly. "Find comfort in the uncomfortable; it is a sign you are on your path! It only feels like anxiety. Don't let fear shut you down and stop your enlightenment!"

"Wow, yes, that's exactly what I needed to hear," I said in mild disbelief.

"See energy, not objects," she said. "You're already learning the secret to the universe: everything is energy."

As the session ended, I wasn't sure what I felt or was supposed to feel. *Was my energy cleared? Did anything heal? Did anything really happen?* All I knew was that I was exhausted. I quickly got ready for bed, silently rejoicing when I slipped between the sheets of my cozy bed. Once I laid down, my body felt too heavy to move. My body and brain felt completely drained. Whether I knew what happened to me that night, I did know that this was just the beginning of something big.

# Chapter 16

## November 2016:

## A New Path

My dad's death was the final wake-up call I needed to fully step onto the path of healing and fulfillment. It sprung a new passion within me to relieve stress and heal myself. It led me to deepen my yoga practice and explore energy work through my thoughts, the Law of Attraction, and the Chakras. But now that I found effective healing methods that felt really good to my soul, I couldn't stand to sit back and watch others move through life without any freedom from their own stress. Especially after losing my dad, I also refused to see anyone else endure a fatal heart attack and learn the hard way like I did.

Looking back now, it's funny to see how quickly the Universe responded to my requests. Almost immediately, I found myself being volunteered to help build an employee wellness program for my company. I dove right in, creating activities and collaborating with others in the wellness industry to bring information and experiences to our organization. After its first year, my company celebrated lower insurance costs and higher employee morale, and I felt prouder of that accomplishment than any other along my engineering path so far.

Little did I know, helping create this positive and healthy change was only the beginning of a major transformation.

One month later, I stumbled upon a local Wellness Coach certification training, surprised by how intriguing it was to me. A few days later, I attended my company's Wellness Committee meeting, and the CEO and I were last to walk out of the room. It must have been a good day for us both, because the question spewed out of my mouth if the company would sponsor my Wellness Coach certification, you know, so I could better support the Wellness Program. The CEO smiled and said, "Sure! Go for it. We support you one hundred percent."

Suddenly, I was studying a two-inch-thick book of anatomy, kinesiology, nutrition, and coaching to first become a Personal Trainer as a prerequisite to Wellness Coaching. And as those certifications were accomplished, I learned that the certifying organization was just launching their new 200-hour Registered Yoga Teacher (RYT-200) training program.

*I might as well give this one a shot, too!* I thought, and asked the CEO to sponsor me again. "Sure!" she responded. "That would be great to have yoga right here on site!" After completing the first foundational thirty-hour workshop, I prepared to teach yoga for my organization and local communities. When I walked into the building for my first community class, something caught my eye. Sitting just inside the door on the front office desk was a small jar filled with water and a handful of daisies.

"Alright," I said with a smile in the warmth of Cody's surprise visit. "I guess I am meant to do this."

My realized passion for sharing yoga and inner healing with others was overwhelmingly fulfilling. I couldn't get enough of practicing yoga and meditation with others and helping them return to their breath and free themselves from the heavy burdens of daily stress. I stepped into another world in every class I attended and taught, accessing a blissful state of refuge through each inhale and exhale. I loved feeling and sharing the yoga high that filled me with so much gratitude for all I had and who I was.

Though my heart and soul were awakened by my dad's heart attack, my body and mind were still caught up running in my hamster wheel of life. I could settle in the peace within me during yoga classes, but it was back to running the race in my career and single-mom life as soon as I walked back out the door.

I found myself resenting my job and the constant energy-sucking firefighting that every day required. I had no passion for making cable and found myself more focused on teaching yoga and helping others get engaged in wellness than the corporate responsibilities that came with my high engineer salary. I started dreading going to work each day; my heart was calling my attention somewhere else, but I couldn't allow myself to follow it.

I mean, I was living the dream, wasn't I? A young single mother and engineer able to provide for her daughter and travel the world, with an upward path to more promotions? That was success right there, wasn't it? *How could I not be happy living this way?* I wondered. It took me a few more years of overworking and raising my own blood pressure to realize the deeper message my father was sending me:

*Don't wait until "when" to do the things you truly love. There's a way to live that NOW.*

I realized I was still clinging to a false sense of importance through the full schedule of work and activities. I noticed my conversations in the workplace and gym revolved around to-do lists. *Do we all feel obligated to "prove ourselves" through our accomplishments?* I wondered. But what we weren't talking about was how difficult it is to actually do those things!

Looking around me, at work, while traveling, in the gym, and at my daughter's school, suddenly all I could see was how busy everyone was. And no one had time to acknowledge the need for, much less engage in, relieving stress. Carrying stress was so normal; we were used to it. We had forgotten that we didn't even have to hold it. We might even cling to our stress like a child with a helium balloon as if it's part of our identity and can't possibly be let go. *What will I be if I let that balloon go?* My stress made me feel important. *Who would I be without it?*

Feeling my dad's presence, I knew I had to let my stress balloon go. I knew that letting go, slowing down, and focusing on my breath could help me live longer... but would I still choose to stay too busy? I had chosen business for too long already; it was time to make a change. And thank goodness I had manifested someone like Kelly in my life to show me how.

Kelly was the angel who magically appeared into our lives exactly when we needed it. A few months after my dad's death, school started for Jaelyn. A new year at a new school with new friends, Jaelyn did amazingly well with her transition. We felt like everything fell perfectly into place, and we had everything we needed to thrive in our new little town. That is, until Jaelyn got sick for the first time. Suddenly, it hit me that I didn't have any help in this new town. My parents were now two-hundred and fifty miles away, and I was even further from my close friends in Houghton. I had no one to call for support, so I called into work and took the day off. That day, I searched care.com for a babysitter, and that's how I found the angel named Kelly.

Kelly's profile was the only one that fit my criteria to a T, and I couldn't wait to meet her. Immediately, her energy was attractive, grounding, and calming. I knew this was the perfect person to trust with my child. We tried a few short babysitting sessions during evening dinners for work and outings with friends, and Jaelyn came to agree that we both really loved Kelly's energy!

Kelly was a true hippie and a supernatural free spirit. I think those things are what I loved about her and needed most. Her kids were my age, and she appeared to be living her passion for nannying children and supporting entire families. That's exactly what she did for us. She was a familiar old soul, one that I must have known over many lifetimes. And wow, over the next few years, I would certainly learn a lot.

As I got to know Kelly, and put more trust in her, I started accepting more work trips. Naturally, Jaelyn started spending more time with Kelly the more I worked and traveled.

They spent many hours and days at Kelly's sweet little lakeside cabin nestled within the trees along the water. Her cozy cabin always smelled like sage, incense, and all the amazing herbs and spices she cooked with. White Christmas lights sparkled in the dark, cozy room in the evenings, illuminating the blue glass bottles that decorated her shelves. Handmade benches and stools made from tree branches and stumps surrounded an oversized white couch. The breeze gently blew in the large picture windows, making the sheer white curtains dance over the hardwood floor. Stepping into Kelly's cabin was like stepping into a magical fairy house, and magic sure seemed to happen there.

At the time, I thought Kelly was my trusting babysitter and growing friend, though I didn't yet realize that she was also my confidant and spiritual teacher. Her naturally slow and calm demeanor mirrored the exact opposite of my busy, fast-paced lifestyle. Our opposite energies appeared to balance each other out well; she offered the quiet, grounding energy I needed, and I happily gave her excess active energy to help her accomplish more physically demanding goals that she frequently procrastinated.

Kelly opened my eyes to many new spiritual concepts and ways of connecting with Spirit, including angel oracle cards. I had used my friend's tarot cards a handful of times back in high school with a mystical excitement for the means of communicating with the other side. The traditional tarot cards always made me a little anxious, though; I was nervous about using them right, and the dark images gave me an eerie medieval-age feeling. However, something felt different about these oracle cards. They were warm and comforting.

I asked Kelly to do readings for me, and she often answered, "You are fully capable of drawing your own. It's a better way to put your energy into the cards. Trust your intuition and listen to what comes up."

We started playing with oracle cards regularly, and each reading blew my mind with accurate insights and advice. It was always exciting to see what the cards would say next, and often, they said a lot of the same things.

After a long work trip, I drove the thirty miles from the airport to Kelly's cabin in the dark. Following her dim porch light down the stone path, I took a deep breath, inhaling the mouth-watering fumes of cooked vegetables and curry coming from her kitchen. A huge smile spread across my face. *God bless this woman,* I thought.

I looked down as I walked up the wooden steps to her little green cottage, noticing a daisy growing between the boards of the first step. I paused to smile and take another deep breath before opening the squeaky white door and entering the kitchen. Jaelyn ran into my arms, and I teared up, as I usually did after long, stressful work trips. It felt so good to return to my daughter, and at the same time, I felt terribly guilty for leaving her again. Then, with another deep breath of the sensational aromas, I was filled with gratitude for the nurturing free spirit who gave Jaelyn space and freedom to learn and be herself.

Kelly could offer Jaelyn the calm, stable energy that I couldn't at the time. She was the mom I didn't know how to be. I didn't have time to be as patient as she was. I was too busy chasing money, because that's what I needed to do first as a single mom, right? It was my duty to make something of myself so I could provide for her. But what I couldn't yet provide was my focused attention, and luckily, that was the most valuable thing Kelly had to offer. She seemed to live in eternal presence, with no anger of the past nor worry of the future. Her positive energy never seemed to get depleted, and it recharged my drained batteries when I needed it. Kelly's presence was the flame that kept relighting my candle whenever the chaos of the corporate world blew it out.

Jaelyn and I sat on backless wooden stools around the island that divided the tiny kitchen and living room while Kelly poured and placed steaming bowls of curry in front of us.

"Oh my goodness," I exclaimed. "This smells like heaven!" We eagerly devoured the delicious food over stories of their adventures while I was away. They made fairy houses and jewelry, explored in the woods with her dog, visited other children Kelly nannied, and baked cookies. I couldn't believe how active they were. I took another bite of curry goodness, swallowing guilt down with it.

My eyes started wandering down the countertop, spotting an open box containing a deck of angel cards. "Ooh," I said. "Let's do card readings!" After we cleaned up dinner, I took the deck in my hands, closed my eyes, and said a little prayer, "Please infuse my energy into this deck. Angels, please deliver me the messages I need to hear to fully heal, grow, and create happiness in my life." I took a few deep breaths, then began shuffling the cards. *What do I need to fully heal, grow, and create happiness?* I repeatedly asked in my mind. Eyes still closed, I slowly stopped shuffling, picked up the deck, and started sifting the cards loosely in my hands until a few fell out. "I guess those are what I needed!" I said out loud. I laid the three cards in a row face down.

"Perhaps that's for past, present, and future," Kelly said, looking over my shoulder.

"Funny," I replied. "I was thinking the same thing!" *My intuition must have been right,* I thought with a smile. I reached for the cards and began flipping them over one by one.

*Healing, Emerging, Manifestation.* The same three cards appeared the last time I had Kelly do a reading for me. "Are those the exact same?" Kelly asked with a laugh. "How awesome. I love when Spirit does that. Clearly, these are the only messages you need right now. You've been healing in your old and recent past. In the present, you are emerging, coming out of the closet, if you will, as you find yourself and discover your truth. And there is abundant manifestation in your future. You create what you think about; think only about what you want, no matter how crazy it seems, and you have the power to manifest it."

"Wow," I muttered quietly. "It's so spot-on and just what I needed to hear. Well, to hear again, apparently."

"Your highest self always attracts the right cards," she said with a smile. "It knows what you need. It knows what answers you seek. And when you listen, it tells you exactly what to do. The cards just help get your attention when you've lost it."

The truth, reassurance, and sense of connection this card reading gave me filled me with inspiration to dive deeper into my own card readings. It was an experience that recharged my energy and willpower. And it worked. I wanted to get my own deck at home and commune with my guides whenever I needed to. Suddenly, a random question popped into my head, *What would my mom think of card readings? She certainly would disapprove. Would she think this is like witchcraft or something?* My excitement was temporarily halted by fear of disobeying the rules and being punished for it somehow. Noticing my own resistance, I took a deep breath in. *Wow, perhaps that's something that still needs to be healed,* I realized. *Let go of what other people think. If this is healing for me, do it. I have to trust my gut and stay true to myself.*

The next morning, I woke up as I usually did, stretching in bed and taking deep breaths in and out, asking myself what my intention would be for the day. Suddenly, a flash of my dream hit me. Cody was in it. I grabbed my journal and scribbled down everything I could remember.

11/20/17

*Dreamt of Cody last night. In a crowded waiting room, a woman approached me and said, "Cody will be here for you soon." It was very unexpected. When he came in, we sat, we kissed – there was an explosion of energy between us. But I knew he was young. It was time to close our romantic chapter. I hesitated. I didn't want to let go of the comfort of his familiar memory. But then he started shrinking, and I slowly lost my physical attraction to him until he disappeared. I am ready to move on. I am ready to let go!*

-Kris

I got up and continued through my routine, contemplating the significance of that dream while determination grew to get serious about moving on. *I can't keep living and dreaming about an 18-year-old boy anymore,* I thought in mild shock and embarrassment that I was still hanging on a decade later. Suddenly, I remembered a comment made by the Medium five years ago. "You'll have a dream in five years," she said. I counted my fingers... *Holy shit!* I couldn't believe it. *It's been exactly that!* It's really time to let go of the physical and move on.

My close friends had tried convincing me to try dating apps for some time, but I ignored and avoided men altogether since my previous dangerous encounters. Not only did I still miss Cody terribly, but I felt terrible about myself and the situations I got into a few years ago.

I lost all hope in the possibility of finding a man who could genuinely respect and admire me and that I even deserved it. After what I did to my friend in Houghton, I punished myself into believing I was meant to be alone and just needed to stay away from men. *He probably has a wife or girlfriend,* I assumed whenever I made eye contact with a new man. *I'm nothing but the hot young mom to conquer. Another notch in the belt of self-serving assholes.*

As low as my self-esteem sunk in the love department, after that dream of Cody, I could feel in my bones something pushing me to give it a shot. "Just give it a try," I felt from my guides. "It's time to move on and open your heart." So, one day, I finally downloaded an app. It was a terrifying decision. I was immediately overwhelmed by making a profile. *What the hell do I say about myself?* I wondered. *How much am I supposed to say? What pictures do I post?* "Keep it simple," my best friend Mel reminded me, excited that I was finally giving it a try. "Don't take it so seriously; just let it be fun! It's about time you meet someone new!"

Once I survived the grueling profile creation process, I was horrified when I immediately received messages from all kinds of men, most of them opening with lines like, "Hey sexy, what are you doing tonight?" or "You have a gorgeous smile. Can I get your number?" *Oh my God!* I thought in horror. *I just exposed myself all over the internet for any creep to hit on!*

"Relax," reassured another friend, who had met her husband on the same dating site. "Don't worry about the creeps. Just give it a shot. It took me a while, but once I found him, I knew."

With a doubtful sigh, I continued swiping left through profiles, and occasionally to the right. Over the next week, I answered very few messages, ultimately finding that the men who didn't initially come across as creepy were just waiting for my response before laying on the heavy pick-up lines. *This is disgusting*, I thought. *Is there anyone honest on here who's actually looking for a relationship and not a hook-up?* Then, almost as quickly as I had the thought, a new message popped up. "Hey there, it looks like we have a lot in common, and your smile is contagious. What type of engineer are you?"

I was shocked. *No sleazy pick-up lines, and asking about engineering? What a relief!* I looked up the screen to his profile picture, and my heart skipped a beat. *No way*, I thought to myself. *Blond hair, blue eyes. He kind of looks like Cody!* I couldn't stop my curiosity from scrolling down, my jaw dropped to the floor as I read. *A photographer, wow! That was my dad's passionate hobby,* I thought, heart beating faster. *Not a carpenter, but I have always often wondered what my dad might have been like as a professional photographer.* I kept reading. He didn't smoke, never married, had a kid, and dreamed of living and traveling with his future partner while building his business. *Is this guy for real?* I wondered. *It almost seems too good to be true!*

I scrolled back up through his pictures. *Hm,* I thought. *He doesn't have a squared-off jaw like my Spirit guide said my man would.* I quickly dismissed the thought. Everything else looked great!

I excitedly replied to his message, and we hit it off talking about our current jobs and homes, working our way to the basic details of names, hometowns, and birthdays. "My birthday is April 21st," I answered to his question. "When is yours?"

"December 30th," he responded. My heart stopped again. *You're kidding*, I thought to myself. *That's Cody's birthday! He looks like and shares the same birthday? This has either got to be a major warning or a blessing!* What were the odds of meeting someone so similar right after my significant dream with Cody? *It must be a blessing*, I concluded. We continued chatting on the dating site for another week before I shared my phone number, which quickly led to daily texts and phone calls.

"I'd really love to meet you," he said. "When can I take you out for dinner?"

My heartbeat skipped. *Oh shit,* I thought. *I haven't gone on a date since... forever!* My nerves immediately knotted my stomach. I swallowed and said, "Well, we're really busy, and it's hard to get a babysitter, but I'll let you know when I can get one." I put it off for another two weeks, with the excuse that I needed to get to know this guy better before I put effort into arranging a babysitter for a date.

*The Daisy Diaries* | 189

So far, everything was checking out. He was polite, respectful, and tastefully flattering. He had a daughter close to my daughter's age, with no apparent drama with his ex. He had a good job, spent a lot of time with his daughter, and had an immense passion for his photography business. Talking to him was a refreshing experience. To have intelligent conversations with a man who seemed to be most attracted to my mind was like a fairy tale. So, after his endless asking and proven patience, I asked Kelly to come over one night after work to meet him for dinner.

That evening, I stood in my closet with a glass of wine, slowly sipping away the ping-pong ball of nerves bouncing around in my gut. *What the hell am I going to wear?* I wondered. The greatest dilemma of every woman on a first date. And as usual, after about five different outfit changes and another thirty minutes later, I was back in the first outfit I tried on and scrambling to finish getting ready on time.

Kelly arrived while I nervously brushed my teeth and checked my make-up for the last time. She was beaming with excitement for me, "Your first date! How exciting! You go have a good time, and we'll be here when you get back." She sent me out the door with a warm hug, and I was on my way.

Heart beating, body shaking, I slowly stepped into the restaurant, scanning my eyes across the room for his familiar face. Suddenly, toward the back of the restaurant, I saw him sitting at a booth. *Wait a minute,* I thought. *Is that him? I thought he was taller.* He noticed me with a smile and waved. *Yep, that's him!* I walked to the table as he got up from his seat, reaching his arms out for a hug. With my heels on, we were the same height. *Woah, he is way shorter than I thought. Didn't his profile say he was 6'1"?* I shook my head of the thought and refocused on his introduction. *Whatever, I need to let go of my fixation on the man being a lot taller than me anyway,* I concluded to myself. *It's not a big deal.* We quickly jumped back into our month-long conversation, and just as quickly, I forgot about his height and got lost in those pretty blue eyes.

After dinner, we took a walk down to the river nearby. It was getting dark, and I could feel the mom-guilt alarm going off in my gut. "It's been a couple hours, it's time to get back to Jaelyn!" it called. *Just a short walk and I'll go home,* I decided. Once we reached the river, we stopped and looked at the view. "Isn't this gorgeous?" I asked him with a smile.

"It really is," he replied, looking across the moon's reflection over the flowing water. "But not as beautiful as you." Suddenly, he stepped in close, reaching one hand behind my waist and the other behind my head, pulling me in for a kiss. Before I could react, his lips were on mine. *Woah, that was fast!* I thought in surprise. But dang, I forgot what it was like to kiss someone again. I embraced the kiss for half a moment before he slipped his tongue in my mouth and let out a quiet moan. Now pulled in close against his body, I could feel his erection hardening.

"Woah," I pulled back with a fake smile and gentle laugh. "I better get home to my daughter."

"Oh, can't you stay longer?" he asked, arms still wrapped around me and pulling me in for another kiss. "Or can I come over?"

Nausea set it. *Is he really trying to sleep with me on the first date?* I wondered in mild panic. To hide it, I laughed again and replied, "No. As much as I'd love to, I need to get back. A kiss is great, but that's all you're getting for now."

"Oh, you're just so sexy, though," he whispered in my ear, now kissing my neck. Chills of excitement and anxiety ran down my spine.

"Don't worry," I replied, pulling away again. "If this is going where I think it is, it'll be well worth the wait." I smiled again, looking into his eyes, and gave him one more quick kiss. "I really need to go, but I'll call you tomorrow."

He agreed, though I could sense his great disappointment in not getting further. We walked back up to our cars, gave one more hug and kiss goodbye, and I drove back home, heart still fluttering wildly between excitement and anxiety. Letting out a deep breath, I consoled myself. *Okay,* I thought. *At least he didn't push it, and he let me go. I should be flattered that he's so attracted to and turned on by me. And man, good for me for not giving in. It's been a long time! I wonder how much longer I can hold him off.*

The next day, he was eagerly asking to get together again. "I just can't get a babysitter all the time," I told him.

"Well, you don't need to get a babysitter," he replied. "Don't worry about that. Why don't I come over there?" I hesitated for a moment. *Come over here?* I panicked. The idea never crossed my mind. *What if he tries to sleep with me?*

"I don't know," I finally answered. "I don't want things to move too fast. Especially not with my daughter sleeping here."

He let out a soft giggle. "Oh, don't worry about that, babe," he reassured me. "I just want to see and be with you."

I finally agreed to let him come over after I got Jaelyn to bed. Anxiety pulsed through my veins until then, unsure of what to prepare myself for.

*The Daisy Diaries*

I was so excited by this new and intriguing man, but something about that first date kiss still made me uneasy. When he came, we first chatted on the couch and picked out a movie to watch. Before long, we were cuddling, then laying down. Now spooning in the warmth of a man's embrace for the first time in three years, I took a breath of comfort and relief, wiggling into the cozy puzzle pieces of his body and the couch. He moaned softly, hugging me closer. Suddenly, I could feel something poke me from behind. *Uh oh,* I thought. His hand slowly ran up and down my side as I felt his warm breath on my neck. He moaned again, now leaning in and kissing my ear. Chills ran down my spine. *Oh no,* I thought, unsure if I felt good about my body's natural arousal to his touch. *What am I going to do?*

He gently turned me to my back and kissed me passionately, running his hand up and down my other side and pressing his body against mine. I got swept into the kiss for a moment, then the mom-guilt alarm went off again. *Jaelyn's here. It's too soon. Shut it down,* my mind panicked.

"Ooh, as much as I want to," I said softly, pulling away from his face. "I just can't yet. And Jaelyn's here. I should get to bed anyway."

After a few attempts to seduce and change my mind, and a few more increasingly concerned and irritated no's from me, he finally gave up and agreed to leave. "Can I see you again tomorrow?" he asked before giving me another passionate kiss. Swept up in the moment and relief that he respected my wishes, my only answer was, "Of course."

I survived just one more night of after-bedtime movies and attempted seduction on my couch before my body and mind couldn't handle it anymore. *Oh, who cares, Krista,* I told myself. *Let yourself have a good time already. Stop punishing yourself and see where this goes.* Plus, his argument became more and more compelling.

"You just need to open your heart back up, Krista," he told me between passionate kissing and groping on my couch. "Let someone in to love and care about you. I'm crazy about you. But you've got to let me in."

His words stung like a bee. *It's true,* I agreed. *I did close off my heart. And I do need to let someone in again. Let my guard down. Let myself have fun...* As he kissed my ear and neck, I felt my guard fall with the chills down my spine. "Let's go to my bedroom," I whispered.

From that moment, I dove straight into my first relationship in over five years. It was equally exciting and terrifying, but he was crazy about me. Plus, he had so many bizarre things in common with Cody and my dad that I couldn't deny the serendipity. As the days and weeks went on, though, the pressure to get serious was building heavily. He called more often, asking to come over nearly every night and starting to make plans to bring Jaelyn and me to his next visit to his daughter and meet his family.

"Woah," I said in response to his plans. "This is moving really fast. Are you sure you want me to meet your daughter already?" He hadn't met Jaelyn yet, either. All his visits had been after bedtime, and I wasn't sure I was ready for it. I had protected Jaelyn from any man I encountered besides her father. Until I knew it was real and serious, I didn't want to risk introducing her to any man who could potentially hurt either of us. But every day, his plans grew more urgent.

"Well, this is obviously going to last a while," he said. "I have to go back and forth all the time anyway, and I want to spend more time with you, so why not meet my family? They'll love you!" I was still hesitant. "Krista, it's time to let that guard down. Let me in. I think I'm falling in love with you."

I went silent, stunned by hearing the words that scared me the most.

"Oops," he said. "I guess I shouldn't have said that."

"Wow," was all I could spit out. "I mean, I'm honored that you think that. I just want to give it time to know it's truly right."

Disappointment washed over his face before he disguised it with a smile. "Don't worry about it. Just know I love you. And my family will, too."

His pressure continued into a fast and serious relationship. I still couldn't distinguish between the sensations of excitement and anxiety that both seemed to go wild inside me when I was around him. It was comforting to be loved and admired by someone again, but his persistence and sex drive were getting intense. He wanted to see me every day, have sex every moment we could, and kept planning for his upcoming trip to visit family. "Just let me love you, Krista," he repeatedly said to ease my resistance. "You don't even know how to be in a relationship anymore; just let your guard down and let me show you."

Well, this is what I needed, isn't it? So, I listened to his advice, convincing myself that I was just out of practice and nervous, and it was safe to let my guard down. *Just go with it,* I told myself. *Let it be fun. Stop worrying so much. Plus, you needed to get some. Sure, he might seem excessively horny, but maybe that's just because my libido shut down completely for three years. Let someone bring your sexy back, Krista!*

So, I kept going with it, letting this new man race me down a new relationship rabbit hole. Before I knew it, he had met Jaelyn, and we were both in his car on the way to visit family. The visits all went well; he was right. His family did love me. Though I was slightly put off by what felt like their surprise in me. They kept teasing him, "How did you rope this girl in? She's wonderful!" We all got along great, and I felt warmly welcomed and comfortable in their presence, yet a little knot of anxiety still stirred inside my stomach. *How did he rope me in? What were his last relationships really like?* I wondered. By the end of the trip, I couldn't wait to get home and away from him for a few days. I was overwhelmed and smothered by him. "You still just need to let your guard down," he kept telling me. "Stop resisting and just let me love you."

The pressure kept rising. To move faster. To spend more time together. To be more sexual. To keep racing past each stage of a growing relationship. And the faster we ran, the more anxious I got. *What's wrong with me?* I thought to myself. *Why can't I let my guard down? Do I know how to be in a relationship? Regardless, it should feel better than this, shouldn't it?* He clearly seemed to know what he was doing in a relationship, so what was I doing wrong? I found myself giving in to most of his pushy requests, then resenting his increasingly needy and demanding behavior. After three months of dating, he suggested he move in with me and, for the summer, move his daughter in with us, too. My anxiety skyrocketed.

At the same time, I slowly recognized the disconnect between his real life and behavior and what he portrayed on his dating site profile. He wasn't nearly as far as he claimed to be on his business plan. He also drank a lot more than he claimed, and I was starting to drink a lot more, too. He didn't even exercise, there was no running, hiking, and weightlifting like he boasted about. His past relationships weren't as long as he first said they were either. I learned that his last girlfriend unexpectedly left him after two months of dating. *What made her leave so suddenly? I wondered. What's with this guy and his desperation to lock down a serious relationship? And seriously, what's with his constant sex drive?* I already thought all men were pigs by this point, but did they all need it that often? *Am I really the crazy one here? Or am I being manipulated by the crazy one?*

Within the next few days, his constant pressure to move in with me and solidify plans was not just overwhelming; it started to anger me. "I'm just not comfortable with that yet," I told him honestly. "And it's really bothering me that you won't listen and respect my wishes."

"Come on, Krista," he barked back. "When are you going to relax already and let this be what it's meant to be?"

That evening after work, I cringed to pull into my driveway and see his car sitting there. *Ugh, he's here again already?* I asked. Then I recognized my reaction of disdain. *Wow, what happened here? What happened to my excitement about this man and all the signs?* I took a deep breath, let it out, and gathered our things before leading Jaelyn into the house. It smelled like garlic. He was in the kitchen cooking. Immediately, I felt irritated by him making himself at home in my house when I wasn't there. I tried to shake it off and dig up appreciation. *He's making us dinner,* I thought. *Come on, Krista, lighten up!*

"You do too much; it's time for you to just sit and relax," he said, stirring the pasta. Pour yourself a drink; the food will be ready in a few minutes." He put the ladle down and pulled me in for yet another passionate kiss. I quickly pulled away, still irritated.

"Woah," I said. "Take it down a notch; Jaelyn is right there." *You really have no control over your sexual drive,* I thought in disgust. *No regard for where we are or who we're with.* It was constant. Anytime, anywhere, and in front of anyone. Plus, he got mad whenever I wasn't in the mood, which was increasingly more often.

"What's wrong with you?" he asked me on numerous occasions. "It's human instinct. It's normal to want it all the time. What's not normal is your lack of it."

I shook my head of our mildly disturbing sexual encounters as we all prepared to sit down for dinner. I tried to swallow down my nerves with my dinner and wine. *Be grateful, Krista,* I told myself. *He's trying to be helpful to you. Let him in. Let him cook and clean the kitchen. Just relax.* But I couldn't. I felt restless. Though he took care of the meal, I was still pacing around, picking up, finding any little task that needed to be done. I could feel myself inching closer to the edge.

"Would you just relax, babe?" he asked. "The point of me doing this is so you don't have to do anything. Would you just stop and sit down?"

After getting Jaelyn to bed, I finally did sit down with my third drink in hand. *I didn't used to drink like this,* I thought while taking another sip. *Gosh, I don't even like who I am right now. And I really don't like him anymore. The Cody imposter. He's not nearly as genuine as the real Cody. And far less spiritual. What am I doing? I said I wouldn't settle for less than a deep spiritual connection.* My thoughts were suddenly interrupted by the imposter, who sat down next to me and drew me in close. I felt like I might vomit in my mouth.

"You know, I'm exhausted," I said, trying to hide my disgust. "I'm going to go to bed." I tried going to bed alone, but he followed, and made his usual attempts at seduction. Clearly sensing something was off, he finally rolled over to the other side of the bed and fell asleep. I, on the other hand, laid there all night with eyes wide and heart racing.

*I can't stand being next to this imposter any longer,* I ranted in my mind. *He's not at all who he portrayed himself to be. He's controlling and manipulative. He makes me question my sanity. This is crazy. It's only been four months, and I feel like I've been ripped around on a ridiculous rollercoaster ride.* I knew deep in my gut that I was better off and safer alone. I needed to get out.

The next morning, I slipped out of bed in the dark to get ready for work, moving as quietly as I could without waking him up. I went out to the kitchen, started the coffee machine, and stepped into the bathroom. A second later, I heard him get out of bed. *Oh no,* I thought. *Here he comes.*

Out he came through the kitchen, where he saw me and sauntered over. I set my hairbrush down and took a deep breath, turning to him and holding him back from a kiss. I didn't know what was about to come out of my mouth, but I couldn't hold it in.

"I can't do this anymore," I blurted.

"What?" he asked in surprise. "What do you mean?"

"This," I said sternly. "With you. I can't be with you anymore. This is crazy. You've pushed me too far too fast, and you're nothing like what I thought you were. I don't want you here when I get back from work today."

Shocked and clearly upset, he rebutted, "What are you talking about? You haven't been in a relationship in so long; you don't even know how one works. I've just been trying to break your damn guard down, but you won't let me in. This isn't crazy, you are for not wanting it."

"Then I'd rather be fucking crazy," I spat back, feeling my temper rising. "Get your things out of here and don't come back. I don't want you manipulating me and my life anymore."

In a mild rage, he gathered his things and stormed off just before I woke Jaelyn up. As she sat down for her breakfast, she asked, "What was all that noise earlier?" My heart sank. I felt sick and disgusted with myself. I had let another dangerous man into my life, and this time, I let him meet Jaelyn.

"Well, honey, he won't be coming back anymore," I said calmly. "He didn't turn out to be right for me, and you and I are better off just us together." I gave her a hug and a kiss on the top of her head.

"Oh, okay, mommy," was all she replied, quickly turning her focus back to her apples and peanut butter.

I turned to pack our lunches. *I can't believe it,* I thought. *Another dangerous man snuck his way in. And this one got in deeply!*

"Protect yourself by surrounding them in white light," I heard, remembering the advice from my Spirit guide. I took a deep breath and closed my eyes, imagining surrounding him in white golden light. *May you find healing. May you be free. May I be protected,* I recited in my mind.

After that day, I never saw him again. Just like the other dangerous men, after surrounding him in white light, he disappeared from my life. And once again, I dug my heels even deeper into my independence. *All men really are pigs*, I concluded. *Are all of them dangerous? There are no normal, honest, good ones left! They all lie, manipulate, and want nothing but sex. I swear off all men for good!*

A few days later, I still felt sick to my stomach about the wild mind game that was just played on me. I couldn't believe I let another man into my life to manipulate and take advantage of me. I was warned about this so long ago! How did I keep forgetting the warning every time? *It won't happen again,* I promised myself.

I couldn't seem to shake off the unease within me no matter how many sun salutations I did on my mat or meditations I listened to. I needed something more. I needed a change. Initially, I thought I just needed a change of environment, so after nearly three years of occasional searching, I found a new house in the suburbs of St. Paul, Minnesota. Though it added forty minutes to my daily commute, I felt it was worth moving to a larger community where I might find other like-minded yogis. This was true, I quickly found a new yoga studio and made friends with other yoga teachers. Plus, just like I wanted to manifest years ago, a dance studio around the block offered classes for both Jaelyn and I! But I still felt something was missing. I still needed to dive deeper into my spiritual practice.

Then, one evening, it hit me that I hadn't received Reiki healing for over a year. My energy felt unbalanced. I had gotten pulled so quickly into the whirlwind of the Cody imposter that I had let my spiritual practice fall to the wayside. It was time to rededicate myself to my healing and growth.

Melissa, the Reiki Master, immediately came to my mind. After seven sessions, our schedules pulled us in different directions, but for some reason, she suddenly kept popping in my head over the next several days. After a week or so, I finally picked up my phone to text and see how she was doing. I craved more knowledge and energy healing and just knew she had exactly what I needed. And I was right; her response revealed her upcoming Reiki Level One Attunement. With no hesitation, I signed up. *If I want to heal myself, I might as well learn how to do it myself!* I concluded.

On the day of my attunement, as usual, I had no idea what to expect. All I could do was go in with an open mind and trust that I was being led to exactly what I needed.

As I drove to Melissa's house for the training, I noticed "Thunderstruck" by AC/DC playing on the radio. My dad was a big fan and took me to a concert with him just a few years before he died. Hearing AC/DC always made me feel his presence. I suddenly had a feeling that he was sitting next to me and had something to say, like he wanted to pump me up for this new journey I was on.

Following Google maps for directions, I forgot about the music for a moment to make a few quick turns. Before I knew it, the lyrics to "Listen to the Music" by the Doobie Brothers sang through the speakers. My attention was immediately drawn back to my dad's presence, this time so strongly that it overwhelmed me. Tears welled up in my eyes, and I choked them down with a surprised laugh.

"Wow, Dad," I said out loud. "I really feel you right now. Thank you for being here with me."

"I'm so proud of you, Dots," I could hear his voice say in my mind. Pops and Dots, those were our nicknames. Dots for daughter, he always called both my sister and me that. Though I couldn't see signs of his presence with my eyes, I could feel his love vibrating through the entire vehicle, blanketing me with comfort and encouragement.

"Keep following your heart," I heard his voice continue. "Don't listen to what anyone else says. Just keep being you."

A tear rolled down my cheek. "Thanks, Pops," I whispered. I took a deep breath in and turned into the long driveway. Just a few other cars were already there. I sat in my car long enough to finish the song, embracing every second of my dad's loving vibration.

"I miss you so much," I said sadly. "Thank you so much for visiting." I shut my car off, gathered my things, and got out of the vehicle.

As I stepped out, I saw a patch of daisies growing along the edge of the driveway. "Wow," I said out loud. "I hear you both loud and clear!" The warm breeze seemed to hug me with my dad's and Cody's presence all at once. My eyes automatically welled up again, and my heart overflowed with gratitude. *Wow,* I suddenly thought. *I never felt their energies together before. They definitely know each other now.*

"Thank you both so much," I whispered while stepping up to Melissa's front door.

A small, intimate group helped me quickly feel comfortable in Melissa's already warm, welcoming, and non-judgmental home. We dove right into her training manual, learning about the origin of traditional Usui Reiki, the benefits and risks of Reiki healing, and the difference between Reiki levels one, two, and three. Melissa walked us through each of the seven Chakras, or energy centers of the body, and I lit up learning more about them and their energetic frequencies. Then we learned about the different symbols, hand positions, and how to perform Reiki healing on ourselves, the goal of Reiki Level One.

The group sat in a big circle in the living room. I sat with my back to the enormous picture window behind me, feeling the warm sun on my back. As we were each attuned by Melissa, we practiced hand positions and sensing the warm energy between our hands. Instructed to hold our hands in front of us as if we were holding a ball, we pulsed our hands further and closer together to feel the energy increasing. At first, I had no idea what I was doing. *Am I really supposed to feel something between my hands? Like a real ball?*

"It may be very subtle at first," Melissa cued. "You may not even notice it at all. Just keep breathing and focusing your attention on that orb of energy between your hands. See it. Imagine it expanding and contracting with the movement of your hands. Feel the heat building and pressure rising as you bring your palms closer together."

Suddenly, as I drew my palms close, I felt an energetic resistance, almost like a magnet forcing my hands back apart. I continued pulsing my hands and could feel the energy growing, and literally felt warmth emanating from between my hands. I imagined a bright golden light there. It got brighter and duller with my pulsing palms. *Wow, is that it?* I wondered in excitement. Melissa noticed my reaction and seemed to read my mind. "Yes, that's it," she said with a chuckle. "That's the healing life force energy that's now activated within you. You are a Reiki healer."

# Chapter 17

## January 2019:

## The Leap of Faith

The day after my blissful high of Reiki attunement, I, unfortunately, had to go back to work. Just as quickly as the Reiki training came, it left, and I slipped right back into my busy over-achieving routine. The more I worked, the more drained I became, and the more I wondered what the hell I had gotten myself into. It suddenly dawned on me that I had been paying other people to raise my child for me while I overcommitted and stressed myself out. I realized that the price I was paying for my prestigious social and economic status was growing much higher than I bargained for.

As a single mother, my life was ruled by the open hours of childcare. I raced against the clock daily to accomplish as much as I could with my available time. This meant tortuously long days for my daughter. Her day had to be just as long as mine, but it was worth the great money I was making, wasn't it?

As my work experience grew, so did my workload, but I couldn't make the hours in my day grow with them. So, I raced faster, packing in as much as I could within my limitations of childcare coverage. And after the work and school day was done? I raced faster. Through the checklist of dinner, homework, baths, chores, and bedtime, I dragged Jaelyn along, praying she'd get enough sleep to be rested for the next early morning's race. I grew more drained and exhausted by the day, but every new raise or exciting work trip was enough to convince me I was doing the right thing to advance my career and provide for my daughter. I had it all, didn't I?

Plus, I wasn't the only one racing tirelessly. The dis-ease of stress and overworking plagued my workplace, along with the rest of corporate

America. The more I traveled, the more I recognized the normalcy and praise of the overachieving multi-taskers. I felt surrounded by living zombies running through the motions of the "American dream," many operating on fumes of caffeine, nicotine, and cocktails.

For a while, though, I must admit that I was seduced by it. I quickly let myself get swept into the glamour of my career, and my ego inflated a little more with every praise for my work, pay raise, and travel opportunity. I bought more expensive work clothes, strutting my stuff around the office, manufacturing floor, airports, and conferences. My confidence grew in a new way, and I know it didn't go unnoticed.

The more I traveled, the more people I met along the way. Working in a male-dominant field, more people meant more dangerous men. Most were obvious, as they were swanky older men with wedding rings. The few younger ones, though, were harder to see clearly.

I slowly learned that no ring meant nothing; they easily came off. I even once met an attractive young man at a conference who flirted with me very openly and suggested that we meet at the after-party that evening, all while holding his left hand in his pocket. We chatted long enough for me to notice his unusual posture. Then, his hand flew out in a grand gesture, flashing the gold ring in front of my eyes for a brief second before diving back into his pocket. *Of course*, I thought in disgust before politely ending our conversation and walking away. *Surround them in white light,* I remembered.

I felt proud of myself for my growing strength around these dangerous men. I had kept them all at bay for another three years now. By this point, any man who looked at me with the slightest interest triggered my wall of protection. I was beyond uncomfortable and awkward around men, as if I had forgotten how to interact with them at all. And after three years, I also felt extremely deprived in the love department. In my late twenties, I was in my prime! *This was the time I should be having the most sex, not none!* As I traveled more often, I became more intrigued by the attractive men I passed. Well, my body did, at least. My mind and my mouth were still awkward as all hell.

Until I crossed paths with the sexy engineer, that is. From across the bar on the last evening of a conference, we locked eyes. He smiled and immediately started walking over. *Oh God, it's the same cute guy I've met at many conferences now,* I thought to myself. I thought we had hit it off a time or two but learned in a group conversation that he had a girlfriend, so I dropped it and hid behind my guard wall a few conferences earlier. *Why is he coming over here now?*

"Hi, remember me?" he asked with a bright, cheesy smile. "I couldn't help but notice you and had to say hello."

I blushed. "Hi," I replied softly. "Yes, I remember you."

He offered to buy my next drink as we got to chatting. My mind raced through all the old and familiar worries. *Does he still have a girlfriend? Is he crazy? Is he dangerous?* I wondered. I checked his left hand, no ring. *That doesn't mean anything,* I thought. After a few minutes, he leaned in closer. "You know," he admitted. "Since I first saw you, I was insanely attracted to you."

"Don't you have a girlfriend?" I asked suspiciously.

"Unfortunately not," he replied, looking down. "That ended a while ago."

"Oh," I said, trying to hide my mild excitement. "I'm sorry to hear that."

"No, no, don't be," he replied. "I feel much better now that I crossed paths with you again."

*Is this guy for real?* I thought. *Should I run?* I had gotten really good at that, and it's all I knew how to do at that point. *But he's so cute and dreamy, and it's been so long...* My mind wandered for a moment to an erotic romance of meeting the perfect man on a work trip. A glass clunked on the bar in front of me, snapping me back into the moment. "This is for you," he said, nudging my arm softly.

We hit it off, learning we were similar in age and reminiscing over nostalgia from our generation. Though he initially came across as a pretty boy hot-shot, he seemed surprisingly down to earth the more we talked one-on-one. We dove deep into personal conversations of our pasts, sharing the losses of our fathers and the impact that made on our lives. There was something very familiar about him, and as the drinks kept going down, so did my guard.

Before I knew it, I had a heavy buzz and total lust for this pretty boy engineer. *You're on a work trip, Krista,* my guilty conscience reminded me. *Get your act together. Be professional.* But I worked so hard all the time. I deserved to have a little fun, and nobody needed to know. Plus, that's what was happening at these events all the time anyway. An escape from home and the "real world," corporate travel and events were like temporarily living in a parallel universe. And who knew where this could

*The Daisy Diaries* | 203

lead? Maybe there really was something between the pretty boy and me. And if not, I was deprived and drunk enough not to care.

"Here, let me walk you to the elevator," he said, smiling coyly. My heart skipped. I nodded, smiled back, and took the last sip of my drink. We made our way to the elevator and patiently waited, keeping our distance and making polite conversation. Finally, the gold elevator doors opened, and we stepped in, turning around as the doors closed in on us. I hit the button for my floor. "No kidding," he laughed. "I'm on that floor, too."

"How convenient," I joked with a smile. We locked eyes again, suddenly realizing we were completely alone. He swiftly stepped forward and kissed me, wrapping his arms around my waist. I was immediately consumed by lust until we heard the ding of the elevator arriving at our floor. I pulled away, and we both chuckled softly. His hands slid down my outer arms and down to my hands. Grabbing my left hand into his right, he led me off the elevator. "Your room or mine?" he asked.

"Let's go to mine," I said, also thinking that whatever happened, I would not be the one sneaking back to my room in the wee hours. We quietly entered my room, turned on the TV, and set down our phones and wallets. We sat on top of my bed and chatted for a few minutes between drunken giggles, and he started slowly rubbing my leg. Before long, we were kissing again, the heat rising quickly. We messed around for a while before crawling under the covers.

Exhausted, I was ready to doze off in the comfort of someone's embrace for the first time in over three years. *Damn, I forgot what this was like,* I thought.

As we drifted off, a phone started vibrating. I looked up to the table to confirm whose phone it was. It was his. "Call from Amber" it read. My heart sank as I said out loud, "Hey, um, Amber is calling."

"Oh," he said awkwardly. "Don't worry about it."

"Is that your girlfriend?" I asked, not wanting to hear the answer.

"Well," he started. "She was. It's been falling apart for a long time. Don't worry. It's over. She's probably just drunk."

"Holy shit," I said with my heart sinking deeper. "I can't believe we did this."

"Seriously, Krista," he said, pulling me back in closer. "I'm not cheating on her. I'm not fooling you. I promise. I find you so fascinating and impressive, and wow, so sexy." He kissed my neck and hugged me.

"Let's go to sleep." I didn't have the energy to continue an argument. Was it worth it? *Just enjoy the moment,* I told myself. *I'll be gone tomorrow.*

So, I laid there, letting him spoon me while my mind raced in contemplation. *Did I just do it again? Let another dangerous man in? How do they blind me until after they rope me in?* I wondered in amazement. Though I felt sick to my stomach, I also felt a reassuring presence within me. Perhaps it was my Spirit guide, and she reminded me to wrap him in white light.

*Oh wow,* I thought. *I never did this practice in their presence before. Maybe he needs healing, too.* I had noticed a sense of insecurity in him throughout our evening together; it even stimulated part of my attraction to him. His first impression was a hot-shot know-it-all, but once we got to talking in private, a whole new person came out. A soft, vulnerable one that felt like a young soul, curious about exploring deeper parts of himself, but too tangled in the webs of the material world to do so. *Maybe he's just attracted to my spiritual nature,* I thought. *He just needs some white light energy to heal and figure himself out.*

As I lay there in the pitch-black darkness, I closed my eyes and imagined him surrounded by white light behind me. I breathed deeply in and out, concentrating on that healing energy. A few spontaneous prayers flowed through my mind. *May you find the healing and clarity you seek. May you find the confidence and courage to create a life for yourself and no one else. And may you embrace true love and give your woman the honesty, love, and loyalty she deserves.* As the words came, I realized that I needed this healing, too. My vision of white light immediately expanded and enveloped me within it. Breathing deeper and slower as I relaxed in my own healing light, I drifted off to sleep.

When my alarm went off just a few hours later, I was surprised to wake up still in his arms. I rolled away, waking him up, and he attempted to pull me back in. "Good morning," I whispered with a smile. "I need to get up, and I think it's time for you to go." With one last hug, I imagined the white light around him again before he slipped out the door and out of my life, again, as quickly as he had entered it.

After that experience, reality slapped me in the face. Again. *What the hell am I doing in this world?* I asked myself. I was slipping away from myself. *Who the hell am I?* Did I really want to be some hot-shot engineer, traveling, wining and dining on the company's dime, and getting hit on and seduced by more dangerous men? What was this corporate world turning me into? And all for what? To make a lot of money in exchange for my time, energy, and morals? To join the rat race and burn myself out? To climb the ladder higher than everyone else? *Whose ladder am I climbing anyway? And why?*

I was suddenly sick and tired of participating in business dinners, where boasting over corporate status, workloads, degrees, and awards was the status quo of conversation. *Do you ever see your children?* I wondered as I realized how little I saw my own. Probably not, but bragging about our children's over-achievements was also a hot topic at the elaborate dinner tables.

My heart kept asking, *What the hell are we in such a hurry for? Why do we need to compete against and be better than everyone else? Are we all that afraid of lack, of not having it all? Since when do we need to have so much and be so busy around the clock? And train our kids to become just as overworked as we are? Does this really bring anyone genuine, lasting happiness?*

I realized that at the rate that corporate America is building our stress levels while tearing each other down, the only thing we were racing to was our graves. Why would I want to win that race? Thank God for my yoga practice, and a little calming cannabis, to remind me so.

Yoga training was an opportunity I stumbled upon with no idea that I'd become serious about teaching it. But when I started guiding classes for my fellow colleagues, I discovered a sense of fulfillment within me that was much stronger than any of my academic or corporate achievements. That fulfillment came from cultivating a sense of inner peace with my class. My heart overflowed in even the briefest moments of relief and calm within my students and fellow co-workers.

One day, during yoga class in our conference room, I felt suddenly struck with my life purpose: to spread this peace and calm with others. The world didn't need another money-hungry engineer to burn themselves out in the rat race to "win" the game of life. Instead, the world needs more people to show how accessible inner peace is for us all, and that it's always waiting for us to access it. Not after we reach that next goal, but right here, right now.

Having this realization was great and all, but how was I supposed to put it into action? How could I possibly leave my high-paying job to teach yoga? How would I still be able to support Jaelyn by myself without the security of my engineer salary?

"Take the leap," I heard in my mind. "Trust the process."

Still unsure of what exactly I needed to leap to, I let thoughts and ideas circulate through my mind over the next few months, often consulting with Kelly over my potential options, who now lived with us in our new Minnesota home.

"I should just get another engineering job at a better company," I suggested. "One that has a good employee wellness program. I could still teach yoga there, and in a better environment!"

"But you would still be in the corporate environment," Kelly reminded me. "Is that really where you want to be? Learning another new, hard, time-demanding job? Where? In the cities? Adding to your commute? You're a yoga teacher now; you can teach anywhere. What if you let yourself let go of the engineer title?"

I shuddered. A sick little pit swirled in my stomach. *But I worked so hard for this engineering degree,* I thought. *How could I let go of this title I worked so hard for?* As much as I wanted to resist Kelly's advice, something in my heart knew it was true. I had to take a major leap. I couldn't play it safe and just move to another company. If I did, I'd still have to work just as many hours, spend that much more time learning a new business, and travel just as much. What would I really be gaining? What was I really seeking? The fulfillment of teaching yoga, relaxation, and inner peace. Not engineering. I had to take the leap.

I stepped outside onto our back deck for some fresh air. I took a few deep breaths, taking in the crisp fall air, and closed my eyes, soaking up the sun that shined on my face through the large maple tree branches above me. Opening my eyes, I looked around the deck, my eyes settling on a small pile of rocks that Jaelyn had painted. The one on top had a big white and yellow daisy on it. I smiled as a chill ran up my spine, letting out a soft giggle of amusement and relief. I heard Kelly open and close the door behind me.

"I hear it's really easy to start an LLC," she said, stopping next to me to close her eyes and face the sun. "You can run your own yoga business. You can even still teach in workplaces if you want. You can do your wellness coaching and help people one-on-one. Who says that you need to work for someone else?"

"Wow, that sounds amazing and intimidating," I replied in wonder. *Could I really run my own business?* I asked myself. "I suppose that runs in the family," I realized out loud with a soft chuckle. "If my grandpa and dad could run their own businesses, it must be in my blood!" At that moment, my bold decision was made. I was going to quit my job and start a new business. Now, how to put in my notice…

It took me another few weeks to build up the nerve and heart to hand in my notice to my boss. I was loved at work. I was respected. I had a lot of responsibility and autonomy. I was paid very well. I got to travel the world. On paper, I had the perfect job. How could I explain that I wanted to quit and risk everything to work for myself in a completely unrelated field? I set goals to talk to my boss on certain days, yet I kept putting it off.

I had no doubt that my energy was shifting at work, though, and it didn't go unnoticed. My boss started avoiding me more, and I noticed resistance from some coworkers, as if they were bracing themselves for me to leave. I had to admit, the signs were becoming evident. I lost concern for arriving to work early or staying late. I prioritized my breaks for the gym. I left work more often for my daughter's school events, and I let myself have way more fun (and alcohol) on work trips than I ever had in the past. Part of me felt careless with one foot already out the door. I needed to get out but didn't know how to build the courage. So, that night, I pulled out my journal.

Nov. 11, 2018

*What's the consequence of not speaking my truth? Feeling trapped back in my psychological prison. Ego says stay safe, you're not good enough to take such a huge leap, you could fail! I don't have time for that nonsense.*

*"Speak what you seek, until you see what you said."*

*I protect my energy, soul, mind, and body from all negative sources. I easily and effortlessly speak my truth. It is safe for me to do or say anything at my job. I am unafraid of defining my boundaries. It is not selfish to state what I want and need, and I will not settle. I must rise above the "suffer for the team" mentality to break it down and help others rise. Only by marching a different path can I truly help anyone. They need to be exposed to another alternative. Otherwise, they won't know it's even an option!*

*My soul is screaming for me to focus my full attention to things that fulfill my passion, and to do that, I must go. It is safe for me to express my truth! I am smart, creative, and capable of bringing anything to fruition!*

*Any self-doubt is only fear branching from an inner knowing that I am not fully living my truth. It is easy and effortless to speak my mind and think creatively in any situation.*

*Don't use your energy to worry; use it to believe.*

*-Kris*

The Monday after Thanksgiving, I finally put in my notice with a heart-to-heart with my boss. Shocked, nervous, and somewhat impressed, he honored my decision, grateful for my willingness to stay another six weeks to train those who would fill my position. Those last six weeks were bittersweet, though each day, I walked in feeling lighter, knowing that my time was coming to an end; I was almost free to move on.

My last days were busy with last-minute training and long goodbyes with nearly every employee in the building. Each one reminded me how respected I was, that what I did there mattered and didn't go unnoticed, and that I really was a nice, considerate, and dependable human being who was worthy of being appreciated.

I did exactly what I thought I needed to prove my worth, and now that I had that validation from others, I finally realized the irony: *I didn't need any of it.* Having it couldn't make me happy; only a healed body, mind, and spirit could do that. After finally achieving and obtaining all that I had worked so hard for, I couldn't wait to let go and be free from it all. I celebrated with my coworkers, high on my upcoming freedom, feeling more ready and excited than ever to carve a new path and work for myself doing something I truly felt passionate about.

Though I held the highest hopes for my daring career leap, my first landing wasn't as graceful as imagined. I took my first month off to begin writing this book. I couldn't wait to have free time during my day to sit in my quiet home office and write. However, I had no idea the rude awakening I was in for with the sudden dramatic change in routine. I had been running on a hamster wheel for over ten years, and my legs buckled under me once I stepped off. Anxiety jumped under my skin each morning. I had a pressing worry that I was late and needed to be somewhere. *I should be hurrying and under pressure to complete a task for someone, shouldn't I?* I didn't realize how deeply my old routine had burned into my subconsciousness.

Suddenly, each step through my house felt like sinking quicksand. The walls started closing in on me. I didn't have anyone to report to. I wasn't on someone else's strict time schedule. *Who am I to live so freely?* I started wondering as I sunk deeper into the quicksand.

Plus, it was the middle of January, right in the middle of a record-breaking cold streak. Normally, my go-to mind-clearing remedy was a brisk walk outside in the fresh air. But at negative fifty degrees, I wasn't about to step outside. It was so cold, I didn't want to roll my mat out inside either. So, I let the cold and snow bury me inside the walls that closed in and shamed me for my selfishness to quit my job and write a book all about me.

Not to mention the immense shame I still had for my story. You remember the first half of this book, don't you? Those were the most painful days of my life. Trying to relive those moments nearly did me in, the guilt from my present and past completely drowning me in a surprising relapse of depression.

*What the hell am I doing?* I asked.

"Trust the process," was all I heard. "Go with grace and ease."

But for several weeks during the dark and record-breaking cold of the polar vortex, I found it nearly impossible to trust anything. I was suddenly questioning myself, my motives, and my purpose for life altogether. I learned first-hand what "imposter syndrome" was as I doubted my ability to teach, write, and run a business.

*I'm an engineer, not a yoga teacher,* became a frequently debilitating claim in my mind. *I should just quit now before I fail. Just go back to engineering where I knew what I was doing without exposing all my painful history. Or, maybe I can just stay in this bed forever until I die. No one would even know...*

Though I had just begun the outline and filled in the first few chapters, I put my story aside. It was too painful to relive in such detail yet, and that made it clear that I still had some healing to do.

*How is this possible?* I wondered. *I've done so much and have come so far; I thought I was over my traumatic past.* But as I began writing about it, the head-on collision with my pain-body was not triggered by the obvious tragedies of Jake's paralysis or Cody's death, but the betrayal, revenge, and loss of integrity that led up to their fates.

It didn't hit me until then that perhaps I still had a false idea of healing. Until then, I believed my deepest pain came from my greatest losses and the obvious traumas from my past. I didn't consider how much my relationships and sense of self-worth impacted my circumstances. Until then, I didn't know that most of the trauma stored in my pain-body was from less "significant" events.

As each day showed hope of more warmth and sunshine, so did my spirit. I knew I had found healing before, and this time, I had the tools to heal myself again. Because this time, I realized there was nothing wrong with me. There was nothing to fix, only compassion to be found for my younger self and the pain she so bravely endured. Though it had to come with recognizing my responsibility in manifesting my experiences, this time, I knew I had a golden opportunity to set myself free from old beliefs. After the last decade of experimenting with yoga, energy healing, and all things mindfulness and holistic self-care, the most valuable thing I learned was that *I am not my thoughts.*

All the nasty things I once believed to be true about myself that tormented me into a relentless race of proving and punishing myself were not really true at all. And I didn't have to believe them anymore. No one was proving them true except for my own thoughts. Remembering Eckhart's wisdom that ego created those thoughts, not my true self, set me free. Writing and reliving my story simply triggered my pain-body and many emotions that hadn't been stirred up in over a decade. I knew that these triggers could strike at any time, no matter how spiritually evolved I became, and that it was not about preventing the triggers; it was about my awareness of and reactions to them. I always had the choice to love and nurture myself when facing pain, and this time, I had the tools I needed to help me out of my dip back into the darkness.

"You be nice to my Krista," I could hear Suzanne's voice remind me. She may have been the only person who truly knew how hard on myself I was over the last thirteen years, and she repeated these words through every visit together, now only a few times a year since Jaelyn and I moved away. "Take care of her," her kind voice said.

For the rest of my time off, I dedicated myself to my personal self-care, taking plenty of Vitamin D and making long-overdue appointments with a massage therapist, holistic family doctor, a new local therapist, and an acupuncturist. For the first time in over six years, I decided to solve the hidden mystery of my physical body, as I still hadn't gotten a period since it stopped in college. I had to accept that I clearly had an energetic imbalance that was preventing my body from being able to perform its most important and amazing function, creating new life. I had bloodwork and ultrasounds done all over again, returning me to the same conclusion, that with no physical answers, it had to be energetic. I set a goal to stay consistent with massage therapy, acupuncture, and my own self-healing Reiki practice. For an extra energetic boost, I even booked a Reiki session with Melissa for the first time in another three years.

At first, I felt guilty prioritizing these appointments, especially going to them during the middle of the day. *Shouldn't I be suffering at work right now with the rest of the world?* I asked myself.

"Shouldn't, shouldn't, shouldn't," I heard a guiding voice in my mind remind me. "No following shoulds. Do the opposite. Let yourself be weird."

*Oh, yes, that's right,* I remembered. *What a concept, to believe I should be suffering instead of prioritizing my personal healing. This is a challenge to shift my own mindset and brighten my light so I can light a path for others.* Each day, it continued getting easier to get out of bed, face the day, and put myself first without feeling guilt.

I vowed to keep these special healing activities in my weekly and monthly routine as I prepared to go back to work. Ironically, my first yoga class was back at my former employer, who decided to be my first corporate client and warmly welcomed me back into the building. It took many weeks to shake off the strange guilt that shadowed me after each visit. *You left them here to suffer. You should be suffering with them,* ego repeated in my mind.

*Don't give in to the shoulds,* I reminded myself. *Brighten my light so I can brighten others'.*

My yoga class schedule continued growing into other workplaces and my local community, slowly lifting my vibration and reminding me why I was doing this. I started making beautiful connections with my yoga students and looked forward to practicing with them every week. I could feel my light brightening as I grew more comfortable teaching and found my voice.

Every couple of months, inspiration would strike to return to the story, and I chipped away one painful and enlightening memory at a time. Some days, I'd make pages of progress. Other days, I ran back into a wall of guilt and shame that seemed to corner me into the darkness without warning.

When the darkness from my past crept in again, I leaned harder into my self-care. I practiced Reiki. Sometimes, I listened to guided meditations and positive affirmations for hours at night or before getting out of bed in the morning, just so someone else could feed positive words and energy into my soul when I couldn't. I continued fitting massages and acupuncture in my schedule, which felt easier once I started to feel the healing impact from them both. The better I felt, the deeper fulfillment I received through my yoga classes and students, though I had to admit, my filling schedule was becoming an escape from writing the book.

*But I'm feeling so good,* I thought. *I don't want to ruin it by facing the book again.*

"Trust the process," I heard yet again. "That's part of your healing."

*Alright, alright,* I felt myself submit. *Spirit, just please help me cultivate the motivation and ability to write without getting pulled into the pain of the story again.*

"Just keep writing," Spirit replied. "Grab your journal. Write the emotions there to be released, and the story will get easier."

*Ugh, journaling,* I thought to myself. *Don't I have enough to write already?* I knew it always made me feel better after. I already had a collection of four filled journals by that point. But after falling out of my regular writing habit, it felt impossible to get back into it. "Just write," was all I heard. "Let cannabis soften resistance when you need it." So, occasionally, I listened to their voice, and after putting down my one-hitter, I picked up my pen.

*What do I write?* I had no idea. So, I started with writing the date, where I was, and what I was physically doing. From there, I wrote how I was feeling. Suddenly, once a few strings of words got started, the pen would take over. My emotions flooded out, my writing getting sloppier

*The Daisy Diaries*

and jumping off the lines of my page. Then, insights started sparking within me.

3/12/2019

*What you feel is what you need to share with the world. No one will know if you keep it in your head. Only you will suffer. Tell your story and set yourself free. It will give others permission to free themselves, too. This is just the beginning. Keep trusting. Keep feeling. Keep writing. Keep sharing. It's all coming together in perfect order.*

-Kris

That moment lifted me back on the saddle, and I began journaling more frequently, not realizing that my "brain dumps" were really channeled messages from Spirit. They sure made me feel better, though, like someone out there supported me through my crazy new venture. It didn't matter who or where it came from. Journaling became my sacred time with my soul, where I could release all the emotions triggered within me, confess my guilt and judgment, and cultivate a sense of peace and knowingness that everything really was working out for me.

The more I felt this Divine connection while journaling, the more I felt that connection elsewhere, especially while driving. Songs on the radio were constantly catching my attention again, shocking me with the loving presence of my dad and Cody. "I'm so proud of you," I could hear them say. "We're right here to support you. Call on us anytime. And don't forget we're here whenever you take a drive."

Their presence was often so sudden and overwhelming, I'd burst into tears of joy. Tears of overflowing unconditional love. In their presence, I felt loved and supported in ways I hadn't felt from other humans walking this earth. I felt complete and confident. After receiving their messages and listening to their songs on the radio, I often felt like I could fly.

I looked forward to driving for this reason and often took a ride whenever I needed connection and support. We had conversations together where I literally spoke aloud in response to the words flooding into my mind. "I'm crazy for talking to myself, aren't I?" I laughed out loud to myself.

"Keep talking," they answered. "You're really communicating with us, and you're going to teach others how to do it, too." In those moments, my heart gushed with overwhelming resonance. Though it sounded completely crazy in my mind, my heart couldn't agree more that that was something I was capable of and passionate about doing. *But how do I get started?* I wondered.

"Don't worry about the how yet," they reassured me. "Trust the process. Go with grace and ease."

Ironically, as my spiritual practice took leaps and bounds into another plane, a discomfort started growing within me around my business and teaching yoga classes. *What am I missing?* I wondered, though a tug in my heart signaled it knew the answer that my mind was ignoring. I felt my passion pour through teaching yoga, but I didn't feel like I was connecting enough with my students and serving them as much as I felt called to. My class schedule filled up, yet I found my confidence sinking down. *How the hell do I connect deeply with my students like I do with my guardian angels?* It took another month or so to realize I had let yoga classes consume my schedule, leaving no room for one-on-one coaching clients or more intimate workshops. So, I slowly reduced classes to create space and finally took the time to build my coaching program and new workshop content. Through word of mouth and minimal social media posting, I led my first public and private self-care workshops and booked my first paid client.

All of it was terrifying. I didn't realize how hard it would be to promote and market my business. *Selling myself? I was an engineer for damn good reason,* ego reminded me. *I don't know shit about marketing. It's selfish to brag about what I do and ask people to pay me for it. Am I really worth it? I'm an engineer; do I really know what I'm doing now?*

The self-defeat could strike at any time without notice, and I often let it knock me out for a day or so. But something in my gut kept driving me forward. *I just know I'm on the right path,* I reassured myself. *I might not be quite there yet, but I'm on my way.* Through all the ups and downs of self-doubt, blind faith, and inspired action, I was reminded every day, sometimes every hour, even every minute:

"Trust the process."

# Chapter 18

## March 2020:

## When the World Stopped

To those of you who remember the year 2020, I need not say more. The coronavirus pandemic brought the entire world to a stop. Right when I was getting comfortable with my new schedule and steady income, everything shut down. I could no longer teach yoga and coach in workplaces, or anywhere. Conveniently, I had made a small yoga studio in my house, so it was easy to join the rest of the world and go online.

I started teaching online yoga classes and found it surprisingly peaceful teaching yoga from the comfort of my own home. No more commuting and hauling yoga equipment around; all I had to do was roll out of bed, into the next room, and turn on my phone or computer. *Wow, this is nice!* I realized. I quickly got accustomed to the new routine and recognized two golden opportunities with all this new free time: to focus more time on one-on-one coaching and finally start a few DIY home projects!

The DIY was easy; I knew exactly what I wanted to do since I bought the house almost three years earlier. I started with refinishing and painting my ugly cabinets in my tiny kitchen. Next, with the help of a few friendly neighbors, I refinished and decorated our back deck into a sweet and private oasis. Last, I brought back to life the old garden plot behind our garage, surrounding it with an adorable gate and planting peppers, tomatoes, and cucumbers.

As for focusing on my coaching program, that was another story. *How the heck do I get new clients while everyone is stuck at home?* I wondered. I had to take it online. Teaching yoga online was already helping me soften my love/hate relationship with screens and technology, but promoting myself online was still a daunting task. *Okay, I need some help with this. I need to connect with other people somehow.* I was thirsty for more knowledge and training, and I was ready to learn right now!

With my newly flexible schedule, I had the freedom to invest back into myself and my business. I had been following Tara, a business coach and yoga teacher trainer from my hometown area, for the last year, after meeting her in person at a ski hill just weeks before I first left the corporate world. I immediately felt a connection and knew we would work together. However, at that time, I was hyper-focused on launching my business and teaching classes and dismissed the idea of hiring her yet.

Well, in the isolation of the COVID-19 shutdown, it was time to get a new coach. I contacted Tara and jumped right into her ninety-day Transformation Program *and* her Yoga Teacher Training (YTT). Even though I had already done a 200-hour YTT, I desperately craved connection with others and a deeper personal yoga experience, and was eager to experience the course again in a completely different format.

My mind was blown by the coaching program; there were so many things to do to build and promote my online business! I quickly got practice with Zoom meetings for my weekly coaching and yoga training calls, where I found myself genuinely connecting with each like-minded group through the little Brady Bunch boxes on my computer screen.

Though I felt locked inside my house and separate from the entire world, I embraced this new cyber connection with others from the serene space of my newly decorated backyard. I also started noticing that the less connected I was to the busy, fear-stricken world around me, the more I connected with Spirit. Random insights and impulses came to me more often. I more frequently felt tingles from the presence of Cody and my dad. Music lyrics caught my attention more than ever, along with the pair of cardinals and blue jays that visited me and our bird feeder multiple times a day.

Coins were popping up everywhere. So were butterflies and dragonflies. Signs from Spirit were flashing in front of me all day, every day. I felt reassurance from Spirit, telling me that I was on the right path and not to fear what was happening in the world. As each sign presented itself, I felt overwhelming joy and gratitude wash over me.

"You're here to do great things," I heard.

*What do I need to do? And how do I do it? Where do I begin?* I kept asking.

"Grab a pen. Just write," replied Spirit.

*Well, what the hell am I supposed to write?* I wondered.

*The Daisy Diaries* | 217

"Don't think about it. Just write." After finally releasing my reluctance, one day I picked up my journal and pen. What came out was this:

4/20/2020

Evening Channel

*I am safe. It is safe to trust that I am always safe. It is safe to unlock my doors. Physically and emotionally. The angels are asking me to release ALL fears of danger. They are with me always. Everywhere. By releasing my fears of safety, pain, deception, loss, criticism, and failure, my "shining armored" man will appear and offer the ultimate sense of safety. He's closer than you think. Move forward with your ideas without hesitation; he'll appear along the liberating journey and join you. Jaelyn will flourish, too. You'll both develop a deeper community on the move than staying put. It's time. Trust the movement. Let old doors close, better ones are opening!*

After I stopped writing, I sat and reread my words. *Did I really just write this?* I thought to myself. *I already don't remember it, but these words are amazing!* I continued flipping back through the pages of my journal and was amazed to notice that most entries included a shift in tense and words of wisdom that didn't seem like my own. *Wow, seriously, did I write this?* I asked myself again. *And what does on the move mean? Where are we going?*

I spent the next hour reading through the pages of newfound gold in my journal, blown away by the brilliant comments and insights I wrote many months earlier that resonated perfectly with my current situation. *Holy shit!* I thought to myself with sudden realization. *Have I been channeling Spirit the whole time?*

*Just keep writing,* an intuitive thought spoke to me. *By letting the pen flow, you can bypass the tough filter of the ego. Don't think or analyze what you're writing. Just write. The words will help heal you and the world.*

A few days later, I felt the pull to my pen for more channel writing. This time, I felt a warm rush of my father's presence. *Oh my God, can I get direct messages from my dad?* I wondered in doubt.

"Just pick up the pen," I heard.

8/15/2020

Channel Time

*Dad: I love you. Your tribe is here. Keep imagining; it WILL come. You will be able to clear things soon.*

*I'm excited for you.*

*Stay open to receiving, it's ALL coming NOW. Only listen to what you are called to do in the moment. You have the perfect amount of time. Focus on you right now. Be where you are, be present to YOU. Inspired action will fill you effortlessly when you leave, not any sooner. No step needs to be rushed, just let it flow through you. It's all coming. I can help deliver it to you. Yes, even money. To create it all. It comes together with each step of inspired action. The more you relax into you, the easier it flows.*

*It doesn't matter how anyone reacts, I am proud of all that you are and all that you do.*

*Love, Pops*

From that moment, I felt a spark of inspiration and trust ignite within me. *This shit might be crazy,* I thought to myself, *but it feels too right to ignore.*

"The weirder it gets, the closer to your truth and abundance you become," I heard from something, somewhere.

Still in global lockdown and isolated from the "normal" world, I continued to talk to people less and Spirit more. Some days, I felt completely crazy living in my own little world, literally talking to Spirit and my guides out loud and giggling with joy from our discussions. But on those days, I felt my best. Joy radiated from me. The more I let myself be weird, the more I felt myself glow.

With the support of my new coach, mastermind group, and fellow yogis in training, I set off on building my online business and strengthening my teaching skills. I started attracting new coaching clients, building confidence, and noticing old beliefs and identities falling away. *I am not what people think I am,* I thought. *I'm not here to do what anyone expected me to do.* Though almost painful to accept at first, these realizations started to settle in my soul. *Just keep being weird.*

By the time the final intensive of yoga teacher training came, I could hardly contain my excitement to be with other humans in person. The eleven days of intense all-day learning and teaching were mentally, physically, and emotionally draining, yet at the same time utterly fulfilling to my soul.

Meeting that group of beautiful souls, and their entire bodies outside of the boxes on my computer screen, filled me with the greatest sense of belonging. These people accepted me exactly as I was and loved me for it. This was my tribe of like-minded souls who had also found yoga on their own spiritual path.

By the end of those eleven epic days, I felt a surge of energy pushing me forward. It was time for major change. I was craving it. It was time to go through a new door and close the old one behind me. But where to? *Everywhere*, is what I heard.

After both Jaelyn and I survived the transition to the online world of work and school, I started questioning where we lived. I no longer had physical work ties to the area, and we were constantly driving back and forth between our home in Minnesota and our family's cottage in northern Wisconsin to enjoy the lake and take care of maintenance for my grandfather.

Perhaps from being secluded at home, my itch to travel grew. *How the heck can we travel during this pandemic, though?* I wondered. My previous work trips to Europe inspired my desire to travel internationally. Part of me wanted to pick up and move overseas altogether. That wasn't an option during a pandemic, but suddenly, I realized: *Wow, this is a big ass country we live in. What if we drive and travel The States?*

During yoga training, I mentioned my itch to travel and free myself from the burden of homeownership in the suburbs of the Twin Cities. I shared my love for my family's cottage and realized that if I was going to put more money and energy into a home, it had to be my cottage, not the house I owned.

"Why don't you sell your house and move to your cottage?" a fellow yogi suggested.

"That's exactly what I want to do! Except I can't live in northern Wisconsin all winter," I replied. "I want to just buy an RV and travel through the cold months!"

Excitement burst through my pores at this thought. How freeing it felt to let go of our Minnesota house and go wherever we wanted! Big eyes and smiles of yogis lit up around the table.

"Oh my God, that sounds amazing!" they responded. "You need to do it, and share your journey!"

I had never camped in an RV before, but that was just a minor detail. The support and encouragement of my fellow yogis filled me with confidence and validation, and by the time I left that yoga training, I was ready to take off.

After returning home, I worked out an agreement with my grandpa to move to our cottage. Though I tried to convince him to sell it to me, he wasn't ready to give up ownership yet. Instead, he was willing to let us move there in exchange for taking care of the place for him. Now, I just needed to get out of my house in Minnesota.

I was able to teach a few last yoga classes outdoors that summer, and at the very last class, I happened to meet a new yogi there. I learned she was a realtor and immediately sensed that she was who I needed to work with to sell my house. We chatted briefly about my plans, connected on Facebook a few days later, and within a week, I had researched her website and scheduled her visit to our house. From there, the rest was a whirlwind of pieces falling into perfect place. She told me everything I wanted to hear, that the house was in great shape, and that we could list it as is, including the master bedroom, which I had turned into my yoga studio with a Yoga Trapeze® hanging from the ceiling.

I scrambled to clean out the house and prepare it for pictures; it was listed for sale within two weeks. My heart raced with anxiety and excitement throughout the first day of showings. *Will it sell? Am I crazy? How is this going to go?* My questions were answered almost immediately. We accepted the second offer on its first day, quickly sending us speeding to the finish line to close the sale in less than a month. As the pieces flew and fell into place at lightning speed, all that repeated in my mind was:

"Trust the process. Go with grace and ease."

# Chapter 19

## August 2020:

## Off We Go

It was a mad race to empty our house. Moving to our cottage, we didn't need any furniture; it was already full to the brim! So, I made my way around the house taking pictures and selling nearly everything we owned online. People and furniture were constantly in and out of our house every day. I filled about six carloads with donations of clothes, decorations, and miscellaneous items. And as more things disappeared from our house, the more anxious and excited I became.

Going through every possession and deciphering what was absolutely necessary was certainly an awakening process. One night, while looking in our storage room for what felt like the millionth time to pick what was next to go, I realized I automatically bypassed a life-long collection of gift bags and tissue paper every time, as if it were obvious that we needed to keep them.

I mean, shit, I had earned those gift bags over a lifetime of birthday parties and other occasions. If I got rid of these, what would I do when I went to another birthday party? I suddenly realized I was clinging to my ownership of these gift bags and laughed. This was clearly my sign to let them go! In reorganizing the containers for their next owner, the words whispered in my mind, "In being willing to own nothing, you truly own everything."

In giving up my attachment to my collection of gift wrap, along with most everything else in my home, I felt free. By being willing to let go of my possessions (and justifications for needing them), I regained possession of something much more important: my life!

I realized that too often, the things we own end up owning us. The more we have, the more we have to take care of, and the more our things control our lives. The fewer objects I owned, the more I owned my life, and that, to me, truly is everything. By letting go of that collection of gift wrap, I was truly ready to let go of everything else and set off on a quest to create a life that gave me genuine happiness without collecting a thing.

Before that moment, I quickly grew tired of going through our house; I just wanted to get it over with! But after that magical moment of releasing my precious gift wrap collection, I felt refueled with inspiration to continue getting rid of everything. The more empty our house, the lighter and freer I became.

As the month of moving, selling, and packing raced on, I looked to obtain just one more big thing. One huge thing. The right RV. The online search seemed endless; every time one that seemed to be the perfect fit popped up, it was gone by the time I contacted the sellers.

"Trust the timing. The right one is coming," I heard Spirit say.

At the same time, I was talking with my friend, Claire, who lived in Mexico. Pre-pandemic, we planned for me to visit her that year with Jaelyn. By this point in October, I had no idea how safe it could be to travel, nor if I could even get Jaelyn a passport in time. My head wanted to argue that it would be stupid and selfish to travel, but my heart kept singing to give it a try.

"Trust the timing, go with ease," Spirit reminded me.

"Ok," I told Claire. "If we can get Jaelyn's passport in time, I'll take it as a sign that it's meant for us to come!"

So, one afternoon while dropping off another carload of donations, Jaelyn and I submitted her passport application. We were told it would take a solid three to four months for it to come in, so I dropped my hope in making our Mexico travel plans and settled with satisfaction that we at least would have her passport for future travels.

A mere three weeks later, I checked the mail and was stunned to find Jaelyn's new passport in our mailbox.

"You're kidding me!" I exclaimed to myself.

I gave Claire a call that evening, and though my ego wanted to scream with guilt and fear in the back of my mind, I gave myself permission to listen to my heart instead and book flights. Before I went to bed that evening, we had a departing flight set for two days after we closed on our house.

"Trust the process," I heard.

Within two more days, the perfect RV popped up at a dealership in the Minneapolis suburbs. It didn't list a price; it only stated to call for pricing.

"Uh oh," I thought to myself. "It's going to be way too expensive." I sent an inquiry anyway, quickly letting go of the outcome based on my recent experiences of getting my hopes up too quickly.

The next day, I received a call back from the dealership.

"Hey, Krista," the salesman said. "You were the first to inquire about this Minnie Winnie, so if you want it, it's all yours."

My jaw nearly bounced off the floor once I heard the price; it was much lower than I was anticipating! Was this too good to be true?

"Trust," I heard again.

I immediately scheduled to see it, about a week before we closed on our house. Upon laying eyes on it, I knew we had to take it. A 2002 Winnebago Minnie Winnie with sturdy bones; everything was in great working order, and the previous owners had recently put new top-of-the-line tires on it. We took the Minnie for a quick test drive, and I was shocked by how comfortable I felt driving it. It was a no-brainer; this was our new home!

"I'll take it!" I told the salesman with excitement. We made plans for us to pick it up the next day after returning from Mexico.

From there, we filled one last carload with the few items we had kept and headed to our cottage. We left our small SUV there, and to my surprise, my mom graciously and supportively drove us back to our home in Minnesota for the last time. After butting heads with my mom through most of my life, enduring several years of pain and tension after my dad's death, and a few more letters and heart-to-heart conversations, I finally felt closer and more comfortable confiding in her more than ever in my life. Though she had certainly expressed her fears and concerns with each big leap, I felt like she finally accepted my wild ideas and free spirit without trying to control or change my mind to keep me safe.

Upon our final return to Minnesota, Jaelyn and I scrambled to get the last of our belongings out of the house within the last twenty-four hours before it was no longer ours. Jaelyn and I slept on an air mattress on the floor on our last night, and my dear friend, Rachel, picked us up within minutes of closing time the next morning.

"This is it, Jaelyn!" I exclaimed with a smile. "Are you ready for the most epic adventure of our lives?"

She beamed with excitement and replied, "Yes!"

As Rachel pulled up, we took one last walk around the house, thanking it for all that it had given us over the last three years, and said goodbye.

I watched our house get smaller as we drove away, partially in disbelief of reality. *Did I really just sell our house to drive around the country? Am I homeless right now*? Well, yes, for two days, we were technically homeless. We stayed with Rachel until our flight departed to Mexico.

That was Jaelyn's first international trip. During a pandemic. I'm not sure if that made me the worst or the coolest mom ever.

"Trust the timing," Spirit assured me. "Trust that you are safe. Go with grace and ease."

We made it to Mexico and back without a hitch, sharing the most memorable week driving across the country with my dear friend, Claire. Upon our arrival, we spent the evening walking the unusually quiet city, admiring all the colorful and fascinating Day of the Dead decorations. Vendors still lined the streets, each with blankets and tables laid out to display their jewelry and artwork.

"Oh, look!" Claire suddenly exclaimed. "Daisy chain crowns!" She pointed to a vendor's blanket covered with flower crowns. I smiled, suddenly feeling safe and protected by my favorite guardian angels.

"Let's each get one," I replied.

For the next five days, we explored adorable cities, ate the most delicious food, hiked gorgeous trails, and splashed in the ocean. We even found a hidden gem on a river where we whitewater rafted for the first time and zip-lined back and forth across the river after.

All firsts for Jaelyn, I burst with love and pride in watching my beautiful 12-year-old girl flourish and dare to try new things within the beautiful culture of another country. I knew right then that this was only the beginning of a great transformation for us both.

Jaelyn and I flew back to The States safely and spent one more evening with Rachel in Minnesota. The next morning, it was time to pick up our new home. We taxied to the RV dealer, and after what felt like forever of shuffling and signing paperwork, we were finally free to go.

Buckling in, I looked back at Jaelyn in the rearview mirror. "Are you ready for this?" I asked.

"Yes!" she exclaimed as a huge smile spread across her face, giving me a thumbs up.

And that was when I made my first real drive in the RV. First, back to Rachel's to pick up our belongings, followed by another four and a half hours to our cottage, where we planned to quarantine, rest, and prepare for our road trip and one more visit with our family over Thanksgiving.

During those two weeks of rest, my mind and heart battled it out. *What the fuck are you doing?* my mind kept asking. *You don't know shit about an RV and don't even have your whole route planned. Plus, how do you know Jaelyn will do well with online home-schooling?* I needed to lean on someone for advice and encouragement, so I made sure to squeeze in a long-overdue visit with Suzanne before we took off.

"I'm so proud of you, honey!" Suzanne said yet again in excitement for our daring new adventure. "Will you just stop and notice how many amazing things you have overcome and accomplished already? You've worked so hard; let this new adventure be fun and easy. Who cares if you've never done it before; I know you'll figure it out. And don't worry about Jaelyn. So many kids are homeschooled these days, and she'll get the best experience learning on the road. Trust the process. Go with grace and ease," she smiled.

"Yes, trust the process," my heart replied. "With grace and ease we go." These words filled me with the comfort and hope I needed to keep moving forward. There was a knowing inside me that was enough to win the battle with my critical doubt. *Just trust the process.*

We hit the road on December 2nd. I had never been so nervous and excited. I once read that both nervousness and excitement are expressed through the exact same sensations in the body, so they're actually the same thing.

"I'm just excited," I reminded myself. "And through all my years of anxiety, I've just been excited!"

Our journey over the next six months was nothing short of empowering, overwhelming, exhausting, and exhilarating, often all at the same time. Though I was happily surprised to realize that driving and operating a motorhome by myself was much easier than I anticipated. It was only the planning that nearly did me in.

I spent excessive hours during our first months on the road researching our routes, reserving campsites, and planning our driving days. Part of me felt sickly anxious that I didn't already have the entire route planned, but almost as soon as I had that thought, my heart would remind me, "Trust the process. What would the point of freedom be if you had it all planned?"

So, I took on the challenge to do just that: let go of plans. For the first time in my life, it was time to completely let go of control and trust that I was in safe hands. The more I leaned into the Universe, the more terrifying it felt at first, but the more magical our days became. We started stumbling upon campsites I would have never found, snagging beach-front sites on cancellations, and meeting some really interesting people everywhere we went.

It took what felt like forever before we started meeting "our people," though. We chatted and shared stories with our neighbors at every campground along our eleven-thousand-mile trip, but we traveled across about nine states before we met others who truly felt like our "tribe."

By that point, I questioned my sanity daily for taking us on such a wild ride. *What did I do but separate myself further from our family and friends?* We were seeing so many amazing places, but I was really starting to miss the people who knew me well, and I knew that Jaelyn was, too.

And honestly, I was beyond sick of introducing myself to everyone we met on the road. Every. Single. One.

Ok, I get it that seeing a young single mom and her daughter driving around in a motorhome from Wisconsin may be intriguing. But man, was I tired of telling my story over and over on repeat, especially to those kind people that were just making small talk without a real connection.

I had even given in to downloading a dating app on my phone just to satisfy my coach, who declared it was time for me to refocus on my love life, in an attempt to increase my odds of meeting someone on the road. Yet, to say the least, the app was a wash. When I actually "swiped right," I consistently connected with men who were either deeply rooted in their local area, or hopeful for a quick hookup while I was in town.

The potential of my dating life outside the app didn't prove successful either. I rarely met other single men on the road, and I met many new people every single day. Older couples, young couples with small children, everyone seemed to be paired up already, leaving me feeling more and more lonely in the evenings.

Here and there, we'd have cool campground neighbors to connect with around a fire. Most of the time, the group consisted of married couples, all our kids, and me. After months of losing hope, I met a group of cool people, finally including other singles my age. We camped and congregated around a few evening fires together, where one new friend seemed to have a particular interest in me. He was cute and immature, but it felt unbelievably refreshing to talk to a single man my age again.

One chilly and windy night, after Jaelyn was sound asleep in our warm RV and others had retreated into their homes on wheels for the night, the fellow nomad and I found shelter in his trailer to chat. We shared interesting stories from our pasts and laughed over nostalgia from our generation. *Damn, it's really nice to just hang out with a guy again,* I thought. *He doesn't seem my type, but who knows where it could go. I always wanted a man I could be friends with first.*

I stood up to stretch my legs as I finished that refreshing thought. Taking a seat on a larger couch next to me, the energy suddenly shifted. Without warning, he dove at me from his seat, plowing me down into the couch.

"Holy shit," I exclaimed. "What are you doing?"

"Oh, come on, let me spoon you," he said. "How long has it been since you cuddled with anyone?"

I was silent for a moment, seriously trying to calculate the embarrassing amount of time it had been since a man last touched me. "Damn, I don't know," I replied. "But I just want to get to know you as a friend. Maybe it'll go somewhere from there, but I'm not hooking up with you."

"Don't be so sure about that," he said, aggressively turning me towards him. "I bet I could change your mind real fast." He grabbed my face and pulled me in hard for a kiss.

"Oh my God," I said in shock. *Is he really trying to kiss me right now? Are you kidding me?* "Don't ruin it!" I exclaimed, pushing back hard against his chest. I wasn't successful; his lips touched mine in a messy kiss, his tongue already heading down my throat. Surprised by the required strength, I pushed harder until his face was removed from mine.

"Come on," he said, laughing. "You know you want to."

"Are you serious right now?" I asked, growing concerned for my safety. *Is this dude going to rape me in his RV?* "I said I'm not hooking up with you," I repeated firmly, though my body was shaking. I pushed myself completely away from him and the couch, stood up, and adjusted my shirt. "I just want to be friends and get to know everyone here."

"Alright, alright," he said, still chuckling. The wind howled outside. "No one would hear a thing, though," he added. Now sick to my stomach and in mild shock of the sudden turn of events, I didn't know what to do or say. I tried to play it cool for the last few minutes of talking my way out of the RV. I stepped out into the windy darkness and ran back to my own vehicle, locking the door behind me.

As I crawled into bed, still nauseous and confused, I thought, *It's true; all men really want is sex.* Suddenly, it hit me, *Woah, this is another dangerous man!* Yet, for the first time, I resisted the mind game. I stood up for myself and said "No." *Thank God,* I thought.

"Wrap them with white light," I heard. I closed my eyes, pictured the nomad, and surrounded him with white golden light. *May you find happiness within yourself and with someone who brings out the best in you,* I prayed silently in my mind.

Just like every other dangerous man in my past, the nomad disappeared just as quickly as he came. We carried on in separate directions, and I didn't cross paths with him again. Though I was sickened again by men in general, I was still proud of myself for not giving in to the moment and finally learning the lesson my Spirit guides had given me so long ago: "Protect yourself by surrounding dangerous men with white light."

Plus, I met a lot of other cool people, and to finally cross paths with other kindred souls was a huge reassurance that, yes, I was meant to do this! I knew I was going to meet important people on my path, I just didn't realize how long I'd have to venture before doing so. But just like anything worthwhile in this life, it's always worth the wait.

Making friends on the road boosted my confidence, and I really needed it. I was starting to feel burnt out and concerned that I was doing it again, trying to do too much all by myself without anyone to lean on or even speak to about it. By the time we made it to Utah, I had made many new friends and stumbled upon a few more.

This time, we met a nomadic crew that felt so good to be around, we decided to reroute our return to Wisconsin and travel in a caravan for the first time. I initially thought I had completely lost my mind for making the huge change in plans. Regardless, I finally learned to completely trust the process. This time, I couldn't resist it if I tried, a powerful energy was pushing me away from our original route and toward the flow and ease of this caravan.

In doing so, I made new connections with the first other single women and moms I ever met on the road. Instead of making any plans, for the first time, I was able to simply follow a train of buses and vans, all driven by those badass women. Jaelyn and I had found our tribe, and I felt for the first time in many decades that I had finally found myself.

# Chapter 20

## April 2021:

## The Intuitive Guide Revealed

Month by month, day by day, even hour by hour, I felt a slow peeling away of the many layers that made up my former self. The self that thought she needed to redeem and prove herself to the world. The one who faked it 'til she made it. As each false layer withered away, they disappeared behind us on the road.

I resisted the urge to plan out our schedule in detail and fearlessly trusted the Universe to guide us where we needed to go each day. I consciously chose to feel excitement over nervousness when I woke up each morning and prepared us for another drive further into the unknown.

I didn't initially notice that I had stopped wearing my old clothes, styling my hair, or even wearing make-up, which I had clung to tightly during the acne years of my twenties. Back then, I concluded that I would never set foot outside without make-up or fixing my hair. My skin, hair, and confidence were so weak and frail then. But now, my skin cleared up and I started glowing from the inside out. And what do you know, after seven years of self-discovery, energetic healing, and letting myself gain back weight, my period finally returned.

The beautiful irony I suddenly realized was that my healing never came from finding and controlling the "right" remedies, it came from the exact opposite: letting go of control and shedding the fake layers of perfection I once believed I needed and hid behind.

Shedding layers went much deeper than the masks I wore on the surface, though. I shed layers of old identities. My identities as an engineer, a yoga teacher, and an independent single mama suddenly dropped their ability to define me.

Oh, those precious identities that I once let define how I lived and how others perceived me. I once strived to prove myself through those titles, but suddenly, as I transformed on the road, I knew with all certainty that there was never anything to prove. There was only one thing left to be found: a lot of unconditional love for my true self and the beautiful world around us.

I learned so much on the road, from every challenge, breathtaking view, and new person on our path. By living in simpler means, I found how much more joy can come from having much less. By letting go of self-judgement, I was finally able to stand confidently in my skin, embracing the power of my own self-healing and the all-natural support of cannabis that I had denied for so long. And by loving myself unconditionally, I set myself free.

Free from the limits of my old beliefs, I channeled spirit more clearly and often than ever before. As Spirit spoke to me, most often while driving, I realized that I had a lot more weird and amazing shit to do on this Earth; I hadn't even touched the surface of what I needed to offer the world.

I realized that the journey I felt so alone on wasn't just for me, it was for all the people I was meant to help along the way. I couldn't keep this magical experience I was having every day to myself. I had to share the words I received from Spirit with others. I had to share my special bond with my oracle cards, too, for they were the easiest way for me to directly communicate with Spirit.

*But what will people think of me?* My ego chimed in to strike me with doubt. *They'll think I'm crazy. And what about my mom? She'll worry that I'm going straight to hell!*

"Go with grace and ease," again came to mind. "Trust the process."

*Dang,* I thought. *Could I get a glimpse of this "process" already?*

"Keep writing," was the answer.

So, I started writing down my intuitive impulses regularly and accepting that the words were not just my own imagination, but messages from Spirit that needed to be shared.

I realized that the angel oracle card readings I already shared with my Facebook community were also a direct expression of my channeling and passion for sharing Divine messages with others. *The cards, of course!* Giving guidance intuitively to others is all I truly needed to be doing.

My purpose suddenly became so crystal clear that I had to ask myself, "What the hell else was I even trying to do until now?"

I was trying to keep everyone else comfortable. All the people, environments, and societal structures that I once slaved and strived to prove myself to. Since I became a young mom after enduring public tragedy, loss, and shame, I absolutely believed that I had to redeem myself and earn recognition and praise from all those who ever judged or doubted me. And to do so, I had to fit in, something I might have once appeared to achieve, but never felt.

I spent most of a decade achieving all the things I thought I needed to be happy, accepted, and successful. I seized and conquered an engineering degree, exceptional physical fitness, a new car, a home in the bougie city suburbs, and the corporate career that paid big, let me travel the world, and feel important. I received the accolades that I dreamed of; I reached all the goals that I was so stubborn and determined to achieve. But none of those things gave me the peace I was ultimately searching for.

Not even the leap of faith from my corporate job to start my own business fulfilled me to the soul-calling level that I anticipated. It physically launched incredible progress, but didn't close the gigantic mental and spiritual gap between where I was and where I was going. Though I was able to break away boldly from corporate structure, I still clung to familiarity and people-pleasing.

Initially, it was "weird" enough to become a yoga teacher and wellness coach; I wasn't mentally ready then to comprehend the deep levels of consciousness and connection with Spirit that I needed to reach with my clients. Plus, I started my yoga business by teaching classes in very stressful and toxic work environments, where I was often urged to avoid using the Sanskrit language and anything that could potentially be found "offensive" to anyone person's particular religious beliefs. "Make it comfortable for everyone," I learned early on. I was just happy for the opportunity to reteach people how to breathe and relax their minds and bodies in environments that desperately needed it, so I contained my "weirdness" and stuck to "politically correct" basics that kept others relatively safe inside their comfort zones.

Though I genuinely loved teaching yoga and connecting with students, it always felt like something was missing. There was no lasting gain inside the constraints of the familiar. I had to risk making others uncomfortable. I couldn't continue toning myself down and being "normal," it wasn't serving anyone. It even made me feel fake. I had to take off the mask I was undeniably still wearing, the mask that I once thought would make people like me more, that helped me fit in and hide my fear of judgment.

Thank God for the blessings in disguise. The pandemic cut my cords to every establishment that I toned myself down to teach in. It also offered me the opportunity to teach online, in my own environment, where I finally felt like I could be my true "weird" self.

I didn't even notice that I had started adding spontaneous card readings to the end of my online yoga classes. I also didn't realize how much people enjoyed them. It wasn't just another strange thing Krista was doing, it was a natural expression of my truth and the messages from Spirit that I was meant to share.

The pandemic also allowed me to step fully into coaching. I developed deep and meaningful relationships with my former yogis and new clients. And without direct intention or much effort, I found Spirit channeling through me for them.

Until then, I was just getting used to the fact that my dad and Cody communicated with me regularly. It never crossed my mind whether I could channel anyone else, for anyone else. Not until it "just happened." Hearing and feeling the urge to pick up my journal and pen, I found myself writing messages for a client from their loved one.

After the first time I shared one of these Divine messages, I could no longer deny my true calling in channeling Spirit for others. The message for my client from her late brother was so profound in her coaching experience, I couldn't believe that I had deprived myself and others of these Divine gifts for so long.

Suddenly, it was shocking that I hadn't been channeling from the start. The more I used oracle cards and shared my written channeled messages with clients, the more aligned I felt with my purpose and progress I saw within them.

It was no longer an option to hide my intuitive skills; it was time to fully step out of the closet and offer to the world what I really left the corporate world to do. I changed and announced my online services and opened my schedule for card readings and intuitive guidance.

Before and during each new call, I found myself bursting with excitement to play with the cards and find out where our conversations would lead us. Both my clients and I frequently felt our hair stand on end as we dove deep into their life situations and found each card validating the guidance already flowing out of me intuitively. For the first time, I finally felt like I was serving others to my fullest capability.

*Now, this is the yoga I was meant to teach*, I realized. Beyond the Asanas, or physical postures, I was made to guide others inward and practice Dharana, or focused concentration, away from the external and back to the internal. To the eternal light and wisdom within. By connecting others with Spirit through the cards and my own open channel, they too, were able to connect to their highest self on their own life's journey towards Samadhi, or ultimate bliss and fulfillment. With booming confidence, courage, and zest for life, my clients made tremendous leaps of progress, and being part of their journey fulfilled me more than I could have imagined.

It took two years of transformation for me and my business to climb, one step at a time, to the peak of my soul-driven purpose here on earth. Yet every single step needed to be taken at its own pace, every experience needed to be had at its own time, and every lesson needed to be learned from them to discover this level of self-awareness and purpose.

To get here, it took not only time but much patience and deep love for myself. And for me, it also took a daring journey around the country in an RV to peel away those old layers and reunite with my truest self.

By this point on the journey, it was time to make our way back home to Wisconsin for the summer. My first niece was born during our travels, and I made a promise to return and meet her. But which way would we go? Originally, Jaelyn and I planned to cut east from Utah through Colorado, but our new nomadic friends were heading north to Yellowstone National Park.

"Go to Yellowstone," I felt in my heart. "Trust the process."

Yellowstone was at the top of my list of national parks to see, especially because I knew it was my dad's favorite. I compared routes multiple times, delaying our decision by staying with the group for another day, and then another day, and another, until there were no more days left to procrastinate and still get back to Wisconsin as planned.

I spoke to my life-long best friend, Mel, on the phone that morning to consult with her over which way to go. "Go sit and meditate about it," she advised me. "Your intuition will know what to do."

"You're right, I need to meditate on this," I replied before rambling off a list of everything else I needed to do that morning. "And I need to…" My voice and focus trailed off for a moment. "Holy shit, Mel," I suddenly exclaimed. "I was just about to say I need to go call my dad. That was weird!"

"You need to go meditate right now and talk to him!" she concluded with excitement.

"Yep, you're right. I'm heading down to the river right now," I said. We hung up the phone and I made my way down to a huge log that had fallen over the bubbling creek. I carefully stepped across it and took a seat in the middle. Sitting up, I closed my eyes and listened to the water rushing below me, the birds chirping above me, and the wind sweeping through the trees all around me.

"Which way do I need to go, Dad?" I asked aloud, eyes still closed. A warm breeze brushed my face and tickled my spine.

"Go to Yellowstone," I heard in reply. "Do what makes you nervous."

*What makes me nervous?* I questioned. Immediately the answer came to me: "do what people don't expect."

"Go to Yellowstone," I heard again.

I suddenly felt deeply in my heart to continue north through Yellowstone, and although I didn't know why, I felt confident enough in trusting my intuition. "I guess we're going to Yellowstone," I concluded out loud with a smile.

The actual events at Yellowstone weren't anything spectacular. We even ran into a snowstorm that covered our tightly parked rigs with eight inches of snow overnight. That evening, I wondered why the hell I came there. But by morning, the magical winter wonderland we woke up to was enough to refuel my faith in my decision. The snow melted quickly that day, and we took in gorgeous sites of geysers, hot springs, and herds of bison. Still, nothing out of the ordinary happened to us in Yellowstone. We couldn't even stay long enough to enjoy the whole park, nor did the rainy weather agree with it anyway. Still, I trusted that we needed to take the detour.

But now the grand detour was ending, and it was finally time to bring our first adventure on the road full circle and back to Wisconsin.

# Chapter 21

## June 2021:

## The Curtain Close

As the day approached for Jaelyn and me to part ways with our new nomadic friends, I felt anxiety swell in my chest. *I don't know if I want to go back*, I thought. *I'm having so much fun on the road with these people. If I go back, what if I get stuck there?*

While sitting in Bozeman on the last day with our new traveling tribe, I realized this was it. A mental movie of highlights from our last six months on the road played through my mind. I reviewed my list of hopes and expectations for our trip, checking off one item at a time.

*Epic scenic drives, check.*

*Explore a handful of national parks, check.*

*Oh yeah, figure out how to drive and camp with an RV, check, check.*

*Make new traveling friends, check.*

*Unexpectedly rediscover my true self and stop giving a shit what other people think, check!*

There was just one thing I was hopeful for that hadn't yet come true, meeting and making a genuine connection with a man.

I had driven almost ten thousand miles and crossed paths with hundreds of people. How was it possible that I didn't meet anyone I could truly connect with?

This was on my mind the entire trip, and by this point, I was ready to give up on it altogether. *There's no hope*, I thought. *Every guy I've met has turned out to be a pig and/or an asshole.* Then I caught my thought. *Wait a minute. What kind of belief is that?* I suddenly realized just how negative my thinking had been about men and dating. *How long have I been thinking this way?* My pathetic relationship history flashed through my mind in reverse, all the way to my first relationships with Jake and Cody.

*Holy shit, I've been thinking this way for over half of my life!* I suddenly realized. *No wonder I could never attract the type of man I actually wanted. I've been deflecting him this entire time!* With my phone in hand about to delete the dating app, I set it back down. *I've only got one thousand miles to go, why the hell not keep it until we get back?* I thought.

"Trust the process," I heard.

I decided to grab my journal and start writing. I didn't know what I was going to write, but I knew I needed to cancel all my old beliefs, honor my past relationships and the lessons they taught me, and get super specific about what exactly I did want in a man.

Bozeman, MT

May 23, 2021

*So many lessons learned from my past romantic experiences: saying yes vs. no, bending backwards to please or change them, handing over my power and sense of worthiness. All for what? To make them chase me? To see my worth? To tell me how perfect I am? To worship the ground I walked on? Like Cody did. But I tried to control him, too. Do what I want, so I can feel comfortable. But what if I were comfortable exactly as he is?*

*I know my soulmate's presence always brings me comfort. I'll feel it when I encounter him. It won't just be familiar, it will feel like the most comforting peace, joy, and stability I've ever known. He is my rock. I am his. He is in love with my soul. Our bodies fit together like a puzzle.*

*I step into new relationships fearlessly.*

*I know my GREAT worth.*

*I radiate confidence.*

*I love myself so much.*

*I know I am always perfect.*

*With him, I love being sober. He inspires me to stay present in the moment. Our energy together is stronger than any high. My light is bright and easy for him to find. He's still on my route.*

-Kris

My eyes glazed over the two pages I filled effortlessly, and a smile of peace spread across my face. I took a deep breath. As quickly as this caught my attention, it slipped back out of my mind.

When the day finally came, I felt a little relief as we detached from our new travel family. I was back on my own and had to find our next destination by myself again, but with that came a new sense of freedom. Driving away from our traveling tribe, I was a different woman. Every old and false layer had fallen off, and as I realized that I wouldn't be returning to Wisconsin the same, a smile grew across my face. I cranked up my favorite tunes, looked back at Jaelyn through the rearview mirror, and set off to the east.

We had one stop left on our epic adventure: Billings, Montana, where we spontaneously made plans with my old high school friend.

Jaelyn and I had an amazing visit with my good friend, where I got to see her home and town for the first time, and we spent hours talking, laughing, and dreaming about the future for the first time in over a decade. If we hadn't detoured to Yellowstone on our route, we wouldn't have had such a magical reunion.

"You're trusting the process," I heard Spirit giggle to me.

We ended up spending an extra night in town with my friend. While waiting to meet her for coffee in the morning, I scrolled through my phone checking emails, Instagram, Facebook, and oh, the dating app was still there. I clicked it open and quickly started swiping left, left, left. Suddenly, a profile caught my eye. He was tall, dark, and handsome, and wearing a T-shirt of one of my favorite bands growing up.

*Hm, he's my age,* I thought to myself. I scrolled down to see the rest of his profile. "Hardworking. Chivalrous. Likes to work hard and play hard." *Seriously?* I thought. *Work hard, play hard?* Those were my dad's favorite words of advice.

More pictures, most of him near water and fishing. *Wow, this guy is cute! And what a coincidence, I always wanted a man to teach me how to catch and prepare my own fish.*

I kept scrolling. More pictures. *Very interesting,* I thought as an old reminder from my guides popped into my mind. *He has a squared-off jaw.* I kept reading. "Swipe right if you're looking for a gentleman that's not afraid to go on adventures." *Um, yes, please! Is this guy for real?* I couldn't believe it. Part of me wanted to dismiss him, rattling excuses through my mind like he's too young, he must be full of crap, he's probably never leaving the state…

I scrolled back up to the top of his profile. His smile made me smile.

"Well, what the hell," I thought out loud.

I swiped right.

Again, the thought of finding interest in a man passed out of my mind as fast as it came in; it just wasn't something my brain was used to processing anymore. I carried on, met with my friend, and enjoyed another great day with her. Later that night, I checked my phone once more and felt a surprising little rush of excitement to see that I had matched with the guy I swiped right on hours before. So, I broke the ice, and we got to chatting. It was a slow start, and by the time he asked where I was, we were already making our way into the next state. *He'll give up in no time,* I thought. *I'm already gone.*

"That's a bummer you're not around anymore," he replied. "But that's really cool that you are able to live and travel like that. I've been preparing to do more traveling myself."

*Interesting. Could he really be interested in our nomadic lifestyle?* I concluded that was probably too good to be true.

Our conversation grew more interesting. The more I learned about him and what he did, the more surprised I became. He was essentially listing everything from my every journal entry of positive affirmations and declaring what I wanted in a partner. A carpenter to teach me how to build and make things, check. A musician to inspire me to get back into playing the drums, check. An adventurer to go camping and travel with, check. A fisherman to teach me how to catch and eat my own fish, check. A kindred soul who's walking a similar spiritual path, check.

*No way could this be,* I thought. Seriously, was I even talking to a real man? My ego, remembering my last online dating experience, wanted to doubt and sabotage the too-good-to-be-true chance encounter.

"Trust the process," I heard again. I didn't know where it was going or why, but each day got a little more exciting as I learned about this mysterious Montana man.

As the landscape flattened and we crossed the border into Minnesota, the reality of returning "home" sunk in. Part of me wanted to turn around and head back to the mountains; I wasn't ready to come back. Yet something in me said, *this is only temporary, we'll be back on the road soon. Enjoy this much-needed break and time for rest with our closest family and friends.*

Much to my surprise, arriving at the cottage filled me with a fresh perspective and clarity. As soon as we turned down the familiar tree-covered road, my heart swelled with nostalgia. Turning down the hidden gravel driveway, my eyes filled with tears. It suddenly felt as if all my guardian angels were there to welcome us home. As the trees cleared our view of the house, I was astonished to find the tall grassy field next to the garage covered in wild daisies.

"Welcome home, indeed," I whispered with a smile.

I could feel Spirit's presence over the next several days and weeks, and with it came an unexpected closure to all the darkest and most painful parts of my past. I shared the first chapters of this book with Jake for the first time. And, for the first time, I felt that sharing my unfiltered truth with him brought closure to many things left unsaid between us over the last fifteen years. I felt a new sense of peace with our unusual history and evolution of our friendship, and though we didn't discuss it at the time, we were both stepping into new relationships.

Even Logan suddenly reappeared, and for another first in over a decade, the opportunity to rekindle our old romance appeared. Though tempting and entertaining at first, I felt in my deepest heart of hearts that our past needed to stay in the past. *Perhaps we had or will have better luck in other lifetimes, but not this one,* my heart spoke to me. Plus, I found myself refreshingly intrigued by the Montana man and felt that, no matter where this new relationship went, it was already worth so much more to open a new door with him than turn back and reopen an old one with Logan. A door I thought was shut ten years ago was still open a crack, and a new sense of closure brought my story with Logan to its final close.

Within the next day or two, I sat on the dock writing these pages and ran into writer's block. I pulled out a new deck of cards that I started using to remedy just this type of case. Each card had a journal prompt with it, and I used them to help spark my creative writing when I needed a boost.

The card I pulled asked me, "What greater meaning can I now see coming from my greatest suffering?"

*Well, that's convenient,* I thought. *I'm writing a book about my greatest suffering!* And that suffering had always pointed straight to exactly what I needed to share with the world.

The card prompted me to continue writing about five different experiences that cracked me wide open, what I learned from them, and what wouldn't have without those experiences. I began writing, surprised by the immediately effortless flow of words. My five experiences of suffering listed themselves clearly:

1. *"You selfish little brat." – Mom*

Through my strained relationship with my mom, I finally learned that I can't make others understand me, and most importantly, that I never needed to. Without that lesson, I wouldn't have deep compassion for self-love and helping others embrace it, nor would I have such a close bond with my own daughter, that ultimately came full circle and helped my mom and I heal our relationship.

2. *Being cheated on by Jake and experiencing his accident.*

If it wasn't for Jake, I would have never learned how much we can unknowingly give our power to others. Without my rollercoaster relationship with him, I wouldn't have discovered the strength within me to walk away from what doesn't serve me, no matter how much I think it would serve someone else, nor discover the freedom of forgiveness and letting love evolve from romance to life-long friendship.

3. *The car accident.*

Easily the hardest experience of my life, it taught me more about forgiveness and mortality. I now value every day I'm given and consider motives and consequences of my decisions. I learned the impact of not only forgiving others, but especially myself. Had I not lost Cody, I wouldn't have learned how to release physical attachments and prioritize spiritual connections with him, my guides, and other people.

4. *My "broken" family.*

Having a baby before age nineteen, out of wedlock, with no hope for keeping our little family together, showed me how perfect imperfection really is. Without letting go of Logan and what "could have been," I would have never found independence, empowered myself to create the freedom and life that I truly wanted, nor have such a strong bond with Jaelyn.

5. *My dad's heart attack.*

His death was the ultimate wake-up call that forced me to relieve my own stress, prioritize self-care, and teach it to others. Without losing him so suddenly, I wouldn't have the passion that fueled my determination to leave the corporate world and create a wellness business.

As my pen scribbled all over my journal pages, I was suddenly interrupted. I felt an immediate knowing that someone was near, and their energy was strong.

"Hey, baby," I heard from what seemed like somewhere behind me. Without a doubt, I knew it was Cody. Intense energy tingled through my body. *Wow*, I thought. *What do you have to say, Cody?*

"Just keep writing," I heard in reply. I picked up my pen and started writing.

6/8/2021

Cody's Goodbye

*You can still call on me. Anytime. It's just time for you to focus on him now. I'm so proud of you. Don't be scared. Just let yourself take it slow and trust the process. He's not going anywhere this time. Enjoy it fully. This time, the spiritual first. It'll be the best, I promise! See you when this game's over. Laterz.*

Suddenly, I felt the most intense wave of energy rush up through my body from my toes and all the way out of the crown of my head. I instantly felt lighter, almost as if I were floating, like a genie that had just been released from a magic lamp. Before I could register what was happening, tears burst out of my eyes, and a profound knowing came to me. Cody's spirit had left my body.

*Wow, I didn't know we were still attached, and certainly not like that!* I thought to myself in surprise. For a second, I felt a sadness for him leaving, before quickly remembering the words I just wrote. "I can still call on him anytime," I reminded myself. "It's just time to move on now, and damn, I'm finally really ready to let go." The tears stopped and a smile spread across my face. I took a deep breath in, still floating in thin air. I sighed with a big exhale of release, "Thank you."

I looked back down at the words like gold on their pages. *This is what I lived this for, and this is what I need to share with the world.* Forgiveness, gratitude, and overwhelming love coursed through my veins, and each breath left me feeling lighter and free. Right then, I felt the curtain close on each of those five experiences.

And with my next breath, I began a whole new story.

# Chapter 22

## August 2021:

## The New Story

I spent the rest of the summer finishing this book and serving my new clients online alongside the gorgeous lake of my childhood. Surrounded by the private and peaceful woods and the loving spirits of my dad, I found myself often bursting with joy and gratitude each time I sat down with my laptop to write or connect with a client on Zoom, soaking in the heartwarming views.

I could feel the loving energy of my surroundings flow straight into my work. New clients contacted me, and my excitement overflowed each time I signed on for the next call. Now that I had stepped fully into my purpose as an intuitive guide, I couldn't wait to see what Spirit and the cards had to offer and had never felt so fulfilled by my work.

Between calls and writing breaks, the love of my dad overwhelmed me. He once dedicated himself to maintaining this magical place and sharing its magic with friends and relatives. And for the first time in my entire life of growing up here, I shared his overwhelming love for this place. Everything about it suddenly seemed to sparkle brighter, often filling me with so much unexplainable love and peace, I cried.

As I closed each chapter of this book, their stories came to a final close in real life, and they all came to be laid to rest at none other than the most cherished place I knew on earth.

After traveling the country, chasing a dream to get away and see all that there is to see, I had to laugh that my journey came full circle to my family's cottage. The perfect place to peacefully rest, contemplate, dream, and write. Suddenly, I knew that no matter where my love for travel takes me, this lakeside cottage will always be home, and it will always be in my heart.

The cottage was where I experienced many memorable firsts. Here, I learned how to swim, dive, fish, bake, knit, sew, paint, rake, mow, and most importantly, dream. And now, for the first time in over a decade, I learned how to re-open my long-closed and guarded heart and step fully into a new relationship.

Much to my surprise, the Montana man cracked me wide open by doing what I believed was impossible. Before we met in person, I felt as if I had already known him for many lifetimes. I finally felt the connection I had waited so long for. A spiritual connection, one of electrifying proportions that penetrated far deeper than physical attraction.

We spent hours on the phone, losing all sense of time. We learned and grew more fascinated by one another and the courageously lonely journeys of self-discovery we each took. It suddenly became obvious that we had to find and love our true selves before our paths could finally cross. Even though I felt like I had waited forever for this, I knew without a doubt that we couldn't have met any sooner. I wasn't ready before, nor was he. We had been preparing our entire lives for this Divine meeting, first needing to learn, suffer, discover our truth, and evolve into the most authentic versions of ourselves. And now, I was finally ready to meet my mirror and step courageously into uncharted territory. This independent woman was suddenly faced with her hardest challenge yet, to vulnerably re-open her heart to give and receive love from a man.

About six weeks after we first met online, I met the Montana man in person for a camping trip in Minnesota. The last week leading up to our trip felt like another month; I could hardly wait any longer to see this man in person and discover whether we had the same magical connection in person as we did over the phone. My heart raced faster as I counted down the hours and minutes of my drive; it nearly beat out of my chest as I pulled into the campground, where I knew he was already setting up our campsite.

I slowly weaved down the winding dirt road through a tunnel of trees, my eyes scanning back and forth for his familiar face. As I turned the last corner, he appeared down the road. *Oh my God,* I thought nervously. *There he is. This is it!* I slowed down, part of me wanting to turn around and run away until a familiar thought came to mind. "Go with grace and ease."

I took a deep breath and watched him turn and face my direction. An electric spark lit up my soul as we recognized each other. Huge smiles spread across our faces. I scrambled for a fresh piece of gum and my favorite essential oil blend. *Oh my God, do I smell okay?* I wondered. *Do I have anything in my teeth? I can't believe this is it!* Nearly shaking in excitement, I pulled into the campsite. *Oh my God, oh my God, oh my God,* raced through my mind at lightning speed. Taking another deep breath to slow my fluttering heart, I slowly opened the door and stepped out of the vehicle.

"Wow, it's so good to finally see you," he said with a beaming smile, immediately stepping in close and reaching his arms for my waist. Electric tingles rocked up and down my spine as a magnetic pull drew me into his arms. *Wow, this feels more intense than I could have imagined,* I thought quickly to myself before I could register that he was leaning in to kiss me.

Before I knew it, his big, soft lips were on mine, igniting fireworks around us. *Wow, okay, now this is way more intense than I imagined.* Time and space stopped. I lost myself in his kiss and wrapped my arms around his neck. And it was just that, just a kiss. No tongue protruding down my throat or hands seductively groping my body. Just an innocent kiss. And the best one I had ever experienced.

I slowly pulled away, looking into his dark brown eyes. There was something so comforting and familiar about him. Though I had relentlessly waited for a connection like I once felt with the blond-haired boy so many years ago, this was completely different. It contained an even deeper, and far more mature, understanding and appreciation. For the first time since I was a teenager, through the eyes of this Montana man, I truly felt seen and admired for my entire being.

"I can't believe you're finally here," I said softly.

"I know," he laughed. "This is amazing. I'm so happy to finally be with you right now."

"Oh my gosh, you have no idea," I said. Suddenly, my ears caught wind of music playing in the distance. I turned my head to search for the sound coming from his speaker on the picnic table. My heart skipped a beat as I recognized the unlikely song that played, "Telephone Line" by Electric Light Orchestra.

A song that I never heard until after my dad died, it became the ultimate signal of my dad's presence for my mom, sister, and me. Only hearing it on rare occasions, "Telephone Line" became my dad's way of checking in, reminding me how proud he was, and reassuring me that I was safe and on the right path. Being a lesser-known oldie, none of my friends had ever heard the song before. *How the hell was it playing from the Montana man's speaker?*

"Oh my God, I can't believe this song is playing," I said in surprise.

"What, 'Telephone Line?'" he replied. "It's a great song."

"I can't believe you know it," I said. "You have no idea how much meaning this song has for me!" Already aware of my past and father's death, I quickly elaborated for him on the song's significance. "I'll take it as a good sign," I concluded. "He clearly knows I'm here, and he's happy about it."

Hearing that song immediately calmed my nerves and helped me relax and enjoy the moment. Knowing I had my dad's support in this new and terrifying adventure was all I needed. The Montana man and I indulged in the most magical four days of my life. We enjoyed perfect weather at the perfect campsite. We went hiking, fishing, and paddling around the serene lake through the day, and in the evenings, we made the best cooking team I could imagine before sharing insanely delicious meals and listening to his dreamy voice sing and play guitar around the fire.

I couldn't believe how easily everything fell into place and how miraculous our chance meeting was. *Now I really know why I was detoured through Yellowstone this year,* I suddenly realized. If I hadn't listened to my intuition, let go of control, and trusted the universe to guide me, I wouldn't have crossed paths with my Montana man.

We lived in bliss for several days, reveling in every pleasant surprise of sharing the same ideas and finishing each other's sentences. "Get out of my head!" I kept joking. *But seriously,* I wondered. *How is it possible for us to have so much in common?* As my excitement grew, so did my old triggers. *Is this too good to be true? Where's the catch?*

By now, you know my story. Accidents, tragedy, shock, and loss, no problem. Been there, done that; I found my own way to heal those wounds. But be vulnerable and trust a man with my heart? No way. That required becoming a team and depending on someone other than myself, and in a relationship, that was something I had never succeeded in doing. Every one of my past relationships ultimately ended with betrayal and heartbreak, ingraining my belief that I couldn't depend on anyone but myself.

I knew that my happiness had to come from me first, and I had also learned that a lot of my suffering came from trusting the wrong people with my heart. I had finally figured out how to guard it against all the "dangerous men" of my life, and now, I was faced with a decision I had avoided for many years. Do I try again and trust this Montana man?

*What if he turns out to be a backstabbing liar?* I suddenly worried, beginning to doubt my ability or worthiness to manifest a truly healthy and fulfilling relationship. *Am I being stupid? Should I run and protect myself?*

"Trust the process," Spirit responded in my heart. "It's safe to trust this one."

As my new relationship grew serious, old triggers and fears continuously slapped me in the face, many that I had long forgotten about. Fear of intimacy. Fear of being myself and "too weird." Fear of not being smart, pretty, or normal enough. Even fear of saying "I love you," as it once signaled my weakness and openness to manipulation and lies. "But I love YOU, Krista," I could still hear the voices of betrayal say from my past. One by one, I learned to face each fear by confessing them out loud to my new partner and finally dissolving the shadows that had followed me for so long.

"Open up. Go with grace and ease," Spirit continued to say.

Sometimes trusting the universe more than myself or my partner, I vowed to continue leaning in and opening myself up, no matter how uncomfortable it got. *Is it really safe this time?* I worried. "Speak your truth and find out for yourself," Spirit challenged me. *Oh God,* I thought. *I really must be vulnerable, yet another foreign concept for me.* Though it sometimes took hours or days to build up the nerve, I slowly opened my fears to my Montana man, only to realize the scariest part was only in the first word. The rest opened new channels of communication and connection between us, ultimately filling us both with surprising amounts of comfort and relief.

Though I thought I had already dissolved much of my pain-body through years of personal healing and self-care practices, I was shocked to discover there was much yet to dissolve through this new and healthy relationship. Every step forward seemed to trigger even deeper fears from my pain-body. Changing plans triggered me the most, setting my ego off on wild tangents of "what ifs" and "he must bes." *He's lying to you. He's not actually interested. He's not what you think. He's going to flake out.*

Both of us self-employed and avid travelers, our flexible schedules changed a lot. It was easy to let ego run wild with judgments and comparisons to the failures of my past relationships and assume that, like them, this too must end in some form of betrayal or disappointment. But each time our plans changed, I felt Spirit console me. "Trust the process, and him, too." None of my ego's projected doom ever manifested, only better plans and understanding of my partner and release of control and worry.

Every day, I felt the wall around my heart slowly crumble down. The vulnerability I once deathly feared began to fill me with empowerment and excitement for more growth and connection with my partner. I finally embraced the comfort and safety of our connection, letting my true self shine brighter each time we came together.

For the first time, I openly spoke about my career and spiritual work, even to the point of following impulses to share my channeled journal entries that suddenly appeared to feed me with encouragement and advice in our relationship. Spirit had made it very clear that this new partnership was important and that we came together for a very specific purpose. The channeling and instructions poured out so clearly, I had to share them with my Montana man. So, for another first, I shared my journal with him, and was met with surprising relief of his interest, understanding, and appreciation for the important messages to us both.

Sept. 5, 2021

*You've noticed that you're always connected (Yes, it's okay to show him this!), and the energy changes. It's going to. Always. The trick is in how you react to various levels of discomfort together. Old habits reactively come up. That's exactly why you came together now: to mirror each other and bring to the surface the dis-ease, stored pain, and demons that your goals are to release. That means the highest openness and vulnerability. Yes, you'll have get to cry in front of him.*

*Your purpose isn't to ride unicorns and rainbows 24/7, it's to help each other break the chains of your past and rise to the next level of spiritual consciousness. You spent 32 human years climbing at a slightly different pace, preparing to meet at this specific level for a very specific purpose. It's easy to get lost in your stories, insecurities, logic, and analyses. If you didn't know how important this relationship is, you'd ruin it by now. That's why we told you.*

*Old ways of thinking are irrelevant. This is like NO other; stop comparing. Your human logic wants to analyze and classify your experiences into familiar buckets. That is impossible here. Let it go (every old version of yourself) and be fully present in your time together. You're finding balance, no mistakes, no time lost. Trust that all is in perfect order.*

*Say goodbye to your former selves. You'll never be the same now that you met. You don't want to be anyway. Let go of old stories of who you are and what you're deserving of. It's time to start fresh with a brand-new life. It does not matter where you've been, what you did, what you have, etc. It's all about choosing your strongest desires and creating them now. You are a team. The more you open yourself to each other, the better it gets!*

- Kris

So, here I sit, from the cozy seat of my motorhome's dinette table, now known as my "mobile office." Looking out the window, I admire the long willow branches flowing all around the RV and this beautiful land where my Montana man and I are working. My daughter just returned from a walk along the river trail nearby. She just held out her open palm. A tiny daisy was in it.

"Here, this is for you," she said, smiling.

"Thank you, love," I said, kissing her on the forehead.

Now, as I take in the views of this little slice of paradise, my heart is full. I've never felt so complete. Though I don't know where this new story will take me, I've never felt so stable and safe in my life. Thanks to the loving support and guidance from Spirit and my guardian angels, I made it. I successfully crawled out of the deepest depths of darkness and settled into the warm light of my truth. I learned how to accept my heartbreak and loss, discover radical self-love and connection with Spirit, and manifest an unbelievably fulfilling and magical life.

Now, my dream life is no longer a dream. I'm living it right now. I finally live my mantra to go with grace and ease. And it's all because I let myself recognize and listen to the voice of Spirit that continues to remind me.

"Trust the process."

# Acknowledgements

***In loving memory of***

Cody Mitchell Southwell
*December 30, 1988 – March 22, 2007*

Brian Kenneth Lindquist
*January 22, 1956 – July 15, 2014*

My deepest gratitude goes to every single person who took part in these pages, especially my daughter and inspiration for life, Jaelyn Rae. Without her, this book would not be in your hands to read today.

A very special thank you goes to Jake Gertz, who graciously supported me in sharing our painful past and continues to be a pillar of inspiration in my life today. My deepest gratitude goes to Alan Simmons, Chad Southwell, and especially the late Cody Southwell and his mother, Deb Danielson, for allowing me to tell their part of my story to the world.

Thank you to my best friend and mentors, Mel DeTray, Suzanne Scheldroup, Melissa Jolly-Graves, Kelly Doran, and Tara Nolan, for their relentless support, guidance, and encouragement for me to step fearlessly on my own path.

A special thank you also goes to the amazing people that helped me write this book behind the scenes, including my phenomenal book coach, Nicole Washburn, editor Caroline Barnhill, and graphic design and formatter, Elijah Toten.

I forever thank my late father, Brian, mother, Marie, and sister, Monica, for seeing me through the darkest of days and always giving their love and support through my wildest adventures.

Lastly, so much love and gratitude goes to my Montana man, Kevin Couch, for surprising me with the happiest end to this epic story.

# Connect with Krista

Krista continues traveling the country by RV with Jaelyn while giving book talks and motivational speeches, guiding clients through her *Manifesting Miracles* Intuitive Guidance Program and online course, and hosting nationwide workshops and yoga retreats on a life-long mission to help others make peace with their past, connect with Spirit and their own intuition, and learn how to manifest the miracles of lasting healing, happiness, and fulfillment.

Contact and learn more about Krista, current programs and services, and upcoming events at: **www.jaeraewellness.com.**

Krista would love to hear from you and learn about your experience in reading her story and how it may have impacted your own personal journey. Simply fill out the "Contact" form on her website or send a message over social media.

You can follow Krista's adventures at **@jaeraewellness** on Instagram and Facebook.